THE TRAVELER'S ATLAS

Edited by Vivian Lewis

Agora Books
824 E. Baltimore St.
Baltimore, MD 21202

ISBN# 0-945332-13-0

THE
TRAVELER'S ATLAS

Publisher: William Bonner
Editor: Vivian Lewis
Copy Editors: Marian Cooper, Dianne McCann,
and Kathleen Peddicord
Artist/Cartographer: Alex Nosevich
Production Manager: Wilma Vinck
Production: Denise Plowman
Editorial Assistant: Christoph Amberger
Assistant to the Publisher: Jane Lears

Researchers: Christoph Amberger, Anastasia Hudgins,
Josh Kendall, Dave Robinson

Contributing Writers: Christoph Amberger, Josh Kendall,
Jane Lears, Paul Lewis

Cover Design: Jack French
Cover Photography: Richard J. Quataert

INTRODUCTION

Travel has changed a lot since the days when Mary Kingsley sloshed her way through unexplored West African swamps, collecting beetles and fishes. She once fell into a game pit with 12-inch ebony spikes designed to impale large animals. She was scarcely injured, however, protected by her large, thick Victorian-age skirts.

One of her contemporaries, Isabella Bird, set off for Asia and traveled to virtually every corner of it, covering some 8,000 miles in China alone—enduring almost unimaginable hardships. She visited places where the presence of a white woman in the full travel regalia of the late 19th century was such a novelty that locals asked if she were human. Those were the travelers about whom Kipling remarked, "Being human they must have been afraid of something, but one never found out what it was."

These intrepid travelers often didn't know where they were going, for there were no maps or literature to guide them to their destinations. So, they created their own "travel atlases" as they went along—hand-drawn maps showing the important features along their route—together with personal comments to describe what they saw and remind them of helpful travel details.

That is the spirit to which this *Traveler's Atlas* is dedicated. For even though the hardships are fewer today, a traveler still needs maps and the wisdom of on-the-ground experience to guide him.

Our ideas of how the world fits together may be full of misconceptions. And almost any atlas can correct these inaccuracies.

However, unlike any geography text you used in school, this atlas is dedicated to travel, bringing to light only those parts of the world you'd most like to visit. Also, unlike other atlases, this book is meant to move. The maps are accompanied by just enough text to get you started, keeping the book lean and portable.

We purposely left out large chunks of the earth where people are not likely to vacation: the Persian Gulf, many deserts, Antarctica, Labrador, Greenland, and much of Africa.

The maps do depict places you may not easily find in other books. For example, this guide provides details of the geography of Tahiti and French Polynesia, which often appear merely as a few dots in the Pacific Ocean. We have covered the islands: the Caribbean, St. Pierre and Miquelon, the Canaries, the Azores, and Madeira. You also get the geographic details of places like Singapore, Hong Kong, Monaco, and Andorra—places that may not be world powers, although they are plenty important to the world traveler.

We have highlighted the major European destinations, too. Our map of France is not cluttered with details of the industrial areas. However, we have described the château country, the wine zones, the Côte d'Azur, and the Alps. Our London map is useful not only for getting around the British capital, but for planning excursions around it, too.

We hope you will use this atlas when you travel and that you will take it with you wherever you go.

Bon Voyage!

—*Vivian Lewis*
Editor

AKNOWLEDGEMENTS

This atlas could not have been written without help from the staff of Agora Inc., starting with publisher Bill Bonner, who first decided that the world needed an atlas for travelers.

Thanks are due to Jane Lears for the sections on the Asian mainland, and to Paul Lewis for the sections on East Africa, Japan, and Russia.

The maps were drawn with accuracy and style by Alex Nosevich; and Wilma Vinck and Denise Plowman coped with the demands of production. Also, thanks go out to Copy Editors Marian Cooper, Kathleen Peddicord, and Dianne McCann, and to Editorial Assistant Christoph Amberger.

Appreciation also is due to our interns Anastasia Hudgins and Dave Robinson, and to fact checker Josh Kendall.

Special thanks go out to Mme. Bellière of the *Guides Michelin* headquarters in Paris for showing *noblesse oblige* in providing substantial help from a great map publisher to a fledgling rival.

Yelena Y. Prokudina of the Soviet Union Embassy advanced *glasnost* in her own way by providing us with help in the transliteration and translation of maps. We also had outstanding help from the Mexican and Yugoslav Embassies.

—*Vivian Lewis*
Editor

TABLE OF CONTENTS

ANDORRA

Andorra is a historical anomaly, an area that managed to avoid being gobbled up by the powerful forces favoring centralization in neighboring France and Spain. It is the only sovereign state in the world whose official language is that of the medieval troubadors, Catalan (which is spoken also by minorities in France and Spain).

Andorra was granted autonomy by Charlemagne in the ninth century for its service in the fight against the Moorish invaders of the Frankish Kingdom. Until the French Revolution, the co-rulers of Andorra were the bishop of Urgel in Spain and the Comte de Foix in France; since then the head of the House of Foix has been replaced by the French chief of state.

Travelers flock to **Andorra la Vella,** the capital, for bargains. Because the country does not have value-added taxes, tobacco or alcohol excises, or luxury taxes (as do its neighbors), it is a shoppers' paradise. And, as a result, the city is

1

filled with a bustle of buyers that may spoil your vacation.

The older houses in Andorra la Vella have jutting roofs to protect from the snow and wooden balconies to benefit from the sun—something like Swiss chalets.

Another Swiss-like feature of Andorra is its status as a tax haven. Residents pay no income taxes and no withholding on interest. Both French francs and Spanish pesetas are legal tender in Andorra; as a result, the franc and the peseta are the venues of choice for operations that violate French and Spanish exchange controls when they exist. Once they manage to get their money into an Andorran bank, French and Spanish depositors are able to invest it and to collect interest or

---

EMBASSY: No embassy in the United States. Contact the **French Embassy,** *4101 Reservoir Road N.W., Washington, DC 20007; (202)944-6000.*

SYSTEM OF GOVERNMENT: Co-principality (France and Spain). Sovereignty is exercised jointly by the president of France and the bishop of Urgel. A unicameral General Council of the Valleys submits motions and proposals to the Permanent Delegations, represented by each co-principality.

ETHNIC GROUPS: Catalan, 27%; Spanish, 55%; French, 7%.

RELIGIOUS GROUP: Roman Catholics.

LANGUAGES: Catalan, 30% (official); Spanish, 58%; French, 7%.

POPULATION: 47,000 (in 1985).

AREA: 180 square miles (487 square kilometers); comparable to Columbus, Ohio.

CAPITAL: Andorra la Vella (population 15,000 in 1983).

TERRAIN: High mountains and narrow valleys.

CLIMATE: Temperate and cool. Average January temperature is 36 degrees Fahrenheit; average July temperature is 67 degrees Fahrenheit.

TELECOMMUNICATIONS
  Country Code: 33.
  Time Zone: +6 hours Eastern Standard Time.
  City Code of Capital: 078.

U.S. CONSULATE IN COUNTRY: *via Laitana 33, Barcelona, Spain; tel. (34-3)319-9550.*

CURRENCY: French franc and Spanish peseta. No limit on import or export.

WORK FORCE: Industry, commerce, services, and government, 80%; agriculture, 20%.

OUR QUALITY OF LIFE RANKING*: 66.52.

VISA REQUIREMENTS: A U.S. passport is required to enter the country. You can stay up to three months without a visa.

TOURIST OFFICE IN THE UNITED STATES: Andorra Tourist Bureau, *1923 Irving Park, Chicago, IL 60613; (312)472-7660.*

*This ranking is taken from the Quality of Life Index, which is published annually in *International Living* (Agora Inc., 824 E. Baltimore St., Baltimore, MD 21202; $36/year). The index rates the overall quality of life in 164 countries and territories. Each country's final score depends on its individual scores in eight categories: health care, economic health, political stability, freedom, infrastructure, recreation and environment, cost of living, and culture.

dividends without interference from their home governments. Backing up this system is a strict custom of banking secrecy.

Often overlooked by the busloads of shoppers that invade the city is the beauty of Andorra, a country made up of six deep valleys beneath the peaks of the high Pyrenees. Skiing is popular in the winter on the slopes of **Arinsal,** six miles from the capital.

You can reach Andorra by car or bus from airports in Barcelona and Toulouse or by a 20-minute ride by small plane from Barcelona to Seo-de-Urgel (which is just over the border in Spain). Or you can take a Spanish or a French train to the Pyrenees, then hire a taxi or rent a car to get to Andorra. The local road system is good, but roads can be blocked by snowstorms or avalanches in the winter.

Although you don't need a visa to go to Andorra, if you travel via France remember to obtain a French visa. **Iberia** flies to Barcelona; to get to Toulouse, your best bet is the French domestic airline **Air Inter,** which does not have offices in this country. ❦

ARGENTINA

Argentina is a large country that is subtropical in the north and subantarctic in the south. The **Andes**, which run along the western border, include the highest mountain in the Western Hemisphere, **Aconcagua.** Near **Mt. Tronador,** a high peak with waterfalls and glaciers, is **San Carlos de Bariloche,** a transplanted Alpine village, complete with chalets and Argentines of Swiss descent. In the south, the high snow-covered mountains form glaciers that reach to the sea. **Nahuel Haupi National Park** is one of the most scenic sites in South America.

However, other parts of Argentina are less beautiful. **Northwest Argentina** is semi-desert. The **Chaco,** a fought-over region on the Paraguay border, is a hot, scrub-covered semi-desert. The **Pampas** region is rich and fertile—but like the Midwest of the United States, the land is flat and boring. The **Patagonian Plains** are arid, swept by cold winds.

EMBASSY: *1600 New Hampshire Ave. N.W., Washington, DC 20009; (202)939-6400.*

SYSTEM OF GOVERNMENT: Bicameral congress. Argentina is a democratic, elected federal republic.

ETHNIC GROUPS: Predominantly European, including Italian, Spanish, German, English, and some Mestizo.

RELIGIOUS GROUPS: Primarily state-supported Roman Catholics; Jews.

LANGUAGES: Spanish, 95%; Italian, 3%; Guarni, 1%.

POPULATION: 31.06 million (in 1986).

AREA: 1.078 million square miles (2.792 million square kilometers).

CAPITAL: Buenos Aires (population 3 million in 1983).

TERRAIN: Plains rising to the Andes. Swampy and forested in the north; fertile and rolling pampas in the south.

CLIMATE: Warm over the pampas, where it rains year-round. Arid in the north and west, with high summer temperatures. Arid in the extreme south but much cooler. Average temperature in Buenos Aires in January is 74 degrees Fahrenheit; average temperature in July is 50 degrees Fahrenheit.

TELECOMMUNICATIONS
   Country Code: 54.
   Time Zone: +2 hours Eastern Standard Time.

Code of Capital: 1.

LOCAL/NATIONAL AIRLINES: Pan Am, *(800)221-1111;* **Eastern,** *(800)327-8376;* and **Argentine Airlines,** *(800)327-0276.*

U.S. CONSULATE IN COUNTRY: *Avenida Columbia, 4300 Buenos Aires, Argentina; tel. (54-1)774-8811.*

CURRENCY: Austral. No limit on import or export.

GROSS NATIONAL PRODUCT: $65.4 billion (in 1985).

WORK FORCE: Industry and commerce, 36%; services, 20%; agriculture, 19%.

OUR QUALITY OF LIFE RANKING: 55.94.

VISA REQUIREMENTS: A passport and a visa are required. To obtain a visa, send a passport and a letter stating the reason for your trip to a consulate in Baltimore, Chicago, Houston, Los Angeles, Miami, New Orleans, Puerto Rico, or San Francisco. Visas are valid for four years.

TOURIST OFFICE IN THE UNITED STATES: Argentina Tourist Information Office Inc., *3030 W. 58th St., Sixth Floor, New York, NY 10019; (212)765-8833.*

Mendoza is the country's wine and fruit center, the garden of the Andes. And in **Cordoba,** to the northwest of the capital, stands a beautiful cathedral.

In the **Pampas** you can see gauchos, Argentine cowboys who parade beautiful creole horses decorated with solid silver bridles inlaid with gold, silver stirrups, and intricately braided rawhide gear. The gauchos' finery matches that of the horses: coin-studded belts, silver daggers, embroidered jackets, and the famous broad leather chaps. Parades are held in Salta in mid-June and at the rodeo in Ayachucho (near La Plata) in May.

Argentinians are proud of their cultural heritage—unlike most Latin Americans, they are of almost pure European stock, with only tiny minorities from Africa and a few surviving Indians. The predominant cultural influence, apart from Spanish, is Italian, particularly Sicilian.

This country was one of the richest in the world when the European immigrants chose it at the end of the 19th century—it was known as the corned beef capital of the world. Since then it has suffered from a decline in the corned beef market and gross political mismanagement under both Peronist and military dictatorships.

Argentina fought and lost a war with Britain over obscure little islands in the south Atlantic called the Falklands (you should call them the Malvinas in Argentina). It also has had disputes with Chile over its southern border.

Argentina boasts the southernmost city in the world, **Ushuaia.** Colonial remains grace **Tucuman, Salta,** and **Jujuy. La Plata** has one of the best natural history museums anywhere.

However, in general, Argentine cities have little to offer tourists. **Buenos Aires** is the exception. It was built during the prosperous years and modeled on Paris. It is relatively cosmopolitan, with more than one-third of the country's total population and a European atmosphere. Downtown includes the grandiose buildings of government: the **Congress Building,** too often the home of powerless legislators, and the **Casa Rosada,** Argentina's White House, too often the home of dictators. The magnificent **Teatro Colon** is one of the best opera houses in the world, seating 3,500.

A most attractive area is **La Boca,** a maze of narrow streets around the port. This area is inhabited by the offspring of Italian immigrants, who speak an argot made up of words from Spanish and Italian. La Boca has the best restaurants.

Argentine food stresses steak—which is excellent but served in giant cholesterol-filled portions—and espresso. Argentina developed a distinctive dance form, the tango, which was fashionable all over the world about 60 years ago. In Buenos Aires, you still can see couples dancing the tango to the bittersweet music of torch singers of both sexes.

Countries with economic woes usually offer bargains. The famous **San Telmo flea market,** *Plaza Dorrego,* in Buenos Aires is where the Argentine middle class raises cash. Mauro dos Santos of *Jornal do Brasil* reported that she had seen "an aristocratic-looking woman offering the finest porcelain and crystal" at the San Telmo market. Other stalls sell old clocks, silverware, dolls, coins, jewelry, fur coats, lamps, books, and clothing.

Because of the country's great number of cattle, Argentine leather goods are cheap. You can buy rugs made out of cowhide still covered with fur. Buenos Aires has a large department store called **Harrods** (which is no longer related to the one in London).

The most beautiful natural wonder in Argentina (which it shares with Paraguay and Brazil) is **Iguazu Falls,** the star attraction of **Iguazu National Park** (which is in Argentina and Brazil). These falls are larger than Victoria Falls (on the border of Zambia and Zimbabwe). The area is surrounded by tropical forests, where orchids thrive in the perpetual mist.

What a contrast to **Perito Moreno,** another beauty spot, which is a glacier that bisects Lake Argentino with a wall of blue ice.

Other natural parks in Argentina include **Valdez Peninsula** in Patagonia, where you can see elephant seals, whales, and penguins. 🦐

AUSTRALIA

Founded 200 years ago as a penal colony, Australia is one of the fastest growing countries in the world. Since 1945 its population has doubled; about one-third of the new settlers have been refugees. Just less than 90% of Australia's population lives in cities—despite the myth of the Outback.

Immigration to this large and empty country—the only country in the world that geographers also treat as a continent—is expected to pick up once the economy improves. Australia has suffered from a high rate of union militancy and an experiment with socialism. Since the worldwide recession, Australia has ended subsidies for new immigrants.

It also has ended easy admission. Only New Zealanders are not required to have visas to visit Australia.

Approximately 150,000 aborigines survive in Australia; only one-third of them are nomadic. These dark-skinned people probably migrated across the sea from Southeast Asia some 40,000 years ago. Before the arrival of white settlers, twice as many aborigines roamed Australia.

Australia's kaleidoscope landscape offers every imaginable form of recreation, from bush safaris with latter-day Crocodile Dundees to jazz festivals, from skiing to sailing along the Great Barrier Reef.

Sydney is the starting point for most travelers, a city of 3.5 million that is situated on a 150-square-mile natural harbor with 100 inlets on the Tasman Sea. Around the steep hills of the old town are beautifully restored Edwardian and Victorian homes. Local culture revolves around the beaches (most crowded is

---

EMBASSY: *1601 Massachusetts Ave. N.W., Washington, DC 20036; (202)797-3000.*

SYSTEM OF GOVERNMENT: Parliamentary Democracy. Although Queen Elizabeth II is sovereign and chief of state, she has no power.

ETHNIC GROUPS: European and aboriginal.

RELIGIOUS GROUPS: Anglicans, 27.7%; Roman Catholics, 25.7%; Protestants, 25.2%.

LANGUAGES: English and aboriginal languages.

POPULATION: 15.8 million (in 1986).

AREA: 2.966 million square miles (7.682 million square kilometers).

CAPITAL: Canberra (population 259,900 in 1983).

TERRAIN: Low-lying. Desert plateau in the west. Mountain ranges running north to south in the east.

CLIMATE: Relatively dry, ranging from temperate in the south to semitropical in the north. The wet season in the north runs from November to March.

TELECOMMUNICATIONS
   Country Code: 61.
   Time Zone: +15 hours Eastern Standard Time (Sydney).
   Code of Capital: 62.

LOCAL/NATIONAL AIRLINES: Qantas Airlines, *(800)227-4500;* **Air New Zealand,** *(800)262-1234;* **Canadian**

Airlines International, *(800)426-7000;* **Continental,** *(800)525-0280;* and **UTA French Airlines,** *(800)282-4484.*

RAILROAD OFFICE IN THE UNITED STATES: Railways of Australia, *(800)626-6665.*

U.S. CONSULATE IN COUNTRY: *Yarralumla, A.C.T. 2600; tel. (61-62)705-0000;* **U.S. Consulate General,** *Hyde Park Tower, 36th Floor, Hyde Park Square, Sydney, NSW 2000; tel. (61-2)261-9200.*

CURRENCY: Australian dollar. No limit on import; travelers can export $5,000.

GROSS NATIONAL PRODUCT: $154.6 billion (in 1986).

WORK FORCE: Commerce and services, 63%; manufacturing, 17%; agriculture and fishing, 8%; government, 5%; construction, 7%.

OUR QUALITY OF LIFE RANKING: 82.24.

VISA REQUIREMENTS: A visa is required. To obtain a visa, send a passport, two photos, and a completed visa application to the consulate in Chicago, Honolulu, Houston, Los Angeles, New York, or San Francisco. Visas are valid up to six months.

TOURIST OFFICE IN THE UNITED STATES: Australian Tourist Commission, *489 Fifth Ave., 31st Floor, New York, NY 10017; (212)687-6300.*

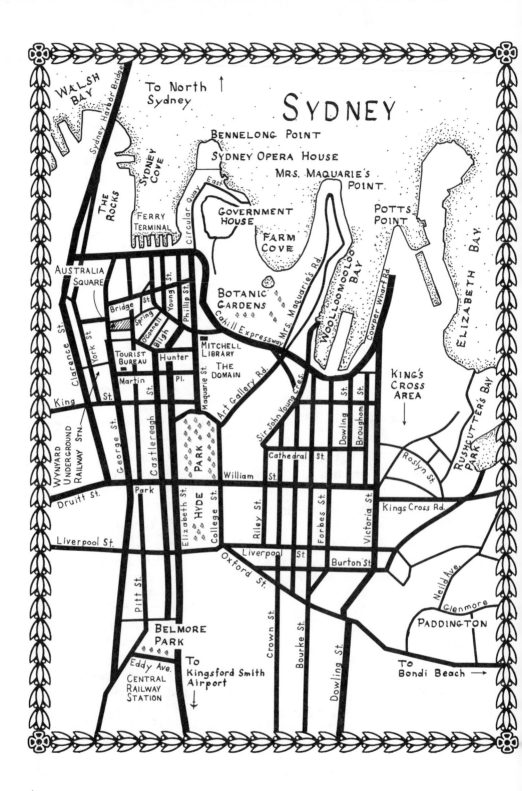

Bondi Beach), with sailing, bathing (including topless), surfing, and windsurfing. The traditional accompaniment to the seaside life is beer. Try Elders XL and Fosters, two popular local brands.

Radiating from its opera house in the harbor (an architectural masterpiece to some, a horror to others) are Sydney's many cultural offerings, including festivals, theater, classical music, opera, jazz, fairs, and carnivals. A great variety of ethnic food and wine adds to the cosmopolitan flavor of Sydney-off-the-beach.

The **Great Barrier Reef** (1,300 miles of reef off the northeastern coast) is one of the great natural attractions of the world, an underground coral garden teeming with marine life and supporting a host of flora and fauna, including sea birds, turtles, and wild orchids. Skin divers and snorkelers can explore without guides.

Melbourne and **Brisbane** are relatively near Sydney on Australia's east coast. But to get to distant **Darwin** (2,533 miles away), **Perth** (2,490 miles away), or **Alice Springs** (1,844 miles away), flying is your best bet. From Alice Springs you also can fly to **Ayers Rock,** the enormous reddish monolith that has mysterious religious significance for the aborigines.

If you have the time, trains are also good ways to travel across Australia. The bargain-priced Sydney to Perth railroad makes three runs a week, each taking three days to travel through the Great Dividing Range, the Broken Hill mining country, and the Dry Nullabor Plains. The Ghan runs from Adelaide to Alice Spring across the Simpson Desert (the Australian salt lake). If you plan to travel by train, buy an **Australpass** from either your travel agent or **Australian Travel/Tour Pacific,** *1101 E. Broadway, Suite 201, Glendale, CA 91205; (818)244-1328.*

Although you can rent a car in Australia, this usually isn't advisable. In addition to the problem of driving on the left, you'll have to deal with the problem of the roads. **Stuart Highway,** which runs from Adelaide to Alice Springs, is made up of 600 miles of badly graded dirt—and breaking down in the Outback qualifies as a bad experience.

Animals are another problem—they wander the roads. Of course, many travel to the Outback for the chance to see Australia's unique animal life. However, a 500-pound kangaroo freezing at the sight of your headlights is another experience that can be termed bad—as is a 100-pound emu (a bird rather like an ostrich) choosing to cross the road while you are rolling down it.

Australia shares the British taste for bed and breakfast accommodations on the farm. For more information, contact **Bed & Breakfast International,** *P.O. Box Q 184, 396 Kent St., Sydney, NSW 2000, Australia, tel. (61-2)264-3155,* or **Islands in the Sun,** *P.O. Box 1398, Newport Beach, CA 92663; (714)645-8300.* ❦

AUSTRIA

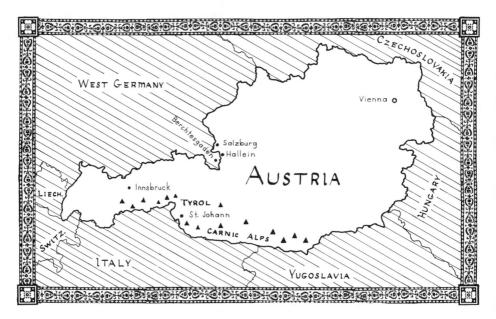

Austria has one of the highest standards of living of all European countries, backed up by beautiful and varied scenery, picturesque villages, and a capital that, although it long ago ceased to be a center of artistic creation, continues to offer exquisite museums, opera, architecture, and coffee shops.

Austria is the home of Mozart, the waltz, the Blue Danube (which is mud-colored), *Sachertorte* (a chocolate cake), *Schlagobers* (whipped cream)—and Hitler. Until the end of World War I, this country ruled the lands to its east, known as the **Hapsburg Empire.** After the Austro-Hungarian Empire lost its hinterland, the rump Austrian state was left with an immense capital in Vienna, a wrecked economy, and dreams of glory that led its population to embrace a merger with Hitler's Germany (or Anschluss) in 1938. Among the Jews who escaped with only their lives was Sigmund Freud.

After World War II, Austria was occupied by the Soviet forces. To stop them from shipping East everything that was not nailed down, the Austrians nationalized much of their industrial and financial sectors. The four-power occupation was ended by the 1949 State Treaty, whereby Austria was granted renewed independence on the condition that it remain neutral in the East-West confrontation. Its neutrality led Austria to develop a profitable specialty as a business and banking entrepôt for former subject territories that had become part of the Soviet bloc. It also became a way station for the refugees, religious minorities, and dissidents from the Soviet Union and its allies. But these preoccupations may have led Austria to neglect studying its own role in the rise and rule of Nazism, the background of the Waldheim Affair.

12

Vienna radiates in a circle whose center, roughly, is **Stephansdom,** the old cathedral with its multicolored tile roof. The old part of town on the right bank has narrow cobblestoned streets that run down to the **Danube Canal,** interspersed here and there by squares, Baroque churches and monuments, expensive stores, monas-

---

EMBASSY: *2343 Massachusetts Ave. N.W., Washington, DC 20008; (202)483-4474.*

SYSTEM OF GOVERNMENT: Parliamentary democracy.

ETHNIC GROUPS: Austrians, 98%; Croatians; Slovenes.

RELIGIOUS GROUPS: Roman Catholics, 84.3%; without religious allegiance, 6%; Protestants, 5.6%.

LANGUAGES: German, 95%; Croatian, Slovene, and Hungarian, 5%.

POPULATION: 7.55 million (in 1985).

AREA: 32.375 square miles (83,851 square kilometers); comparable to Maine.

CAPITAL: Vienna (population 1.489 million).

TERRAIN: Mountainous and hilly. Forests and woodlands cover 40% of the land area.

CLIMATE: Continental temperate. Considerable snowfall. Average temperature in Vienna in January is 28 degrees Fahrenheit; average temperature in July is 67 degrees Fahrenheit.

TELECOMMUNICATIONS
  Country Code: 43.
  Time Zone: +6 hours Eastern Standard Time.
  Code of Capital: 222.

LOCAL/NATIONAL AIRLINES: Austrian Airlines, *(800)872-4282* or *(212)265-6350* in Hawaii, New York, Puerto Rico, and the Virgin Islands; **Air**

France, *(800)237-2747;* **ALIA Royal Jordanian Airlines,** *(800)223-0470;* **Lufthansa German Airlines,** *(800)645-3880;* **Pan Am,** *(800)221-1111;* **Sabena Airlines,** *(800)521-0135;* **Tarom,** *(212)687-6013;* and **TWA,** *(800)892-4141.*

NATIONAL RAILROAD: Austrian Railroads, *500 Fifth Ave., New York, NY 10110; (212)944-6880.*

U.S. CONSULATE IN COUNTRY: Mariott Hotel, *Gartenbau Promenade 2, 1010 Vienna; tel. (43-222)42-67-21.*

CURRENCY: Schilling. No limit on import; travelers can export 15,000 Austrian schillings (in any form of payment medium).

GROSS NATIONAL PRODUCT: $94.7 billion (in 1986).

WORK FORCE: Industry and commerce, 60%; agriculture, 13.8%; services, 25.5%.

OUR QUALITY OF LIFE RANKING: 76.07.

VISA REQUIREMENTS: U.S. tourists can stay up to three months without a visa. Contact the consulate in New York, Washington, D.C., San Francisco, Los Angeles, Chicago, Denver, Detroit, Honolulu, Kansas City, Miami, New Orleans, Philadelphia, San Juan, or Seattle to arrange a longer stay.

TOURIST OFFICE IN THE UNITED STATES: Austrian Tourist Office, *Suite 2009, 500 Fifth Ave., New York, NY 10110; (212)944-6880.*

tic cellars now devoted to eating and drinking, and homes of famous men, including Beethoven, Mozart, and Schubert. The houses of Haydn and Freud are outside the center of town.

The old town is circled by the **Ring** (a series of streets, all of which end with the word *ring* and around which trams circulate). The Ring was built on the site of the former city walls and was graced by the best that the 19th century could produce in the way of impressive neo-Baroque public buildings, including an opera house, museums, hotels, and private residences.

The **Hofburg,** the former city palace of the Hapsburg emperors, fills the western part of the old town, with a series of interconnected palaces now used for government offices. Here you will find three Viennese musts: the **Spanish Riding School** (with its Lipizzaner horses, which walk on their hind legs); the **Vienna Boys' Choir;** and the **Hofburg museums.** The **Schatzkammer** displays civil and ecclesiastical treasures of Austria.

Across the Ring from the Hofburg are the university and museums of art, archeology, musical instruments, drawings, manuscripts, and maps and globes.

Melomaniacs should visit the opera and the **Bosendorfer Hall** (where piano concerts are given in a former piano factory) and keep an eye on the bulletin boards of churches for the incredible array of recitals offered in Vienna.

Outside the old town, the main sight is the Hapsburg summer palace at **Schönbrunn,** which you can reach via public transportation. When you change from the subway to the bus, look for **Karl-Marx-Hof** across the street, the world's first public housing project.

The first thing you will notice about Schönbrunn is that it is not symmetrical—a fact noted by Napoleon when he was staying here to court the lady who later became his empress. In addition to the usual trappings of imperial life (the palace was modeled on Versailles), Schönbrunn includes a few Austrian touches, notably a room papered in porcelain, enameled cast-iron stoves to keep out the central European winds, awful 19th-century apartments (decorated in brown), where the imperial family actually lived, and exercise rooms, where the Empress Sissy (wife to Franz Josef) worked out to get rid of all that *Sachertorte* and *Schlagobers.*

Other sites in Vienna include the **Prater** (seen in *The Third Man,* a great movie set in Vienna), the **Vienna Woods,** the **Danube, Grinzing** (where new wine is drunk), and **Klosterneuberg,** a Baroque monastery, all of which you can get to via public transportation. By car or bus, visit **Meyerling,** site of the death pact of Crown Prince Rudolph and his mistress.

After Vienna, visit **Salzburg,** Mozart's home. The town attracts musicians and music lovers from all over the world during its summer festival (late July to August). Tickets are expensive and difficult to get. But don't despair; you can always go to the puppet theater for a (canned) Mozart opera. Visit the Mozart birthplace, the **Residenz** (palace of the worldly prince-archbishops of Salzburg Mozart served), and the **Hohensalzburg fortress** on the hill—or, instead of sightseeing, you can simply collapse in a café or konditorei. Salzburg is the home of the *Mozartkugel,* a concoction of marzipan and chocolate that has no connection whatsoever with the composer.

Nearby are **Hellbrunn,** another bit of archiepiscopal worldliness, a summer palace with water gardens that can be used to squirt guests, and the **salt mines of Hallein** (which you can tour). Don't let the man who lived there keep you from visiting Hitler's **Eagle's Nest** in Berchtesgaden, which offers a great view of the Alps.

Other things to see in Austria include the ski slopes in **Kitzbühel, St. Johann,** and **Waidring.** Here are lovely Alpine villages, historic inns, and ski runs for all levels of skill. **Sankt Anton am Arlberg** in western Austria, home of the Arlberg technique, claims to be the origin of the modern downhill sport. It was here, in 1909, that Hannes Schneider adapted skiing, which had been invented for crossing flatland in Scandinavia, to the mountains, creating the downhill sport.

Austria's other famous ski area is the **Tyrol.** The leading city of this area, **Innsbruck,** is one of the most beautiful small cities in the world. Walk down **Maria-Theresien-Strasse,** the main street, and look at the glorious mountains around you. The old town here is everyone's image of the Tyrol.

Bad Ischl is a good base for exploring the Austrian lakes, another popular destination. Austrian lakes ban motor boats because of noise pollution, which makes them more pleasant than similar sites in other European resorts. Bad Ischl was where the Hapsburgs spent their summers, dressed up in the same sorts of Tyrolean peasant costumes that you still see on non-aristocratic Austrian holiday-makers.

Hallstatt, on the lake of the same name, is 14 miles from Bad Ischl. It is the most beautiful village in Austria. Between November and February, the sun never shines on this lakeside village, where cars are banned. The site was first settled by prehistoric Hallstatt man (3,000 years ago), who mined salt here. You can visit the ancient salt mine, the oldest in Europe.

The Gothic **Maria Himmelfahrt** Catholic church in the village has a chapel of bones (because people had to be disinterred to make room for those who died after them) and two altars. Hallstatt also has a Protestant church. The nearby **Gosautal** is the most beautiful valley in Austria.

Traditional Austrian foods include *Wienerschnitzel* (breaded veal or pork), *Tafelspitz* (boiled beef filet with vegetables), *Knoedel* (dumplings), and *Palatsch-inken* (a dessert pancake).

Shopping in Austria is nerve-wracking, because of the poor performance of the dollar in recent years. Embroidered shawls, petit-point bags, and rustic woven cotton goods (from dirndl skirts to tablecloths) all tempted Americans a few years ago, but now they are priced out of reach. A few alternatives: scarves or ribbons in typically Tyrolian designs (make your own costume); lederhosen (particularly for girls with good legs); and *Mozartkugeln* or *Sachertorte* (don't buy at Sacher itself; across the Kaerntnerstrasse you'll find cheaper imitations that are just as fattening).

You can rent a car to see Austria, or you can fly on Austrian Airlines. Rail connections between cities are good. Another option is a cruise on the Danube.

The Austrian schilling moves with the German mark. The groschen, 100 of which make up a schilling, is not often used. ❦

THE BAHAMAS

The Bahamas are an archipelago of 700 palm-covered islands set tranquilly in the Caribbean Sea off the coast of Florida (see the map of the Caribbean on page 20). The islands are made of coral limestone, and the Tropic of Cancer roughly bisects the 5,350 square miles of land so that half of the Bahamas are in the tropics and half are in the temperate zone. The islands are warmed by the Gulf Stream in winter and cooled by trade winds in summer, producing an ideal climate. In January 1977, the northern islands experienced a rare snowfall.

Only 29 of the islands are inhabited. Most, like Florida, are flat, with white sandy beaches. The exact date of discovery is not known, but it is believed that Spanish sailors with Columbus in 1492 first explored Walker Cay, one of the islands, which were then inhabited by Arawak Indians. The islands were claimed for Spain and named Bajamar (Shallow Sea).

The British claimed the islands in 1629, but the first European settlement came later, when shipwrecked British Puritans landed in Eleuthera in 1648 and colonized it. This is one of the Out Islands, along with Great Exuma and the Abacos, which are to the north of the range. To boost tourism, the Bahamians now market these as the Family Islands.

Famous as tax havens, the Bahamas are also superb vacation sites, with good restaurants, shopping, and night life. Although 85% of the 210,000 Bahamians are black, you'll notice little tension between them and the predominantly white tourists.

The main reason for this is that tourism accounts for 70% of the gross national product of the islands, 45% of the jobs, and 60% of government revenues. More than two-million tourists visit each year. The islands are the destination of ultra-cheap package tours and exclusive sea cruises—and every price range in between. They offer beautiful beaches, deep-sea fishing, sailing, and duty-free shopping, plus casinos (including the largest offshore casino in the world) and nightclubs with topless dancers.

Nassau, the capital of the island group, boasts beautiful public parks (including **Ardantra Gardens**) and the curious **Queen's Staircase,** a manmade canyon carved into coral. This port city is full of beautiful colonial and Victorian architecture. The Coral World tower and undersea observatory, built in 1988, enable you to view coal reefs 20 feet below sea level without getting wet (you look through 24 picture windows). The city's lovely octagonal building (which was once a jail and is now used to house the public library) is worth a visit. **Ft. Montagu** has great cannons.

Coral World is on Silver Cay just off Nassau, on New Providence Island, roughly in the middle of the archipelago. (Most Bahamians live on New Providence Island.) Nassau is also the financial center of the Bahamas, with brass plaques from just about every major bank in the world displayed on the buildings along Bay Street.

Shopping is fun in Nassau, where you can find locally woven straw baskets, beachwear, and clothes in handmade batik (called Androsia after the island where it is made), pink conch-pearl jewelry, and imported brand-name luxury goods at duty-free prices.

Nassau itself is somewhat seedy, full of junk, wrecked cars, graffiti, and vagrants—but the rest of the islands live up to the image of an island paradise.

Just off Nassau is **Paradise Island,** the center of mass tourism in the Bahamas. Paradise Island is largely owned by real estate magnates, such as Donald Trump, Sheraton, Holiday Inn, and Loews. At the end of the island are **Ocean Club** (in a Georgian house) and the **Bahama Club Med.** Another new development here is **Cable Beach,** with its golf course. This resort is run by the same company that operates the elegant and pink **Royal Bahamian Hotel** downtown.

EMBASSY: *600 New Hampshire Ave. N.W., Suite 865, Washington, DC 20037; (202)944-3390.*

SYSTEM OF GOVERNMENT: Independent democratic sovereign state. Member of the Commonwealth of Nations.

ETHNIC GROUPS: Blacks, 85%; Europeans, 15%.

RELIGIOUS GROUPS: Baptists, 29%; Anglicans, 23%; Roman Catholics, 23%; Methodists, 7%.

LANGUAGE: English.

POPULATION: 235,000 (in 1986).

AREA: 5,382 square miles (13,939 square kilometers); comparable to Connecticut.

CAPITAL: Nassau (population 135,400 in 1980).

TERRAIN: The nearly 700 islands are primarily flat. No freshwater streams.

CLIMATE: Semitropical. Average temperature in Nassau in January is 71 degrees Fahrenheit; average temperature in July is 81 degrees Fahrenheit.

TELECOMMUNICATIONS
   Country Code: 809.
   Time Zone: 0 hours Eastern Standard Time.

LOCAL/NATIONAL AIRLINE: **Bahamas Air,** *(800)465-4329;* **British Airways,** *(800)247-9297;* and **Air Jamaica,** *(800)523-5585.*

U.S. CONSULATE IN COUNTRY: *Mosmar Building, Queen Street, P.O. Box N-8197, Nassau; tel. (809)332-4753; telex 20-138.*

CURRENCY: Bahamian dollar (equal to U.S. dollar). No limit on import; travelers may not export Bahamian dollars.

GROSS NATIONAL PRODUCT: $960 million (in 1984).

WORK FORCE: Government, 30%; tourism, 25%; industry and commerce, 20%; agriculture, 6%.

OUR QUALITY OF LIFE RANKING: 59.70.

VISA REQUIREMENTS: Passports and onward/return tickets are required of U.S. tourists.

TOURIST OFFICE IN THE UNITED STATES: Bahamas Tourist Office, *1730 Rhode Island Ave. N.W., Suite 510, Washington, DC 20036; (202)659-9135.*

Sailing or flying north from Nassau takes you to the **Abacos.** These Out Islands are the sailing centers of the Bahamas, and the villages here often look like New England towns. In the Abacos, you can really get away from it all. Try **Green Turtle Cay** and its colonial inn for solitude; **Man-O-War Cay,** where cars are banned (mopeds are allowed); and **Treasure Cay,** where golf is the most popular pastime.

Or head for **Eleuthera** or perhaps **Harbor Island,** which is the best place for deep-sea diving. On Eleuthera, stay at the **Cotton Bay Club**, which was founded as a private golf resort for top corporate brass. Juan Tripp, president of Pan American, used to divert planes flying to South America to let him off at this resort. Even more chic in this former British colony is the **Windermere Hotel,** which was where British royalty stayed when visiting Lord Mountbatten's (small) beach house.

Also on Eleuthera (at **Tarpum Bay**) is the studio of the best known local artist, Georgia-born Mal Flander, who paints fellow islanders in a Gauguinesque style. Another island treat is Thompson's Eleutheran pineapple rum, which you can find at **Thomspon's Bakery** in Gregorytown—and nowhere else.

New Providence Island was named (although perhaps not discovered) in 1666 by a Bermudian Puritan en route to the Carolinas. The islands were granted to the Carolina Colony in 1670, but during the American Revolution, the U.S. Navy was unable to hold the islands, which became a haven for British Loyalists. The islands were used to smuggle goods to the South during the Civil War and to beat Prohibition.

The national cuisine of the Bahamas is based on the conch, the sea snail, known as *lambi* on the islands. (The conch shell is the one you put to your ear to hear the sea.) The gastopod is tough and can be eaten raw (in salads) or stewed, in which case it tastes like crab. Bahamian ingenuity also produces conch fritters, cracked conch, and conch chowder.

A second seafood favorite is the grouper, a white fish that is usually grilled. Bahamians eat a lot of fish, starting with breakfast, when they eat boiled fish and fish stew.

The best time to visit the Bahamas is **Junkanoo**—which is the local version of Christmas. The parades and dancing reach their peak in a Bahamian spectacle something like Carnival in other places. The festival continues from Boxing Day (Dec. 26) through New Year's Day. ❦

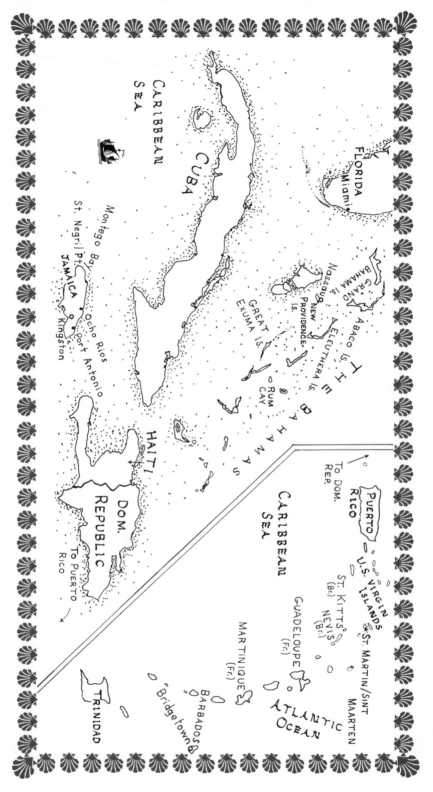

BARBADOS

Barbados is a pear-shaped tropical island (see the map of the Caribbean on page 20), a former British colony with sandy beaches and historic buildings located at the easternmost point of the Caribbean Islands in the Lesser Antilles chain. It was first settled by the English in 1627 and has the second-oldest House of Assembly in the world. Although the island is relatively flat, the interior has hills where sugarcane is grown and a high spot called **Mt. Hillaby.** The temperature is constant year-round, from 72 degrees Fahrenheit to 86 degrees Fahrenheit. The island is

EMBASSY: *2144 Wyoming Ave. N.W., Washington, DC 20008; (202)939-9200.*

SYSTEM OF GOVERNMENT: Independent sovereign state within British Commonwealth since November 1966. Queen Elizabeth II is the head of state.

ETHNIC GROUPS: Africans, 80%; mixed, 16%; Europeans, 4%.

RELIGIOUS GROUPS: Anglicans, 70%; Moravians, 17%; Methodists, 9%; Roman Catholics, 4%.

LANGUAGE: English.

POPULATION: 253,000 (in 1985).

AREA: 166 square miles (430 square kilometers); twice the size of Washington, D.C.

CAPITAL: Bridgetown (population 7,466 in 1985).

TERRAIN: Relatively flat, rising to a ridge in the center.

CLIMATE: Pleasantly tropical. The wet season runs from June to November. Average temperature in Bridgetown in January is 76 degrees Fahrenheit; average temperature in July is 80 degrees Fahrenheit.

TELECOMMUNICATIONS
Country Code: 809.

Time Zone: +1 hour Eastern Standard Time.

LOCAL/NATIONAL AIRLINE: American Airlines, *(800)433-7300;* **BWIA,** *(800)327-7401;* and **Pan Am,** *(800)221-1111.*

U.S. CONSULATE IN COUNTRY: *Trident House, Broad Street, Bridgetown; tel. (809)63574-7.*

CURRENCY: Barbados dollar (equal to U.S. dollar). No limit on import (subject to declaration); travelers can export up to the amount declared on arrival.

GROSS NATIONAL PRODUCT: $1 billion (in 1984).

WORK FORCE: Services and government, 80.9%; industry and commerce, 12.7%; agriculture, 6.9%.

OUR QUALITY OF LIFE RANKING: 62.24.

VISA REQUIREMENTS: Neither a passport nor a visa are required for stays of up to six months. You must have a return ticket and proof of U.S. citizenship.

TOURIST OFFICE IN THE UNITED STATES: Barbados Board of Tourism, *800 Second Ave., 17th Floor, New York, NY 10017; (212)986-6516.*

cooled by trade winds. Humidity is low, but 40 to 90 inches of rain fall during the wet season, from July through November.

Barbados' principal port and capital is **Bridgetown,** on the southwest coast, which has a museum, a cathedral, and the **Garrison** (which formerly defended the island against pirates and naval attacks from foreign enemies, such as the Americans). Bridgetown's main drag is Swan Street.

Holetown is where the first settlers landed in 1627, and it has become a center for American expatriates and retirees (especially around St. James Parish). **Speightstown,** an early trading center on the northwest coast, also boasts a fortress, as does **Maycocks. St. Philip** has Lord Sam's Castle, now a club; another club here, The Savannah, features hard-fought polo matches.

Other sports on the island include surfing, swimming, golf, tennis, hockey, bicycling, water polo, riding, fishing, yachting, and cricket. **Bathsheba** is a famous health spa on Barbados that was once visited by George Washington.

The island was granted independence in 1966. It has more tourists than native inhabitants, but it is less dependent on foreign visitors than other Caribbean sites. Thanks to a hard-working, highly literate population and aid under the U.S. Caribbean initiative and the European Community programs, Barbados has attracted international companies, including TRW, Playtex, and Bayer, to set up plants here.

Local food specialties include flying fish, dolphin, saltfish cakes, and crab; cristaphene, which is a mixture of cucumber and avocado; and tropical fruits, including papaya, mango, and lime. Try locally distilled Mt. Gay Rum and Banks Beer.

The Barbadians call themselves Bajans and speak a dialect of English that is easy to understand. ❦

BELGIUM

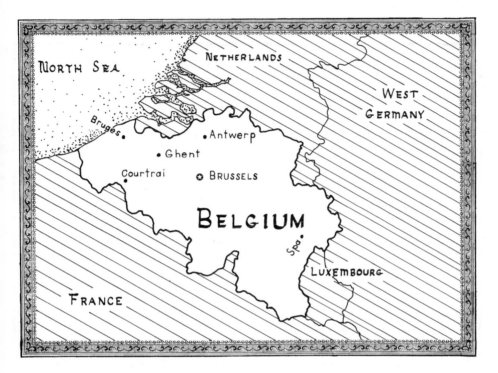

Belgium is an invented country, put together after 1830 as a result of an uprising that began in the Brussels Opera House protesting the country's rule by the Dutch. To create a sufficient counterweight to the Netherlands, areas of Flanders where the people spoke Dutch but were Roman Catholic were combined with Brussels and the French-speaking areas (Walloonia) that had not been captured by either Louis XIV or Napoleon. The created country was held together by religion, colonialism (tiny Belgium ruled huge parts of Black Africa), a dynasty set up by Queen Victoria to help her cousins, and a balance between Dutch- and French-speaking inhabitants.

Today the forces for unification are weak: colonies are passé; religion is embarrassing; monarchy is irrelevant; and the economic and demographic power of the Dutch-speaking inhabitants dominates the country (with the exception of the capital, **Brussels,** which is still firmly Francophone). Unlike other countries with more than one language, Belgium is beset by linguistic disputes. One way around this impasse (particularly in advertisements) has been the adoption of English. As the headquarters of the North Atlantic Treaty Organization and the European Common Market and the European headquarters of many American companies,

23

bilingual Belgium is learning to use English.

Thanks to the linguistic impasse, even Belgians now refer to their country as Belgium (rather than Belgique or België) and to its capital as Brussels (rather than Bruxelles or Brussel).

The linguistic split is also reflected in geography. The French-speaking parts of

EMBASSY: *3330 Garfield St. N.W., Washington, DC 20008; (202)333-6900.*

SYSTEM OF GOVERNMENT: Parliamentary democracy under a constitutional monarchy.

ETHNIC GROUPS: Flemish, 57% Walloons, 33%; Germans, 0.7%.

RELIGIOUS GROUP: Roman Catholics, 97%.

LANGUAGES: Dutch, 56%; French, 32%; legally bilingual (Brussels), 11%; German, 0.7%.

POPULATION: 9.856 million.

AREA: 11,781 square miles (30,513 square kilometers); comparable to Maryland.

CAPITAL: Brussels (population 1 million).

TERRAIN: Varies from coastal plains in the northwest to low plateaus in the center to the wooded Ardennes plateau in the southeast.

CLIMATE: Cool, temperate, and rainy. No extreme temperatures.

TELECOMMUNICATIONS
Country Code: 32.
Time Zone: +6 hours Eastern Standard Time.
Code of Capital: 2.

LOCAL/NATIONAL AIRLINES: Council Charter, *(212)661-0311;* **Pan Am,** *(800)221-1111;* and **Sabena Airlines,** *(800)645-3700* (East Coast), *(800)632-8050* (New York), *(800)645-*

3790 (Southwest and Midwest), and *(800)645-1382* (West Coast).

RAILROAD OFFICE IN THE UNITED STATES: Belgian National Railroads, *745 Fifth Ave., New York, NY 10151; (212)758-8130.*

U.S. CONSULATE IN COUNTRY: *27 blvd. du Regent, 1000 Brussels; tel. (32-2)513-38-30.*

CURRENCY: Belgian franc. No limit on import or export of currency; however, travelers must leave with the same cameras and electronics with which they entered.

GROSS NATIONAL PRODUCT: $112.9 billion (in 1986).

WORK FORCE: Services and transportation, 36%; industry and commerce, 33%; public service, 21%; agriculture, 3%.

OUR QUALITY OF LIFE RANKING: 72.54.

VISA REQUIREMENTS: A passport is required. A visa is not required for U.S. businessmen or tourists staying less than 90 days, but a residence visa is necessary for stays longer than three months. To obtain a residence visa, you simply must demonstrate a job or financial means.

TOURIST OFFICE IN THE UNITED STATES: Belgium Tourist Board, *745 Fifth Ave., New York, NY 10151; (212)758-8130.*

the country are mountainous and beautiful, with caves to explore, game-filled forests, lovely vistas, and spas (including Spa, the watering hole that gave its name to the notion). Flemish Belgium is largely flat and boring, with a few miles of equally boring (and cold) beach, to which the entire population flocks during spring and fall weekends (in summer they go to the Mediterranean along with the rest of northern Europe). However, the Flemish cities, particularly **Antwerp, Ghent,** and **Bruges** (as we shall call them, using the medieval English rather than either French or Flemish), are graced with some of the most beautiful paintings ever made by some of the most talented painters ever to live: Memling, Van Eyck, and Rubens.

Presiding over the mishmash is Brussels, which is beautiful despite the Belgian building boom that has surrounded the old town with high-rise monstrosities to house Eurocrats and corporate America. The best site in Belgium is the **Grand' Place,** the medieval town center of Brussels. Here, during the Middle Ages and the Renaissance, the great guilds, which then controlled the city, put up sumptuous gilded halls around the 14th-century Gothic city hall, competing with each other in splendor and ostentation. Thanks to environmentalists organized by a British journalist in Brussels, cars are banned from the Grand' Place. Have a beer in the **Maison des Tanneurs,** now a café graced with a sheep's bladder and a stuffed horse.

The area to the north and east of the Grand' Place is called the **Ilot Sacré,** a region of great restaurants. The Belgians combine Germanic portions with French gastronomy. **Chez Vincent,** a fish restaurant, is decorated with beautiful 19th-century tiles showing fishermen bringing home their catches. Try sole, *tomate aux crevettes* (a tomato stuffed with tiny shrimp), and raw Zeeland oysters in season.

Other Belgian specialties include *carbonnade* (a beef stew made with beer), *waterzooie* (either fish or chicken in cream sauce), *paling* in *het groen* (eel), and fondu. Belgian fondu is a square of cheese-laden gnocchi, breaded and deep fried and served with fried parsley. However, Belgians are most famous for eating lots of french fries and steamed mussels.

With Belgian food you probably should drink Belgian beer; try Stella Artois. If you're a more serious beer connoisseur, look out for specialty brews, such as *mort subite* (sudden death) or *kriek* (cherry-flavored beer).

To the south of the Grand' Place, on rue de l'Etuve, is a famous statue that symbolizes Brussels and the effects of drinking beer: **Le Mannekin Pis,** which shows a small boy urinating. Other sites in Brussels include the **St. Michel Cathedral** (from the 13th century) and the beautiful **Sablons Church,** with its great stained glass. This is the focus of the Sablons squares, which are near the city's impressive art museum featuring works by Magritte and Delvaux, both important 20th-century Belgian painters.

But true art lovers should go to the **Ghent cathedral** to see the Van Eyck altarpiece; to Antwerp for the world's largest collection of Rubens religious paintings (in the **Onze Liewe Vrouw cathedral**); to Courtrai for the Van Dyck; and to Bruges for the Van Eyck, the Van der Weyden, the Memling, and the other works by Flemish masters that are scattered throughout a series of museums and churches along that city's swan-filled and romantic canals.

In addition to its artistic masterpieces, Bruges also has a famous procession (which is held each year on Ascension Day and dates back to the Crusades) and charming remnants of a *begijnhof* (a *begijnhof* was a part-time convent, occupied by medieval Flemish ladies who took the veil temporarily, with the right to keep their property and to leave eventually and marry). When one of the women left, she sped across the Minnewater (the Lake of Love) to her wedding.

Belgium is a good place to buy a car (you could buy one to drive in Europe and then ship it home, for example). The market is extremely competitive, because the country has no domestic automobile company.

Other Belgian shopping bargains include lace, which is an expensive luxury but cheaper here than elsewhere. Most common is Bruges lace, which is woven in cotton or flax in bands that are then embroidered onto table linens or blouses of the same material. Small basket-liners, which you can use to create little pockets for rolls, are relatively inexpensive.

A cheap Sunday flea market is set up in Brussels in the **Marolles,** a semi-slum beneath the horrible and huge Palais de Justice. Antiques are sold in the area of the Sablons Church at prices that are low enough to attract dealers from Paris and London.

The Belgian currency is called the franc, but it has a different exchange rate from the French franc. It is divided into centimes, which are all but obsolete except in groups of 25. ❦

BRAZIL

The he largest country in South America (larger also than the continental United States), and the only one where Portuguese is spoken, Brazil has a powerful identity. This is the land whose new and ultramodern capital (**Brasilia,** which is a combination of all the mistakes of city planning of the 1960s) governs the great basin of the Amazon River and the undreamed of wealth of the country's natural resources.

Brazil is also the land whose multiracial population has given the world voodoo, xango, candomble, and macumba (all fusions of African and Christian religions); a beach culture based on the almost non-existent string bikini; the most fervent Carnival in Christendom; great soccer players; great television soap operas (*Aguas Vivas*); and a fast-growing population in Rio de Janeiro that exists in the most appalling poverty in *favelas* (slums) within sight of palatial homes on **Avenida Beira Mar.** Homeless squatters bed down for the night on the marble forecourts of the Banco do Brasil.

Red tape, inflation, and nationalization have turned Brazil into a problem country. The poverty you see in Rio is even more visible in the countryside and in the shantytowns of other Brazilian cities.

History buffs love Brazil, because it was discovered in the year 1500—the world's easiest date to remember. However, one theory holds that Brazil was discovered earlier by the Portuguese (who kept quiet about it and let Christopher

EMBASSY: *3006 Massachusetts Ave. N.W., Washington, DC 20008; (202)745-2700.*

SYSTEM OF GOVERNMENT: Federal republic.

ETHNIC GROUPS: Whites, 60%; mixed, 30%; blacks, 8%; Indians, 2%.

RELIGIOUS GROUPS: Roman Catholics, 89%; Protestants, 4%; followers of Macumba, 2% (about 30% of the Roman Catholics are affiliated with Macumba).

LANGUAGES: Portuguese (official); English.

POPULATION: 143.28 million (in 1986).

AREA: 3.286 million square miles (8.512 million square kilometers); almost half of South America.

CAPITAL: Brasilia (population 1.47 million in 1980).

TERRAIN: Dense forests, semiarid scrubland, rugged hills and mountains, rolling plains, and a coastal strip. The largest rain forest in the world surrounds the famous Amazon River Basin.

CLIMATE: Mostly tropical or semitropical with a temperate zone in the south. The average temperature in Rio de Janeiro in February is 79 degrees Fahrenheit; the average temperature in July is 70 degrees Fahrenheit.

TELECOMMUNICATIONS
Country Code: 55.
Time Zone: +2 hours Eastern Standard Time.
Code of Capital: 61.

LOCAL/NATIONAL AIRLINES: Pan Am, *(800)221-1111;* and **Varig Airlines,** *(800)327-2604* or *(800)432-4420* in Florida.

U.S. CONSULATE IN COUNTRY: *Avenida das Nacoes, Lote 3, Brasilia, D.F.; tel. (55-61)223-0120; telex 061-1091;* **U.S. Consulates General,** *Rio de Janeiro, São Paulo.*

CURRENCY: Cruzado. No limit on import or export.

GROSS NATIONAL PRODUCT: $218 billion (in 1984).

WORK FORCE: Services, 41%; agriculture, 36%; industry, 25%.

OUR QUALITY OF LIFE RANKING: 46.87.

VISA REQUIREMENTS: A visa is required. Send a passport, one passport-size photo, an application, and a return/onward ticket to the consulate in New York, Washington, D.C., Atlanta, Chicago, Dallas, Houston, Los Angeles, Miami, New Orleans, or San Francisco. Visas are good for three months.

TOURIST OFFICE IN THE UNITED STATES: Brazilian Tourism Foundation, *551 Fifth Ave., Suite 519, New York, NY 10176; (212)286-9600.*

Columbus sail for rival Spain). The evidence for this is that before Columbus returned from his first voyage, Portugal persuaded the pope to recognize its right to all the land east of 52 degrees latitude, while Spain had to settle for the rest.

Brazil became independent under an offshoot of the Portuguese monarchy in 1822; it got rid of the monarchy in 1889, when the monarch made the mistake of abolishing slavery (which was popular among Brazilian landowners).

Brazil's population is a mixture of Portuguese and African in various combinations (which race-conscious Brazilians are able to differentiate accurately), along with admixtures of Indians, other Europeans, and Japanese. The center of the melting pot is **São Paulo,** the country's financial capital and the largest city in South America.

São Paulo resembles Los Angeles and Chicago—the former for its climate, the latter for its city-center Triangulo, which is similar to the Loop. The city has a 22-floor library, the tallest in the world. The people from Rio de Janeiro, the country's fun and tourism capital, do not think much of the folks from São Paulo, whom they consider too serious and business-like. Neither do bureaucrats from Brasilia think much of São Paulo's inhabitants—which is one reason the country is in trouble.

Rio de Janeiro, a city snuggled into the side of the **Great Escarpment,** climbs up into tall mountains from the shore, giving the city incredible views as well as lovely beaches. Rio's most famous landmark is **Pão de Açucar** (Sugarloaf Mountain), which guards the entrance to Guanabara Bay (you can take a cable car to the top). Another important site is the great statue of **Christo Rey** (Christ the King) on top of the 2,250-foot **Corcovado Mountain** (which you can reach via cog rail).

Yet another landmark is **Copacabana Beach,** where both Cariocas and foreigners take the waters. Rio's lovely tree-shaded streets are covered with mosaics of multicolored stone, and the city is graced by parks, including **Parca Paris. Maracana Stadium** is the largest sports arena in the world, site of hard-fought soccer games.

Then, too, is the mayhem of **Carnival,** a celebration that begins the Friday before Ash Wednesday. The festivities feature parades and balls, during which beautifully costumed dancing and singing groups from different (often wretchedly poor) neighborhoods compete for prizes and glory. Many of the dancers save money all year to afford their spangled, feathered, and brightly colored ensembles.

Almost as exciting is the celebration of New Year in Rio, when just before midnight, white-robed worshippers march with candles to the beaches to make offerings to Iemanja, the goddess of the sea. At midnight, firecrackers are set off, and, amid cries and songs, the followers of the goddess rush into the sea bearing flowers and gifts.

If you can't be in Rio for one of these festivals, you can enjoy the city's other attractions: the beach, the casino, the golf course, and shopping (for fashionable clothing, which is cheap here, jewelry, and plastic surgery, inevitably a big specialty in this land of body-conscious hedonists).

São Salvador da Bahia de Todos os Santos (usually referred to as Salvador de Bahia) has the most interesting culture of any Brazilian city, a melange of Portuguese, African, and Indian folklore. You can watch African voodoo and

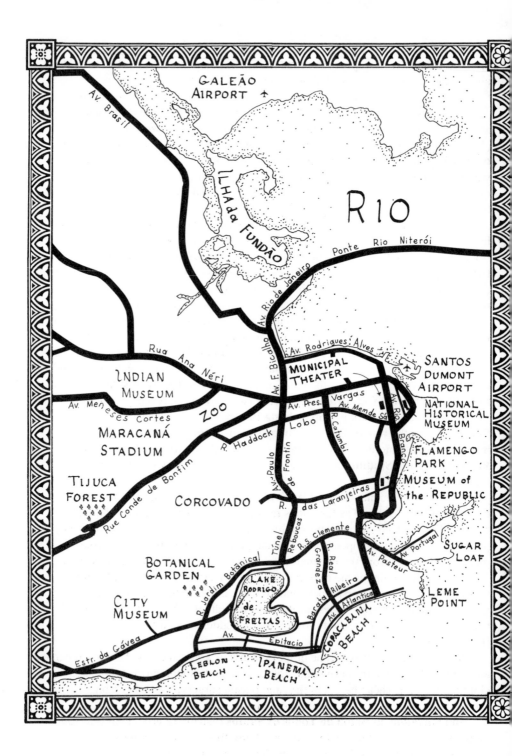

dancing festivals, many of which are held precisely for the entertainment of travelers.

Salvador de Bahia is where the braided string fetish was invented. (You can wear a fetish like a bracelet. Make a wish, then tie the strings around your wrist. If you wear the fetish until it rots, your wish will come true.) The city's primary site is the **Salvador Elevador,** a 234-foot landmark that links the old and new parts of the city.

The strongest remnants of the African culture are in the northeastern part of the country. This is also where you'll find the poorest land, depleted by intensive cultivation of sugarcane, and the most historic cities. Here is **Recife,** the Venice of Brazil, with its canals on three rivers. A suburb of Recife, **Olinda,** is a beautiful colonial town built during the Dutch occupation of this area under Maurice of Nassau.

Portuguese and Dutch Jews fearing the Inquisition fled Recife after the Portuguese recaptured the city and took shelter in Peter Stuyvesant's Nieuw Amsterdam (which later became New York).

Ouro Preto, a gold-rush town, is a baroque architectural treasure house still, full of carved wood and soapstone created by the famous Brazilian sculptor Aleijaninho and members of his school.

Manaus, on the Amazon, is a major inland city, built by the great 19th-century rubber barons (many of whom were partly Indian). It has a huge and deserted opera house and a great flea market.

Brazil's leading export is coffee, which gives you an idea of what you should drink here. Another popular beverage is wine, which is not at all bad; the beer is quite good, too.

The national dish is a stew of beans, meats, and sausages called *feijoada,* which exists in dozens of regional variations, all usually delicious.

Shopping is a pleasure in Brazil. The fashions, starting with the barest of bikinis, are stunning exercises in hedonism. Shoes, handbags, and other leather goods are good quality and inexpensive. Agate, malachite, and marble are carved into bookends, ashtrays, bowls, and vases—perfect souvenirs except for their weight. International entertainers unable to export their fees from Brazil (because of exchange controls) buy huge emerald jewels—which they sell at a profit when they return home. So if you are in the market for emeralds, this is the place—at least according to soprano Beverly Sills.

Shopping at Brazil's handicraft markets can be tricky. Much of the African-inspired carving you'll find is fake, made for the tourist market. Fake, too, are the voodoo charms and intricately assembled pictures and ashtrays made out of butterfly wings, colored woods, and seashells that you will be pressured to buy. But carved wood in the form of bowls is usually a good value. Buy this stuff only if it pleases you—and don't allow the poverty of the surroundings make you feel obligated to pay the asking price. ❧

BRITISH ISLES

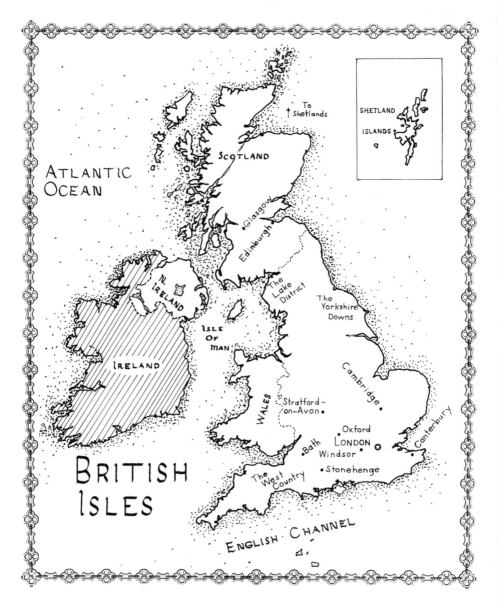

Britain is the least exotic place in the world for U.S. tourists to visit, offering an embarrassment of riches we cannot summarize in a short space. We are ready to send you off on your own, because our common language makes Britain an easy destination for American travelers.

Once in Britain, the place you want to head for depends on which aspect of our common history and culture attracts you. Intellectuals should go to Oxford or Cambridge; thespians to Shaftesbury Road or Stratford-upon-Avon; British history buffs to Blenheim, Hastings, or the Tower of London; U.S. history buffs to Ply-

---

EMBASSY: *3100 Massachusetts Ave. N.W., Washington, DC 20008; (202)462-1340.*

SYSTEM OF GOVERNMENT: Parliamentary constitutional monarchy. Power lies in the hands of the prime minister, not the queen.

ETHNIC GROUPS: British; West Indians; Indians; Pakistanis.

RELIGIOUS GROUPS: Members of the Church of England; Roman Catholics; Presbyterians.

LANGUAGES: English; Welsh; Gaelic.

POPULATION: 56.437 million.

AREA: 94,266 square miles (243,977 square kilometers); slightly smaller than Oregon.

CAPITAL: London (population 6.765 million).

TERRAIN: Meadow or pasture, 50%; arable, 30%; waste or urban, 12%; forest, 7%; and inland water, 1%. Mostly rolling land, rising to the uplands of southern Scotland. The lowlands are in the center of Scotland.

CLIMATE: Generally mild and temperate. The weather is subject to frequent changes but to few extremes of temperature (the temperature rarely rises above 90 degrees Fahrenheit in the summer and rarely drops below 14 degrees Fahrenheit in the winter).

TELECOMMUNICATIONS
  Country Code: 44.
  Time Zone: +5 hours Eastern Standard Time.

Code of Capital: 1.

LOCAL/NATIONAL AIRLINES: Aer Lingus, *(800)223-6537;* **Air France,** *(800)237-2747;* **American Trans Airs,** *(800)225-2995;* **British Airways,** *(800)247-9297;* **British Caledonian Airways,** *(800)231-0270;* **Continental Airlines,** *(800)231-0856;* **Council Charter,** *(212)661-0311;* **Delta,** *(800)221-1212;* **Icelandair,** *(800)223-5500;* **Northwest Airlines,** *(800)447-4747;* and **TWA,** *(800)892-4141.*

RAILROAD OFFICE IN THE UNITED STATES: BritRail Travel International, *630 Third Ave., New York, NY 10017; (212)599-5400.*

U.S. CONSULATE IN COUNTRY: *24/31 Grosvenor Square, London, W.I.; tel. (44-1)499-9000.*

CURRENCY: Pound. No limit on import or export.

GROSS NATIONAL PRODUCT: $554.6 billion (in 1986).

WORK FORCE: Services, 64%; manufacturing and engineering, 26%; agriculture, 1.7%.

OUR QUALITY OF LIFE RANKING: 75.44.

VISA REQUIREMENTS: A visa is not required.

TOURIST OFFICE IN THE UNITED STATES: British Tourist Authority, *40 W. 57th St., New York, NY 10019; (212)581-4708.*

mouth; and archeology history buffs to Stonehenge.

Even if you limit yourself to **London,** the number of destinations is great. Those interested in finance enjoy visiting downtown, with its banks and brokerage houses, while those interested in government go to **Westminster,** for the debates at Parliament and 10 Downing Street. Monarchists go to see the changing of the guard at **Buckingham Palace** and the crown jewels in the **Tower of London.** Flower lovers head for **Kew;** panda and monkey lovers for the **Regents Park Zoo.** Scientists go to **Greenwich** and the **British Museum,** while art lovers head for the **National Gallery** and the **Tate.** Sailors go to **Nelson's Column;** architects to **St. Paul's Cathedral** and the **Wren** churches. Those in search of a good time head for **Soho** or **Piccadilly Circus,** where you can buy bodies of various sexes, drugs, and trouble. Shoppers hit **Harrods** and **Oxford Street**—or posh **Jermyn Street** and **Savile Row,** depending on their purses. Antique hunters hit **Petticoat Lane, Portobello Road,** and the **silver vaults.**

Don't expect London to feel like Dickens or Conan Doyle. **Scotland Yard** no longer is the headquarters of the police. Sherlock Holmes' address on Baker Street does not exist. Hansom cabs are gone, as is the city's infamous fog (it was caused by burning coal). Instead of picturesque cockneys and Jack the Ripper, the **East End** is now home to Pakistanis and yuppie gentrification.

But if London has become less like its literary image over the years, other parts of Britain have changed less. So you must fashion your itinerary to match your tastes. Different parts of Britain attract gardeners and golfers, sailors and fishermen, hikers, hunters, and the horsey set (who can choose from steeplechasing, flat racing, polo, and foxhunting). You can go on photo safari among the lions at **Longleat;** you can visit the ruins of a **Cistercian abbey** amidst the Yorkshire moors. You can ferry down the **Thames** or cross the **Firth of Forth**; you can travel by car or bus or horse and cart or punt or canal boat or airplane. You can visit **Devon** for the primroses at Easter or hit a haunted house at Halloween or spend *A Child's Christmas* in **Wales.**

Wales is also the place for choral singing and castles. For offbeat theater, health food, and old pubs where you can taste vintage Scotch, go to **Edinburgh;** for Victorian architecture and great museums, head for its archrival, **Glasgow;** for 18th-century architecture and great dining, take off for **Bath** or **Brighton.** If you love Lorna Doone or the *Hound of the Baskervilles* or *Tess of the Durbervilles* or apple cider or strawberries and clotted cream, visit the **West Country;** fans of the Brontës and James Herriot and real ale head for **Yorkshire;** Du Maurierians and painters go to **Cornwall;** Wordsworthians hit the **Lake Country;** fans of Dorothy Sayers, bird watchers, and sailors go to **Norfolk;** while those who read Scott and Burns, Boswell and Adam Smith must go to **Scotland.**

Obviously, this guide can give only a once-over-lightly view of British history, which began during the early Stone Age (some 25,000 years ago). Traceable history began with the arrival of the Celts, who had mastered the art of working metal, about 500 B.C., a people whose language lives on in Ireland, the Scottish Highlands, and Wales. Julius Caesar and the Romans came in 55 B.C. and left their marks on the language and the landscape, founding most of the major cities in

England, building **Hadrian's Wall** to stop attacks from the Scots and Picts to the north, and changing the country's land-ownership and building systems. You still can see Hadrian's Wall, as well as the ruins of Roman villas. (Unlike many modern British houses, Roman villas had central heating, piped in from a boiler under the hollow tiles of the floor.)

With the collapse of the Roman Empire, Britain was prey to invasion from Germanic tribes, including the Angles, the Saxons, the Vikings, the Danes, and the Norsemen, whose various linguistic traditions live on in the names of villages throughout Britain (and of course villages in the United States as well). It is thanks to the differences among these tribes that mastering the English language is such a problem. These tribes ultimately united—just in time to be conquered in 1066 by the Normans (descendents of other Vikings who had conquered Normandy in France).

The great power of regional rulers called barons forced the Norman kings to accept the Magna Carta in 1215. It also forced the rise of the first parliament a half-century later and acted as the foundation of U.S. democracy. There followed many wars—to assert claims to France and to decide between rival claimants to the English throne (which you can learn about by reading Shakespeare). Henry Tudor, a Welsh outsider, settled the matter of succession and united Wales to the throne. His son, Henry VIII, broke with Rome and established Protestantism as the dominant religion of his country.

The great age of English literature and naval power came under the daughter of Henry VIII, the first Elizabeth, whose forces defeated the Spanish Armada sent to conquer England for Spain and the Catholic Church in 1588. During her reign, Shakespeare wrote his plays, and explorers laid claim to American lands. The state of Virginia was named for the queen.

Her heir united the crowns of Scotland and England. His son, Charles I, was beheaded in 1649 during the English Civil War, when Britain experimented with a republican government under Oliver Cromwell. During the 1660 Restoration, the monarchy was given back to the Stuarts, who were succeeded by William of Orange and Queen Mary, who conquered Ireland. The juxtaposition of the crosses of St. George, St. Andrew, and St. David (England, Scotland, and Wales) produced the Union Jack, Britain's flag.

The monarchy then passed to obscure German cousins of Queen Mary, good Protestants who could not speak English. These were the Hanoverians, who managed to reduce the moral tone of the country through scandalous liaisons and to improve the musical climate by bringing over great German composers, including Handel. However, this group failed totally to understand the aspirations of Britain's colonialists in what came to be the United States.

Once they were rid of the American colonies, the British got down to the business of having an Industrial Revolution—enclosing land for sheep, dispossessing farmers, and building railroads and dark satanic mills. One result was that a lot of people left for the United States.

Under Queen Victoria (1837-1901), the monarchy cleaned up its act, and some reforms in political and factory systems took effect. Victoria was empress of India,

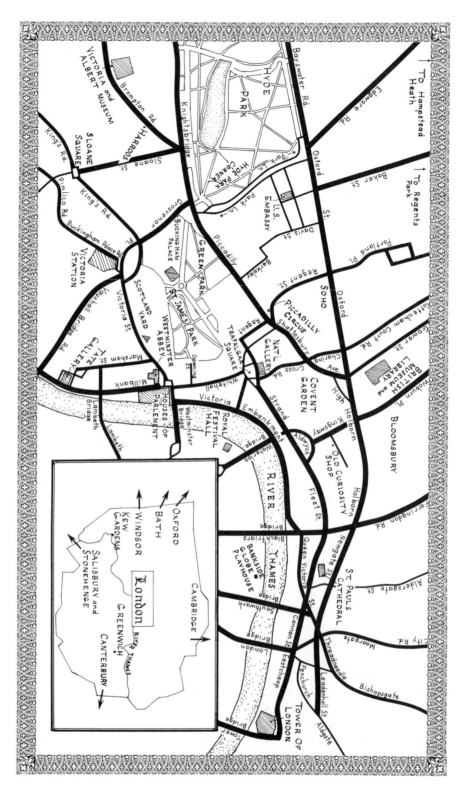

and during her reign the sun never set on the British Empire or the Union Jack.

After Victoria's death and World War I, such innovations as women's suffrage, a Labor Party, and Home Rule for most of Ireland came about. British wealth was further eroded by World War II, after which most of the remaining colonies were given their independence.

Modern Britain is part of the Common Market. It is building a tunnel under the English Channel to close links with the continent of Europe. But the country is far from unified. Regional dialects are pronounced, and you may have trouble understanding people from Yorkshire, Glaswegan Scots, and some Cockneys. The regions where the people speak most like Americans are Norfolk and Devon.

The prosperous and overpopulated southeast around London, where most Britons live, is worlds removed from the rest of the country, which remains rural and much poorer—and generally much more beautiful. However, the poorest parts of the country are the least picturesque: the earliest industrialized areas; the Midlands; the mine towns of Scotland, Wales, and County Durham; the blighted shipbuilding cities of Merseyside (which is where the Beatles came from); and the Scottish west coast. Northern Ireland is another bleak area.

Geographically, Britain is varied, with lochs and glacial mountains in Scotland; incredible hilly relief in the mountains and ports of Devon; flat, sandy land cut with canals in East Anglia; lakes in the Lake District; and wild and rough moors in Yorkshire.

The highest mountain in England is in the **Lake District: Scapell Pike,** topped by Snowdonia in Wales and by Ben Nevis in Scotland, the watershed of the Scottish Highlands, the highest point in the British Isles. But Scapell Pike is only 4,406 feet high—a challenge for climbers, but not the Alps, not a place to ski or gasp—which is why the British invented vacations in Switzerland.

Britain also has islands. Off the southwest are the **Scilly Isles,** where the Gulf Stream warms the climate so much that palm trees grow. But as a general rule, you don't want to travel to Britain to see its beaches. Off Scotland are the **Hebrides** to the west and the **Shetlands** to the north (this is where North Sea oil is produced). Between Britain and France are the **Channel Islands,** which are dependencies of the duke of Normandy (that is to say the queen) with their own separate governments. Between Scotland and Ireland is the large **Isle of Man,** also self-governing. Both the Channel Islands and Man are centers of offshore banking.

British food is generally as bad as its reputation, with a few exceptions. British fast food is horrible. But thank heavens for breakfast, a proper cholesterol-laden meal that gives you a good start on the day, with bacon, eggs, cereal, and tea. Try kippers (a smoked herring), another fine first meal. If you insist on coffee, be prepared for it to be weak, instant, and served already mixed with milk.

Fish and chips are fun and taste good even when made with frozen fish. Great roast beef with all the trimmings can be bought at carveries in several large London hotels and at **Simpsons.**

British cheese is about as interesting and varied as American cheese, which is to say it's boring—with the exception of Stilton, which is a smelly blue cheese you can develop a nose for.

Wherever you eat in Britain, you'll notice bottles of A-1 sauce, mustard, vinegar, and Worcestershire sauce on the table. The reason is that much of the food is unpalatable without these things.

For French cooking, you should hop the Channel and try the real thing. However, chances are you won't be off to Delhi very soon, so we suggest you try Indian food in London, especially the curry. Try *prawn biryani* (rice and shrimp), *tandoori* chicken, or *murgh ghosht* (lamb stew). Eat *chutney* and *papadams* (crisp breads) with your meal.

British teas are world-famous. You do not want high tea—this is what children are served before they go to bed; it's comparable to what we call supper. Afternoon tea involves thin sandwiches made with watercress or cucumbers, splendid rich cakes (fruitcake-like cakes), and, of course, tea. The British drink it with milk, not lemon. If you get to the West Country, try cream tea, which features buttery clotted cream, extra calories that you dollop onto deep dish hot apple pie and other delicacies.

The British are also famous for their beer. They drink it warm. When shopping in Britain, you'll find many clothing bargains for men. British tailoring is world-famous; if you want a posh hand-sewn suit or a made-to-measure shirt, this is the place. However, shopping for women is more difficult. The only real buys are flowered hats, tartan skirts, cashmere sweaters, and tweed suits—which don't fit every woman's tastes.

When shopping for clothing, keep the following guidelines in mind. British sizes are less flattering than those in the United States—an American lady who wears a size 12 needs a British size 14. For shoes, the general rule of thumb is to take two away from your U.S. size to get the British equivalent.

The country's flea markets are good places to look for bargains, especially old silver (if you are serious about silver shopping, invest in a guide to hallmarks from a British bookstore, such as W.H. Smith, and a magnifying glass).

British books tend to be cheaper than American, and secondhand books are great bargains. Bath bridges, trivets, toast racks, loofahs, table pads, wicker shopping carts, floral soaps, fruitcakes, tea cozies, linen towels, and Scottish short-bread are all great British gift items. (If you don't know what these things are, ask—it will improve your vocabulary.)

The British currency is the pound, now mercifully divided into 100 pence, thereby ending a British tradition that forced foreigners to learn higher mathematics when counting their change.

Officially, the British use the metric system. However, they still drink in pints (which are about 20% bigger than U.S. pints), and they still shop in pounds and ounces. ❦

CANADA

$\mathbf{T}$he easiest way for most people from the United States to take a foreign trip is to escape to Canada (and, as a result, Canada is the leading foreign destination for U.S. travelers). Unlike the United States, Canada uses the metric system, making transactions in that country seem foreign to Americans. Canadians drive more recklessly than people from our side of the border. And although Canada's currency is the dollar (and cents), the Canadian dollar is worth less than the U.S. dollar, forcing you to deal with currency conversions.

With nearly 3.9-million square miles of territory, this is the second-largest country in the world. Although it is foreign, it is not terribly exotic (except in the areas where French is spoken).

Most of Canada's 25-million people live within 300 miles of the country's border with the United States (despite the vast reaches of territory), because the border zone has the warmest weather. The only exception is **Newfoundland,** which

39

is warmed by the Gulf Stream. Unless you're interested in wilderness or Eskimos, you probably won't be interested in these frozen northern regions.

Furthermore, in addition to the frozen northern areas, other parts of Canada are of little interest to travelers for other reasons—for example, the Canadian extension of our own Great Plains. If you've seen one wheatfield, you've seen them all.

The first Canadians were Indians and Eskimos, who make up 1.6% of the population today (the Eskimos call themselves Inuit in their language). The date when European settlers first arrived on the Canadian coast is disputed, but both Norsemen from Greenland and Irish carraghs may have arrived more than 1,000

EMBASSY: *1746 Massachusetts Ave. N.W., Washington, DC 20036; (202)785-1400.*

SYSTEM OF GOVERNMENT: Confederation with parliamentary democracy. Queen Elizabeth is the head of state.

ETHNIC GROUPS: British, 44.6%; French, 28.7%; other Europeans, 23%; indigenous Indians and Eskimos, 1.5%.

RELIGIOUS GROUPS: Roman Catholics, 46%; members of the United Church of Canada, 18%; members of the Anglican Church of Canada, 12%; other Protestants, 10%.

LANGUAGES: English; French.

POPULATION: 25.390 million.

AREA: 3.85 million square miles (9.976 million square kilometers); second-largest country in the world.

CAPITAL: Ottawa (population 695,000).

TERRAIN: Varied. Mountainous in the east and west, interior plains, and abundant lakes.

CLIMATE: Temperate to arctic.

TELECOMMUNICATIONS
Country Code: None.
Time Zone: Varies.
Code of Capital: 613.

LOCAL/NATIONAL AIRLINES: Canadian Airlines International, *(800)426-*

7000, and most major U.S. airlines.

RAILROAD OFFICE IN THE UNITED STATES: None. Contact **VIA Rail,** *P.O. Box 1358, Montreal, Quebec H5A 1H2; tel. (514)871-1331.*

U.S. CONSULATE IN COUNTRY: *100 Wellington St., Ottawa;* **U.S. Consulates General,** Calgary, Alberta; Halifax, Nova Scotia; Montreal, Quebec; Toronto, Ontario; Vancouver, British Columbia; and Winnipeg, Manitoba.

CURRENCY: Canadian dollar. No limit on import or export.

GROSS NATIONAL PRODUCT: $367 billion (in 1986).

WORK FORCE: Services and government, 39.7%; trade, 17.6%; manufacturing, 17.3%; transportation and communications, 8.2%; finance, insurance, and real estate, 5.7%; construction, 4.9%; agriculture, 4.2%; mining, forestry, fishing, and quarrying, 2.4%.

OUR QUALITY OF LIFE RANKING: 84.92.

VISA REQUIREMENTS: Neither a passport nor a visa is required for U.S. tourists, but you should carry personal identification (a birth certificate, a naturalization certificate, or a valid or expired passport).

years ago. The first official European discoverer was John Cabot, who in 1497 sailed to Nova Scotia and Newfoundland (which he named). Although he sailed under the British flag, Cabot, like Columbus, was Italian.

The next major wave of exploration began in the 1530s, with French explorers, such as Jacques Cartier and Samuel de Champlain. The latter founded the first mission at **Port Royal,** Nova Scotia (in 1604) and the first European settlement at **Quebec** (in 1608). In 1663, Louis XIV proclaimed Canada a French province, which encouraged French settlers. But a mere seven years later, the Hudson Bay Company was founded to encourage British settlement, laying the basis for the French-English rivalry in Canada that continues to this day. In 1759 (during the course of a war that began in Europe), the British decisively defeated the French on the Plains of Abraham and took Quebec. As part of the Peace of Amiens, the British promised to respect French linguistic rights and freedom of religion. They didn't.

Tories who opposed the American Revolution emigrated to Canada, as did many Highland Scots impoverished by the 19th-century enclosures. More people speak Scots Gaelic in Canada today (usually as a second language) than in Scotland. Although the newly founded United States had territorial ambitions in the north (Montreal was taken by the Continental Army during the Revolution), the border finally was fixed and respected under treaty.

In 1867, the British North American Act granted Canada dominion status, and new provinces were created as the population growth warranted it. However, most of the frozen north (except the frozen north of the historic province of Quebec) is not divided into provinces but handled as two territories: the **Yukon** and the **Northwest** (which accounts for about 40% of the land mass). The 10 provinces have local governments similar to those of U.S. states. The central government is led by the prime minister, who, as in Britain, is the leader of the party that wins the largest number of seats in the House of Commons. Unlike Britain's House of Lords, the upper house is elected in Canada and called the senate. The chief of state is the Queen of England, represented by a governor general for Canada.

A visit to the Canadian capital in **Ottawa** is a good way for Anglophiles to gain a quick introduction to Canadian culture. The houses of parliament of Ottawa's **Parliament Hill,** as in London, are built in pseudo-Gothic style—not the Greek Revival design of the U.S. Capitol (which evokes Athenian democracy). This architecture has a message. Canada, the buildings are saying, is not a democracy but a constitutional monarchy. The guards wear bearskins and red coats and perform a precision drill when they change places. Even the grass looks greener and somewhat British.

Ottawa is a surprisingly rural place, thanks to several public forests and the **Rideau Canal** (which is used by cyclists or cross-country skiers, canoers or ice skaters, depending on the season). The downtown **Spark Street Mall** combines shopping with sculpture and live entertainment with movies. Shop here for Canadian handicrafts. **Byward Market** is a renovated 19th-century market for farmers, craftsmen, artists, ethnic food stores, and restaurants. Mounties parade during the **Royal Canadian Mounted Police Musical Ride.**

41

A trip to the province of **Quebec** (Quebec city, Montreal, and the hinterland, notably the Laurentians) is a way for Francophile tourists to save trans-Atlantic fares and still get a taste of France. Quebecois are fiercely protective of their linguistic rights, which are finally being recognized under Canadian laws. The best time to visit Quebec is June 24, during the **Fête de St. Jean Baptiste,** when parades, markets, balls, and fairs are held.

Downtown **Montreal** has been transformed in recent years, with the construction of a metro, covered shopping malls (remember those winters), and high-rise buildings. **Place Ville Marie** is the oldest underground complex; **Westmount Square** is the center for fashion; and **Place des Arts** is where the Montreal opera and symphony perform. All these spots are linked by the metro and underground walkways. In downtown Montreal, French is spoken, but in some of the outlying suburbs (Westmount and near McGill University, for example), English is more widely spoken than French.

Old Montreal is dominated by the huge **Basilica of Notre Dame,** built in 1827-1829. It has a splendid pre-Vatican II altar with fine wood carvings, stained-glass windows depicting the history of French settlement, and one of the best organs in North America. **Place Jacques Cartier,** a cobblestoned square, by day houses a flower market, by night outdoor cafés and restaurants.

The city of Quebec is less modern, with narrow hilly streets winding down to the water. Around **Place Royale,** near the river, where Champlain built his house, is the best collection of 17th- and 18th-century houses in North America. The two you must see (in addition to the **Eglise Notre Dame des Victoires**) are the **Maison Fornel** and the **Maison Soumandre** (now the tourist office).

In the upper town (**Ville Haute**), the oldest square is **Place d'Armes.** Built into the side of the cliffs (on the site of the original fortress) is **Château Frontenac,** a great hotel and site of the Quebec Conference of World War II. You can visit the citadel and the **Plains of Abraham.**

Toronto, Canada's financial capital, is lively, thanks to the burst of art, theater, and music that has taken place in recent years. It looks much like a U.S. city, with a revived waterfront, a Chinatown, skyscrapers, office buildings, and an ethnic market (**Kensington**). Visit the city's art gallery, with its Henry Moore sculptures, and **Yorkville,** a Victorian neighborhood that is being revived. However, while it is cosmopolitan for Canada, this is not a world-scale metropolis. Of course it is a good entry point for the U.S.-Canadian natural wonder: **Niagara Falls.**

Calgary, site of the 1988 Winter Olympics, is best known for its annual rodeo, called the **Calgary Stampede.** It offers yet another Canadian solution for keeping pedestrians and cars from interfering with each other: overhead ramps. During the Stampede, beer-laden cowboys sometimes forget that the streets are no longer filled with horses.

This is a town for Indian art (at the **Glenbow-Alberta Institute**), for nearly extinct wild animals (at Calgary's natural zoo), and for pioneer villages (at **Heritage Park** or the outlying town of **High River**).

Along with the cowboy image of the Stampede, Calgary's drawling accent and its reputation for lawlessness help sell the city to tourists. However, the city retains some of its authenticity despite all the visitors. It is still possible, for example, to find and haul home a pair of dropped moose antlers in the city's **Fish Creek Park**—should your tastes run to dropped moose antlers.

Vancouver is an increasingly popular travel destination—because of, rather than in spite of, its foggy, damp climate. This climate, which is the result of Vancouver's fabulous situation on the edge of a peninsula with water all around, makes the grass and flowers grow well—and the city's public gardens are magnificent. This city is a sailor's delight, a great place for fishing (salmon in particular), and the site of Canada's best aquarium (complete with killer whales).

Vancouver is relatively newly settled. It has a German neighborhood (**Robson Street**), and in all of North America only San Francisco has a larger Chinese community.

Canada offers skiing at all levels, from the genteel slopes of the country's oldest (and most elegant) resort, **Mt. Tremblant,** in Quebec Province, to **Branff's** blizzard-torn high slopes, which offer powder snow in May. You can cross-country ski in the **Laurentian Mountains** near Quebec, inside the city limits of Montreal, or in the foothills of the **Rocky Mountains** in the **Cariboos,** the **Selkirks,** and other areas of **British Columbia.** Other sports popular among Canadians include golf, fishing, white-water rafting, camping, and climbing.

Eastern Canada is the waterman's delight. Here you can sail, swim, or stroll amidst pretty coves, pine forests stretching to the beach, lobster ports, and villages inhabited by Scottish settlers, refugees from New England, and Indians. In French, *cocagne* means the land of earthly delights, Utopia, the Garden of Eden. The only place in the world the French have been bold enough to name **Cocagne** is the tiny village of that name in **New Brunswick** (13 miles north of Shediac), which was settled by refugees from the expulsion from Nova Scotia in 1755 (if you want to know more, read Longfellow).

If you don't sail, you can spend your time in eastern Canada island hopping. Ferries crisscross among the islands off the U.S. and Canadian mainlands. While ferrying from island to island, you may wind up in France—if you make it to islands off the southern coast of Newfoundland, called **St. Pierre and Miquelon.** (This group of islands numbers eight, not two, as the name suggests.) By the way, Newfoundland is perfectly pleasant in summer, despite its reputation.

St. Pierre and Miquelon have been overseas *départements* of France since 1816 and have long been used for smuggling (most recently during Prohibition) and spying (most recently by the Vichy government of France during the early days of World War II).

It is difficult to give guidelines for shopping in Canada, in part because of uncertainties about the exchange rate. Inuit soapstone carvings (which curiously resemble Japanese netsuke) are the most attractive native handicrafts. Furs are said to be cheaper in Canada than in the United States. Because of the country's strong Scottish heritage, it is cheaper and easier to buy tweeds and clan ties in Canada than in the United States (if the idea of walking around with a tartan tie is unappealing, consider buying a more discrete cravat with only the clan's symbol).

Eating in Canada is similar to eating in the United States, although the steaks are better. In the west, try moose steak or elk pie. Seafood is good, particularly in the east. And no less an authority than the French newspaper *Le Monde* has claimed that the best fish restaurant in the Americas is the **Admiral Fishing Restaurant** in St. Johns, Newfoundland.

Typically Quebecois dishes include *tourte,* a covered meat pie. The Canadians have their own version of bouillabaisse (which has more garlic), as well as their own chowder (with lots of butter and milk). Canadian Camembert is disappointing. Of course, every ethnic gastronomic option you can think of is offered in the large Canadian cities.

Changing money in Canada is no problem, because the city is filled with banks—particularly in Quebec, where sometimes main intersections have four banks, one on each corner. And most banks and credit unions, even in the most out-of-the-way places, are able to change U.S. dollars into Canadian dollars and to cash traveler's checks. ❧

CHINA

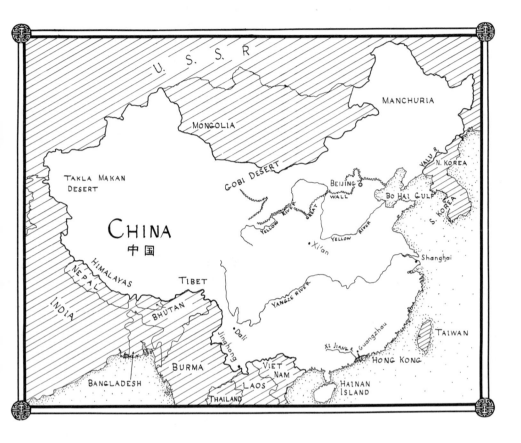

The only man-made artifact on earth that can be seen from the moon is the **Great Wall of China,** one of the seven wonders of Asia. China also has a second of the seven, the **terra-cotta warriors of Xi'an,** which are not visible from the moon, and indeed became visible on earth only after excavations in 1974. Depending on which experts you consult, China may also have a third wonder, the **Forbidden City,** the Imperial Palace of Beijing (formerly called Peking).

Given its multiple attractions, including its huge size (just short of 3.7-million square miles, the third-largest country in the world), population (1.008-billion people, give or take a few hundred thousand, the largest population in the world), and its cuisine (one of the world's best), China is becoming an increasingly popular tourist destination. And the canny Chinese, heirs of one of the world's oldest civilizations, are doing their best to attract more tourists and to separate them from their money. They've set up a system of double prices: one scale for the home folks, and one scale for foreigners. Unless you look Chinese and can speak Chinese, you will be a victim of this system.

The Chinese are like the Russians in claiming to have invented everything; the difference is that the Chinese really did invent a lot. Moveable type, silk, firecrackers, noodles, time-keeping, porcelain, tea-drinking, the compass, paper, and—alas—gunpowder are among the things the world owes to China. This is a tremendously old culture. The first human beings, Peking man, date back 500,000 years. Stone Age man lived in the valley of the Yellow River 5,000 years ago. The oldest written traces of the Mandarin writing system date back to 221 B.C.

EMBASSY: *2300 Connecticut Ave. N.W., Washington, DC 20008; (202)328-2500.*

SYSTEM OF GOVERNMENT: Communist.

ETHNIC GROUPS: Han Chinese, 94%; Mongol, Korean, Manchu, and others, 6%.

RELIGIOUS GROUPS: Confucianists; Buddhists; Taoists; official atheists.

LANGUAGES: Mandarin (official); regional dialects; minority languages.

POPULATION: 1.045 billion (in 1986).

AREA: 3.692 million square miles (9.561 million square kilometers).

CAPITAL: Beijing (population 8,487 million).

TERRAIN: Varied. Two-thirds of the land area is mountainous or desert. Low plains in the lower reaches of the Yellow and Yangze rivers.

CLIMATE: Very cold, dry winters and extremely hot summers. Southern regions have milder climates.

TELECOMMUNICATIONS
   Country Code: 86.
   Time Zone: +13 hours Eastern Standard Time (Beijing).
   Code of Capital: 1.

LOCAL/NATIONAL AIRLINES: Civil Aviation Administration of China, *(212)371-9898;* **United Airlines,** *(800)241-6522;* **Japan Airlines,** *(800)525-3663;* and **Cathay Pacific,** *(800)663-8833.*

U.S. CONSULATE IN COUNTRY: *Guang Hua Lu 17, Beijing; tel. (86-1)52-2033.*

CURRENCY: Yuan. Travelers may not import or export currency.

GROSS NATIONAL PRODUCT: $318 billion (in 1984).

WORK FORCE: Agriculture and fishing, 62.5%; manufacturing, 16.7%; services and commerce, 12.2%; government, 3.8%; construction, 1.7%.

OUR QUALITY OF LIFE RANKING: 42.20.

VISA REQUIREMENTS: A passport and a visa are required. To qualify for a visa, you must show a letter of confirmation from China International Travel Service (CITS) or an invitation from an individual or institution in China. Submit the visa application to the embassy or consulate in Houston, San Francisco, New York, Chicago, or Los Angeles. You also must show a round-trip ticket and a hotel reservation when you enter the country.

TOURIST OFFICE IN THE UNITED STATES: China International Travel Service, *60 E. 42nd St., Suite 3126, New York, NY 10165; (212)867-0271.*

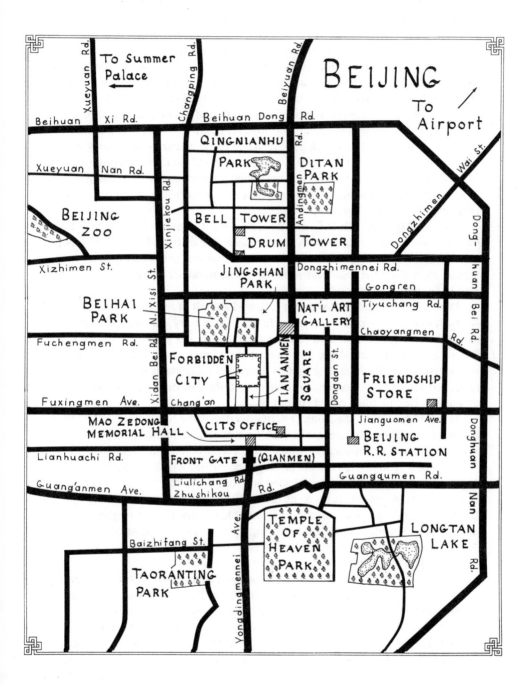

The Chinese writing system is peculiar, which helps explain why it has survived. Unlike most other writing systems, it doesn't use letters to spell out words. Instead, it uses ideograms or symbols, each standing for a word. This peculiarity has helped written Chinese remain the same despite considerable variations in pronunciation over time and place. Communication in writing is easy between Guangzhou (formerly Canton) and Beijing, for example—even though when people talk to each other, their dialects are mutually incomprehensible.

Older than the written language is the system of dynastic rule that used it. The first Chinese dynasty was the Xia (2000 to 1500 B.C.). The first strong dynasty was the Qin (221 to 206 B.C.), which gave its name to the country (the dynasty was formally known as the Ch'in). This dynasty abandoned the idea of burying servants live with their deceased masters and substituted pottery figures—including the Xi'an hoard. During the rule of the Qin Dynasty, the written language was codified, fixing the writings of Confucius.

The Han Dynasty (206 B.C. to A.D. 220) gave its name to the people of China, 94% of whom consider themselves Han Chinese. (Apart from Tibetans, Mongols, and Uighurs, the remaining 2% are members of minority tribes that flourish in the tropical areas along the southeastern border.) The Buddhist religion came to China from India during this period.

During the years of civil war that followed the fall of the Hans, the **Great Wall** was built to protect population centers. In the 13th century, the Mongol hordes under Ghengis Khan began their relentless expansion. His grandson, Kublai Khan, decreed a stately treasure dome and founded the Mongul empire, which stretched from Russia to all of China. During this time, the first contacts with Europe were made, and Marco Polo, a Venetian, visited the **Palace of the Great Khan** in present-day Beijing (then called Buluc).

In the 14th century, the Ming Dynasty overthrew the Mongols. The Mings, in turn, were overthrown by the last non-Chinese rulers, the Manchus, who ruled from 1644 to 1911 and who made Han Chinese men wear pigtails to humiliate them.

The opening to foreign traders produced problems, which resulted in the Opium War in 1839. China was defeated and forced to allow foreign traders and drug importers increased access to its market. The Western powers and Russia collected concessions and territory, including Manchuria, Hong Kong, and Macao—which remain controlled by foreign powers. In 1894, Japan defeated China and won control of Korea. The Boxer Rebellion (1900) was another unsuccessful attempt to drive out the exploitative foreigners.

The republic established in 1912 was unstable and racked by civil war among rival warlords. In 1920, the Kuomintang Nationalist Party, first under Sun Yat-sen and then under Chiang Kai-shek, gradually took power. Initially, the Chinese communists (led by Chou En-lai and Mao Zedong) supported the Kuomintang (at Moscow's orders), but by 1928 Chiang had conquered the country and Beijing and had proceeded to wipe out the communists, who were his major rivals for power.

Meanwhile, Japan was becoming even greedier and more militaristic, and from 1931 it occupied Manchuria and set up a puppet state. The communists were forced to flee to the remote north of the country (Shaanxi) in the Long March of 1934, which few survived. Meanwhile, working down from the north, the Japanese occupied most of the industrial and port areas of China. By 1937, Chiang had begun to fight the Japanese, as had the communists. In 1946, the two victorious Chinese armies began to battle each other. Mao's forces were victorious in 1948, sending Chiang's defeated army to found the Kuomintang state of Taiwan.

Communist rule of China was wracked by foreign wars involving China (Korea, Vietnam, Laos, Kampuchea) and by Mao's revenge for the deal Stalin made with Chiang in 1927, a break with the Soviet Union.

Recent Chinese history has been rendered inscrutable (not only for Occidental observers) by internal upheavals, such as the Great Leap Forward, the Let a Thousand Flowers Bloom episode, the Cultural Revolution and the Red Guards, the Downfall of the Gang of Four, the rise of Deng Xiaoping, and the 1979 Pinyin change in how Chinese is transcribed into Western languages.

China is surrounded by mountains, desert, and the sea. The **Himalayas** to the south include the highest mountain in China and the world, **Mt. Everest** (known in China as Qomolangma), situated on the border of Chinese-occupied Tibet and Nepal. The lowest point in the country is the **Turfan Depression,** 505 feet below sea level. The country's deserts include the **Gobi** and the **Takla Makhan.** Where the border is not protected by some great natural obstacle, it is a cause for worry to the Chinese (which is why they fight with the Soviets). The classic invasion routes are via Mongolia.

Most Chinese live in the basin of land east of and protected by these natural obstacles. This area of land divides into north and south, with different climates, dialects, and agriculture in each of the two regions. Three great rivers flow through the inhabited area, all from west to east. The small **Xi Jang** waters Guangzhou; the mighty **Yangze** (renamed the Changjiang) is navigable by ocean vessels from its mouth (at Shanghai) 600 miles upstream to Wuhan and is the major transport system of China within the Great Wall; and the **Yellow River** (Huang He) has been nicknamed China's Sorrow, because it floods.

China's leading city is not the capital, Beijing, but **Shanghai,** which, with 11-million inhabitants, is the largest metropolis in the world. The air is polluted, the water undrinkable, the population cosmopolitan, rude, and commerce-minded (it had the first advertising agency of China), and the food the most varied in China. (An informant, a loyal son of Shanghai, claims that the city's cuisine, based on vegetables and seafood, cooked in sweet-and-sour sauces, is the best in China.)

People from Shanghai think themselves sophisticated and claim they feel right at home in New York or Paris. The city's sights include the former foreign enclaves of the **Bund,** a broad promenade that runs between the waterfront on the Wusong River and the old town with its bazaars, teahouses, winding streets, and spruced-up houses.

The center of the city is marked by a huge oval public park that has been stripped of its capitalistic racecourse but that still has lovely gardens, a stadium, a library, a small museum, ponds, trees, and promenades. The **Shanghai Museum of Art and History** includes some Xi'an pieces, bronze and porcelain objects of both the Han and the minority cultures, torture instruments, and huge bronze doors—it is one of the best museums in China.

Longhua Pagoda, with its 10-foot statue of Buddha and 14th-century clock, the **Jade Buddha Temple,** the **Jaiding Confucian Temple,** and **Songjiant Square Pagoda** are among the city's historic sites. You can take a ship tour of the harbor. You can visit the home of Dr. Sun Yat-sen, the tomb of his widow Soong Ching Ling, and the garden of Lu Xun, the important modern author. Here is the **Yuyuan Garden,** which inspired the Blue Willow china pattern. You can take tea in the old Wuxing Ting house at the end of the zigzag bridge over the pond, where the star-crossed lovers fled.

Most tourists go to **Beijing.** Here you can see part of the Great Wall and the Forbidden City, a huge area consisting of monastery and temple, storehouse and tower, moats, old houses, willow groves, plum orchards, monumental gates, ornamental lakes, imperial archives, museums, palaces, and **Tian'anmen Square,** the former main entrance, now the site of Red Guard demonstrations and May Day parades. It takes days and strong shoes to see this properly.

Beijing also has pagodas (including the **Temple of Heaven**), markets, shopping streets, the Catholic cathedral, which was established by the Jesuit missionary Matteo Ricci at the start of the 17th century, and the former houses of parliament.

The Great Wall once stretched more than 6,000 miles from the Yalu River to Xinjiang in the northwest, encompassing 16 Chinese provinces. Only about 60% of it still stands, from the Bohai Sea to the Gobi Desert. The section near Beijing is about 50 miles from the city and dates back only to the Ming Dynasty. Ten soldiers can march side by side along its top, as can a fast-moving Citroën.

From Beijing, you can take excursion trains or buses to see the Great Wall and the **Ming Tombs,** two of which have been excavated.

Beijing is also the home of one of the greatest styles of Chinese cooking, which has produced such goodies as the pancake (the basis of Peking duck) and dumplings. This is not rice country, but the land of wheat and millet.

Guangzhou (formerly Canton) is the business center of modern China, but it also has popular tourist sights, including a zoo featuring pandas, the oldest mosque in China, another (more recent) Catholic cathedral, a host of rather didactic historical museums, and a statue of five goats in **Yuexiu Park** (the ancestors of the people of Guangzhou, according to myth). It is from this region that most U.S. Chinese restaurateurs spring.

Visit the street market in Guangzhou. You'll be appalled at what the people are buying for food: baby deer, dogs, cats, snakes, owls, mice. This is not the sort of Chinese food we get in the United States.

Getting to **Xi'an** (formerly Sian) to see the terra-cotta warriors can be difficult. This was the old imperial capital and an important spot on the trade route. In addition to the warriors, the city is full of archeological wonders, tombs and mausoleums, many of which are still being dug out by specialists. It also has a mosque, pagodas (downtown are the **Big Wild Goose** and the **Small Wild Goose** pagodas), and a wall around what was once the old town with two famous towers, the **Bell Tower** and the **Drum Tower.** The city's final attraction is its **Golden Flower** hotel, which opened in 1986 and has been called the best in the country by *Business China.*

50

China's **Silk Road,** which runs through Uighur, Kazak, Kashgar, and other Moslem territories in Xinjiang Province, is an increasingly popular destination for foreigners (this may be at least partially because the local population looks so un-Chinese that you cannot always be spotted as a tourist). This is the area to shop not only for silk, but also for knotted carpets and jade.

Ethnic minority regions in the south around **Dali** and **Jinghong** (in Yunnan Province) are also beginning to attract tourists interested in seeing China off the beaten track. So is **Hainan Island,** the southernmost part of China, which the Chinese plan to turn into a clone of Hawaii. You should visit this island before the metamorphosis has taken place, even if accommodations are rough. As of this writing, you cannot visit another favorite of adventurous travelers, **Tibet.**

Shopping is wonderful in China (even if you do pay special tourist prices). Furs, leather goods, linens, rugs, porcelain, jewelry, scrolls, antiques (of varying antiquity), rosewood furniture, and ceramics are among the goodies to look for.

China's currency is called the renminbi (RMB) or the yuan. However, tourists must use a separate currency, which consists of Foreign Exchange Certificates (FEC). These are renminbi stamped with the letters FEC. Certain shops and other tourist facilities require that you pay with FEC. You also can use Hong Kong dollars (in the Guangzhou area) and foreign credit cards to pay for goods or services in some parts of China.

You should have a cholera shot if you are planning an extended stay in China. 🐌

COSTA RICA

$\mathbf{C}$osta Rica, located between troubled Nicaragua and troubled Panama, is an anomaly in Central America: a stable, democratic, literate country. While not exactly prosperous, Costa Rica has the highest gross national product per capita south of the Rio Grande, and its economy is not marked by the extremes of wealth and poverty common elsewhere in Latin America. As a result, it is less exotic, less Latin, and less touristy than other destinations. It is a favorite among retired Americans, of which at least 15,000 call Costa Rica home.

Because of its high mountains and fertile valleys, some people claim Costa Rica is a little Switzerland—which is going too far. Unlike the Alps, Costa Rican mountains sometimes erupt (several are active volcanoes), and instead of dairy farms, the land supports coffee plantations, banana groves, and sugarcane fields. The Costa Rican wildflower is not the edelweiss, but the jungle orchid. While Swiss neutrality is supported by the draft and the second-largest army in Western Europe, Costa Rica is supported by no army at all—another unusual phenomenon in Latin America.

Costa Rica was part of Spain until 1821. It broke away from the United Provinces of Central America in 1838. It has had democratically elected governments since 1919.

The capital, **San José,** is part of the range of high mountains and plateaus in the middle section of the country, upland from the low-lying Atlantic and Pacific coasts. This is a European-looking city, with neoclassical buildings, wooden houses with gingerbread carvings, floral balconies, public parks filled with statues, formal flowerbeds, fountains, and even a bandstand (**Parque Central**). Its airport, Juan Santamaria International, in **El Coco,** is only 10 miles (25 minutes) from downtown. Domestic flights take you to another airport, Tobias Bolanos at Pavas, three miles west of San José.

The San José opera house, modeled on the one in Paris, was built from coffee profits. It is elaborate, with ormolu and marble, murals and sculptures. In **Bella Vista Fort** is the national museum, which naturally focuses on pre-Columbian artifacts. Costa Rica was the source for two major elements of Mayan culture: gold and bells. The gold artifacts archeologists are discovering in Yucatan, Mexico were made from metal mined here; and copper smelting in pre-Columbian Costa Rica was so advanced that Aztec bells from all over were cast here.

EMBASSY: *1825 Connecticut Ave. N.W., Suite 211, Washington, DC 20009; (202)234-2945.*

SYSTEM OF GOVERNMENT: Democratic republic.

ETHNIC GROUPS: Spanish; other Europeans; Mestizos; Africans; Mulattos; American Indians; Chinese.

RELIGIOUS GROUPS: Predominantly Roman Catholics.

LANGUAGES: Spanish; a Jamaican dialect of English.

POPULATION: 2.714 million (in 1986).

AREA: 19,652 square miles (50,898 square kilometers); slightly smaller than West Virginia.

CAPITAL: San José (population 241,000 in 1984).

TERRAIN: Two mountain ranges run the length of the country. Central plateau; extensive forests.

CLIMATE: Tropical and subtropical. The rainy season runs from May through November; the dry season is from December through April.

TELECOMMUNICATIONS
   Country Code: 506.
   Time Zone: -1 hour Eastern
      Standard Time.

LOCAL/NATIONAL AIRLINES: **Lacsa,** *(800)225-2272;* **Pan Am,** *(800)221-*

1111; and **Eastern,** *(800)327-8376.*

U.S. CONSULATE IN COUNTRY: *cctl. y 1 , avenida 3, San Jose; tel. (506) 33-11-55.*

CURRENCY: Colón. No limit on import or export.

GROSS NATIONAL PRODUCT: $3.7 billion (in 1985).

WORK FORCE: Industry and commerce, 40%; agriculture, 34%; services and government, 25%.

OUR QUALITY OF LIFE RANKING: 54.3.

VISA REQUIREMENTS: Neither a passport nor a visa is required if you obtain a tourist card prior to departure; otherwise, both are required at no charge. Tourist cards are valid 30 days and can be extended for 6 months; they are available from the airline in Costa Rica. For a passport or visa, apply to the consulate in Chicago, Washington, D.C., New York, Los Angeles, Miami, or Ottowa.

TOURIST OFFICE IN THE UNITED STATES: **Costa Rican Tourist Board,** *1101 Brickell Ave., Suite 801, B.I.V. Tower, Miami, FL 33131; (800)327-7033.*

Volcanos to see include **Poas,** the highest in the world, which still bubbles; **Irazu,** a lunar landscape (at 11,000 feet) in the midst of a tropical forest called the Irazu Volcano National Park, 90,000 acres making up the most complete virgin ecosystem on earth; and **Arenal,** which still produces warm lava and red hot rock (the sight is spectacular at night).

For beaches, choose your coast. On the Pacific, you can fly to **Manuel Antonio Beach Park,** which provides sand under jungle-covered cliffs; **Quepos,** which is more difficult to get to (you must take a bus from the airport) but more beautiful; or **Guanacaste,** which is more remote, five hours north (via the Pan American Highway) from San José by road, and relatively primitive. On the Caribbean, choose **Cahita National Park,** which offers coral reefs and a lovely fishing village, Puerto Viejo, nearby; or **Tortuguero National Park,** near the Nicaraguan border, where giant green turtles come to spawn. Costa Rica's climate is perpetually spring-like, but note that the Caribbean beaches are more humid than the Pacific beaches.

The **Basilica of the Virgin of the Angels** in Cartago, not far from San José, is worth seeing. Try to visit on Aug. 2, when a pilgrimage to the site of the Black Virgin's apparition in 1826 takes place. You can hunt, fish, go white-water rafting, and hike in the jungle provinces. Or you can join a hunting safari and go in search of wild boar, armadillo, puma, jaguar, deer, and alligator. ❦

CZECHOSLOVAKIA

Czechoslovakia is a jewel that most travelers fail to appreciate. Of course, Czechoslovakia is in Eastern Europe, which frightens people. However, if you take a good look at a map, you'll realize that this East European country is pretty far west—and geography sometimes determines cultural attitudes.

Czechoslovakia sticks out like a finger pointing at West Germany, between Austria and East Germany. **Prague,** the Czechoslovak capital, is not far from Vienna, Munich, and Frankfurt, for example. It is on the same approximate longitude as Naples—meaning it is well to the west of some West European places, such as Stockholm, Helsinki, Vienna, and all of Greece. The longitude of Czechoslovakia corresponds to that of Yugoslavia. The difference is that, surrounded by strategic East European countries (such as East Germany, Poland, a tiny corner of the Soviet Union, and Hungary), Czechoslovakia wasn't allowed the luxury of choice in the question of alignment.

Czechoslovakia is the East European country with the longest and most genuine democratic past. Perhaps because of this, it has been a rebellious part of the Soviet empire, having resisted communist-controlled government until June 1948; having attempted liberalization under Alexander Dubcek for eight months in 1968 (the Prague Spring, which was put down by an invasion from Russian and other East bloc neighbors); and having again in 1977 produced a movement demanding freedom of expression (the Charter 77 group). In 1988, Czechoslovaks took the lead in Eastern Europe in celebrating the millennium of the conversion of the Slavs to Christianity (by saints Cyril and Methodius)—in defiance of government attempts to let the occasion pass uncommemorated.

The country is made up of plains and plateaus, a watershed drained by mighty rivers such as the **Danube** and the **Moldava,** which flow to the Black Sea, and the **Elbe** (Labe to Czechs), which flows to the Baltic Sea. The eastern part of the country, **Slovakia,** has high peaks and ski resorts.

Czechoslovakia was a center for the Reformation (under Jan Hus, an early follower of Wycliffe), but the Counter-Reformation successfully returned the country to the Catholic fold. But it took the papacy, the Hapsburgs, the Holy Roman Empire, and the Thirty Years' War to defeat the rebellion, which may indicate the determination of Czechs. Today, two-thirds of the population is officially Catholic. A tiny remnant survives of the country's ancient Jewish minority.

EMBASSY: *3900 Linnean Ave. N.W., Washington, DC 20008; (202)363-6315.*

SYSTEM OF GOVERNMENT: Communist.

ETHNIC GROUPS: Czechs, 65%; Slovaks, 30%; Hungarians, Poles, Ukrainians, and Germans, 5%.

RELIGIOUS GROUPS: Roman Catholics, 66%; members of the Czechoslovak Hussite Church, Lutherans, and members of the Russian Orthodox Church, 34%.

LANGUAGES: Czech (official), Slovak (official), Hungarian, German.

POPULATION: 15.503 million.

AREA: 49,374 square miles (127,896 square kilometers); comparable to New York.

CAPITAL: Prague (population 1 million).

TERRAIN: Mountainous and hilly.

CLIMATE: Moderate and transitional. Average temperature in Prague in January is 30 degrees Fahrenheit; average temperature in July is 67 degrees Fahrenheit.

TELECOMMUNICATIONS
   Country Code: 42.
   Time Zone: +6 hours Eastern Standard Time.

LOCAL/NATIONAL AIRLINE: Czechoslovak Airlines, *(800)223-2365.*

U.S. CONSULATE IN COUNTRY: *Trziste 15, Prague 12548; tel. (42-2)53-66-41-49.*

CURRENCY: Koruna. Travelers may not import or export currency. You must change $18 a day.

GROSS NATIONAL PRODUCT: $132.7 billion (in 1984).

WORK FORCE: Industry and commerce, 66%; services and government, 18%; agriculture, 12%.

OUR QUALITY OF LIFE RANKING: 49.90.

VISA REQUIREMENTS: A visa is required. Tourist/transit visas are valid for one entry for up to five months. Apply at the **embassy,** *address above.*

TOURIST OFFICE IN THE UNITED STATES: *Czechoslovakian Travel Bureau (CEDOK), 10 E. 40th St., New York, NY 10016; (212)689-9720.*

Travelers should be sensible. Do not try to bring in anti-communist literature, religious material, or Bibles. Do not insult the regime when talking to people. Be careful not to photograph things that may have military significance, such as airports, bridges, or trains. Be careful when exchanging money on the black market (although you will get a nice premium over the official rate). As in other East European countries, you are required to change a fixed amount of currency per day.

Travelers must obtain visas (valid for five months), which cost $10 per passport per entry. Some organized group visas can be obtained more cheaply.

Czechoslovakia is a cultural melting pot. Its two major linguistic groups are the Czechs and the Slovaks, whose Slavic languages are closely related but different. However, the country also includes German-speakers, Gypsies, Ukrainians, and Russians.

Until 1918, Slovakia was ruled by Hungary, and Bohemia and Moravia (where the Czechs live) were ruled by Austria. Both Hungary and Austria were part of the Austro-Hungarian Empire, which collapsed in 1918, when the Czechoslovak Republic was formed. The eastern part of historic Czechoslovakia was annexed by the Soviet Union in 1945.

Although the language is written using Western letters, it is Slavic, related to Ukrainian and Russian. Unlike other Eastern Europeans, people in cosmopolitan Czechoslovakia can manage English and Western languages. And you can read signs and write addresses all by yourself. The most important things to realize about Czechoslovakian is that the letters L and R count as vowels (which explains why the lingo looks unpronounceable); H is pronounced like the CH in the word Loch; and C is pronounced like TS.

After Prague, popular travel destinations include the cities of **Brno, Spindleruv Mlyn** in the Krkonose Mountains, and **Strbske Pleo** in the High Tatras (both ski resorts), and **Karlovy Vary** (formerly Karlsbad) and **Marianske Lazne** (formerly Marienbad), the famous spas.

The best known writer ever to come out of Prague, Franz Kafka, wrote in German under the republic. Sigmund Freud, another Jew who spoke German, was also born in what is now Czechoslovakia. At that time, about one-fourth of the population, and particularly those in Prague and the Western borders, called Sudetenland, were German-speaking. It was to protect German-nationals—after Britain and France gave him permission with the infamous Munich Agreement—that Hitler's Germany first invaded and then dismantled Czechoslovakia in 1937. German speakers who were Jewish, including Kafka's and Freud's families, wound up as corpses in Hitler's concentration camps. However, Kafka's contemporaries Karel Capek (whose play *RUR* introduced the notion of the robot) and Jaroslav Hasek (author of *The Good Soldier Sweik*) wrote in Czech. Mozart wrote his Italian opera *Don Giovanni* in Czechoslovakia; it had its world premier in Prague. Among 19th-century composers, Antonin Dvorak was Czech, and Bedrich Smetana was Slovak.

Many observers call Czechoslovakia the musical conservatory of Europe; and so beautiful is Prague that it vies with Paris for the title of the most beautiful city in the world. Hitler's conquest of the country spared Prague the destruction that other European cities faced.

Prague is a city made for walking, and you should take time to tramp its seven romantic hills on both sides of the **River Vltava.** The most famous bridge across this river is the baroque **Karluv Most** (Charles Bridge), which has rows of sculptures on either side. The old town center (**Stare Mesto**) is closed to automobiles. Prague is at its best in the spring, during the **Prague Spring Music Festival.** It's not bad in the summer either, when the people of Prague take to the outdoors, lingering in sidewalk cafés along the boulevards, especially the **Vaclavske namesti.** The old town hall on Staromestske namesti dominates the old town's most famous square. The town hall clock features 15th-century mechanical figures of Christ, the apostles, and the Angel of Death (who tolls the hour).

Nearby are the famous **Carolinium** (or Charles University, which was established in 1371), the **Tyl Theater,** where the debut of *Don Giovanni* was staged, and the **Powder Tower,** which is part of a gate to the new town (which is actually old).

Follow either Rariszka or Maislova streets, and you'll come to the oldest Jewish ghetto in Europe, founded in the 10th century. Here you will find the oldest synagogue in the world (still used for worship), the Gothic **Staronova Synagogue.** It was built in 1270. Because Jews read and write from right to left, the builders of the synagogue put up a special clock, whose hands rotate counter-clockwise.

In addition to Staronova, other Jewish sights include the old cemetery, the **High Synagogue,** with its 18th-century Jewish town hall, the **Maisel Synagogue,** with its magnificent ritual objects, and the **Pinhas Synagogue,** with its memorial inscription to 77,000 Czech Jews killed by the Nazis. The ghetto and the Holocaust are also commemorated in the **Statni Zidovske Muzeum** (State Jewish Museum), *Jachymova 3*.

This area also has important Protestant associations, including the restored **Betlemska** (Bethlehem Chapel), where Jan Hus preached. Here is the threshold the martyred preacher crossed more than 500 years ago. The best view of **Hradcany** (Prague Castle) is from this area.

Across the river from the old town is **Mala Strana** (Lower Town), the former neighborhood of the nobility. Here are the **National Gallery,** the Gothic cathedral (dedicated to St. Vitus), the great brooding Prague Castle, and the **Sternbeek** and **Wallenstein** (Valdstejn) palaces, now art galleries.

In Czech cafés, do not drink the unpleasant coffee; order Pilsner or Pils, the national brew, which has given its name to a type of beer all over the world; or Budvar, the original from which American Bud stems. Czech food includes good fish (try carp), goose, sausages with sauerkraut, wild mushrooms and game (served in the autumn), and dumplings and pancakes. The country's delicious strudel and chocolate desserts are tributes to the Hapsburg influence. ❦

DENMARK

Denmark is the odd man out in Scandinavia. Scandinavian countries speak closely related languages (Danish, Norwegian, and Swedish), permit their citizens to hop freely across their international borders, run a common airline (SAS), and operate similar high-tax, high social-benefits economies.

Denmark is different from the other Scandinavian countries because it is a member of both NATO and the European Economic Community (EEC). However, Greenland, a part of Denmark (which is in the process of becoming independent), is not in the EEC. (Because **Greenland** was named that only as a public relations gesture by its discoverer, Eric the Red, and in fact is covered with snow most of the year in most places, we are not going to tell you about its charms.)

The mainland of Denmark is a series of islands; only **Jutland** is connected to the European continent. The **Faeroe Islands,** between Iceland and Scotland, are Danish and great sources of fish. Because **Bornholm Island,** the easternmost Danish island, is off the coast of Poland, it is of great strategic importance, acting as a safe harbor for Polish refugees. It is also a Baltic tourist resort, with sand dunes and beaches, great tide-washed cliffs, and picturesque wooden houses. Denmark's capital, **Copenhagen** (København in Danish), is on the island of **Sjaelland,** the largest in Denmark.

Denmark ruled the whole of Scandinavia off and on until 1523, when Sweden

---

EMBASSY: *3200 Whitehaven St. N.W., Washington, DC 20008; (202)234-4300.*

SYSTEM OF GOVERNMENT: Constitutional monarchy.

ETHNIC GROUPS: Scandinavians; Germans; Eskimos; Faeroese.

RELIGIOUS GROUPS: Evangelical Lutherans, 97%.

LANGUAGES: Danish; German; Eskimo dialect; Faeroese.

POPULATION: 5.116 million.

AREA: 16,631 square miles (43,075 square kilometers); about half the size of Maine.

CAPITAL: Copenhagen (population 633,000).

TERRAIN: Undulating landscape. Average altitude of 30 meters.

CLIMATE: Mild winters and cool summers. Average temperature in February is 32 degrees Fahrenheit; average temperature in July is 63 degrees Fahrenheit.

TELECOMMUNICATIONS
Country Code: 45.
Time Zone: +6 hours Eastern Standard Time.
Code of Capital: 1 or 2.

LOCAL/NATIONAL AIRLINES: SAS Scandinavian Air, *(800)221-2350;* **Council Charter,** *(212)661-0311;*

Northwest Airlines, *(800)447-4747;* **Pan Am,** *(800)221-1111;* and **Sabena Airlines,** *(800)645-3700* (East Coast), *(800)632-8050* (New York), *(800)645-3790* (Southeast and Midwest), or *(800)645-1382* (West Coast).

U.S. EMBASSY IN COUNTRY: *Dag Hammerskjolds Alle 24, 2100, Copenhagen; tel. (45-1)12-31-44.*

CURRENCY: Krone. No limit on import; travelers may export up to the amount declared when they entered the country. Special regulations apply to foreign-capital investments.

GROSS NATIONAL PRODUCT: $57.9 billion (in 1985).

WORK FORCE: Industry and commerce, 46%; services, 13%; agriculture, 8.2%.

OUR QUALITY OF LIFE RANKING: 75.78.

VISA REQUIREMENTS (for Denmark, Greenland, and the Faeroe Islands): A visa is not required for stays of up to three months (period begins when you enter the Scandinavian area—Finland, Sweden, Norway, or Iceland).

TOURIST OFFICE IN THE UNITED STATES: Scandinavian Tourist Board, *655 Third Ave., New York, NY 10017; (212)949-2333.*

broke away. For a while, Denmark ruled England as well (King Canute, the 11th-century monarch, was a Dane). Under Christian IV (1577 to 1648), Denmark became a modern country, thanks to its own cultural Renaissance, mercantile investments, and colonization of such far-off sites as India. Denmark became Lutheran in 1536; it became a constitutional monarchy in 1849. The country was neutral in World War I; it was occupied and heroically resisted the Nazis during World War II.

The best known sight in Copenhagen is the statue of the little mermaid in the harbor (**Citadel Park**). The statue honors Hans Christian Andersen, one of the best-loved Danish writers, who created the character. The poor mermaid has been stolen and vandalized several times, despite the Danes' reputations for being peaceable and law-abiding people. Andersen was a great traveler, as was another Danish author, Isak Dinesen (Baroness Blixen).

Open during the summer only (usually from May 1 to mid-September), the second top sight in the city is **Tivoli Gardens,** which is a collection of parks, restaurants, concert halls offering everything from oompah bands to a symphony orchestra and ballet all Tivoli's own, the only Commedia del'Arte still performing Harlequin, Columbine, and Pierrot theater, and amusement parks.

The most shocking thing about Tivoli is that just getting in is expensive, 60 kroner as of this writing. Despite the welfare state, Tivoli Gardens is wholly private, a 100-year-old for-profit concern. Being blatantly capitalist, its admission prices are what the market will bear.

The same attitude applies to other Danish tourist facilities that the government cannot put the squeeze on, including hotels, taxis, restaurants, bars, and cafés. On the other hand, travel by railroad, domestic airline, and bus; admission fees for museums, art galleries, and castles; and theater, opera, and ballet performances are subsidized, making them more affordable for poor American travelers. Unfortunately, most of us have this awful habit of eating three meals a day—which is very expensive in Denmark.

Other areas of Copenhagen that you should see include the **Nyhavn** waterfront zone, lined with 17th-century houses and warehouses, many of which are now boutiques, antique shops, cafés, and restaurants. This area can be dangerous at night. The center of Copenhagen, the **Strøget,** is called by a multitude of formal names. It is a kilometer-long succession of streets running from **Radhus Plads** to **Kongens Nytorv** (the Royal Theater). These and other streets running parallel to the Strøget, including the Farvergade, Kompagniestraede, and Laderstreaede, are closed to automobiles and are good places for strolling and shopping.

The **Latin Quarter,** near the university and the cathedral, also pedestrians-only, is filled with antiquarian booksellers. Most of downtown Copenhagen is within walking distance of **City Hall Square** and the railroad station.

Copenhagen's cultural sights include **Rosenborg Castle** (with the Crown Jewels), the **Royal Museum of Fine Arts** (Nørreport or Østerport stations), the **National Museum,** the **Royal Arsenal,** and **Trinitatis** (the Holy Trinity Church), with its famous round tower. **Lyngby,** *Frilandsmuseet, Kongevejen 100,* on the northern edge of the city, is an open-air museum of old-fashioned Danish rural life.

In the midst of the **Dyrehaven** deer forest, also north of town, is the world's oldest amusement park, **Bakken,** founded in the late 16th century. This amusement park is cheaper but more difficult to get to than Tivoli. It offers shooting galleries, roller coasters, and taverns, as well as the **Eremitagen,** the royal hunting lodge in the forest.

You can tour the **Carlsberg Brewery,** *Valby Langgade 1,* or the **Tuborg Brewery,** *Stranvejen 54,* (open weekday mornings). The **Royal Copenhagen Porcelain Manufactory,** *Smallegade 45,* is also open to the public. However, the most popular tourist destination is to the area north of the city, called **North Zealand.**

Take advantage of the **Copenhagen Card,** which allows you free rides on city buses, trains, and subways. It even allows you free rides on the ferry to Sweden. Or go one better and purchase the **Nordturist Ticket,** which permits 21 days of unlimited train travel throughout Scandinavia. (You can buy either pass at the Central Train Station opposite Radhuspladsen, off the Strøget.)

Use your travel pass to visit Hamlet's 16th-century **Kronborg Castle** at Elsinore (Helsingør in Danish); the **Humlebaek Louisiana Museum** (of modern art); the 18th-century **Palladian** summer palace at Fredensborg (which is open to the public when the royals are not in residence, unlike Amalienborg Palace in Copenhagen, which is private); **Roskilde,** with its 12th-century cathedral (which houses the tombs of Danish monarchs); and **Hillerød** (Frederiksbord Castle), with its magnificent chapel.

Because, as I mentioned above, eating in Denmark is an expensive proposition, here are a few tips to help you save money. Copenhagen is full of hotdog stands that offer cheap alternatives to formal meals. The Danish hotel and restaurant industry, aware of the problems of U.S. visitors, has set up a system called *Dan Menu.* More than 400 restaurants and eateries in Denmark offer a fixed price two-course lunch or dinner for 69.50 kroner (not including tax, service charge, or tip, to say nothing of drinks). This comes to about $10.

Look for signs reading "café" or "*kolde bord*" or "*smørrebord.*" These places often offer buffets of open-faced sandwiches featuring smoked meats and fishes, herring in 400 varieties, eggs, and cheeses (you know about Danish blue, but also try Tilsit, Havarti, and Samsoe). Always drink the local beer.

Instead of a full breakfast, have Danish pastry, which is very good, along with Danish coffee, which is also delicious. Pastries are sold in places called *konditori* or *conditoriet.*

Denmark's leading vegetarian restaurant is called **Cranks,** *Grønnegade 12-14.* Never tip. Tips are included in all prices in Denmark.

Don't take a taxi to or from the Copenhagen airport. Buses from Kastrup to the railway station cost only 20 kroner, take 25 minutes, and leave every quarter-hour.

Rent a bicycle at the railway station, **Danwheel,** *Colbjørnsengade 3,* or **Cykelbørs,** *Gothersgade 157-159,* and peddle your way through Denmark. Or join a walking tour (July and August only, unless you speak Danish). Contact the tourist information office in Copenhagen for times and itineraries.

Take advantage of the **Meet the Danes** program, which allows you to spend an evening at home with Danes in any of eight provincial cities: Aarhus, Aalborg, Esbjerg, Fredericia, Lonstrup, Odense, Roskilde, and Skive. You can make arrangements with as little as 24 hours notice. You also can make arrangements through the Danish Tourist Board in New York before you leave the United States.

Shop intelligently. Look out for seconds of goodies from **Georg Jenson** (crystal) or **Royal Copenhagen** (china), which sell for half the retail price. Eagle-eyed Danish quality-control inspectors reject things you and your friends will think perfect.

Save on the 22% value-added tax (VAT) by looking out for shops that offer VAT refunds. The minimum purchase to get the refund is 600 kroner per shop. ❦

EGYPT

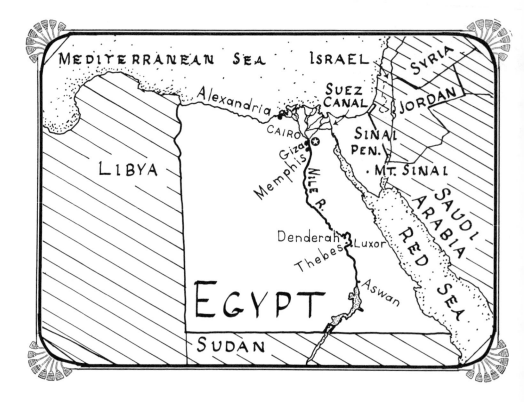

"**E**gypt is the gift of the Nile," wrote the historian Herodotus in 450 B.C. Indeed, this country is a cradle of human history and culture. The **Nile River** brought prosperity to the Egyptians, giving them the luxury to develop one of the first major civilizations. Only 4% of this nation, the land along the banks of the river, is suitable for farming. The rest of the country is desert.

Cairo, the capital, has always been a crossroad between Europe, Asia, and Africa. Today, you can get to Cairo via almost all of the world's major airlines. TWA and Pakistan International both offer direct flights from New York. Pan Am flies to Cairo via Rome. PIA flies via Paris. KLM has service via Amsterdam from New York.

Several steamship companies offer voyages through the **Suez Canal** as part of a Mediterranean or Red Sea cruise. Cruise lines calling at Egyptian ports include Cunard, Epirotiki, Karageorgis, Norwegian America, Royal Viking Line, and Sun Line Cruises.

A problem in Egypt and other Moslem countries is **Ramadan,** a month-long fast during which it can be difficult to have a meal during the daytime. Ramadan does not occur during the same season every year. So before you make plans to visit Egypt, find out when Ramadan will be held, and avoid its dates.

A network of trains connects Cairo with major towns and sites. First-class tickets are cheap. Reserve in advance at the Cairo train station at Midan Ramsis, the Alexandria train station, or through a travel agency.

A voyage up the Nile by steamer is a good way to see the country. Boats offer 3- to 5-day cruises from Luxor to Aswan and 7- to 11-day voyages to Luxor or Aswan from Cairo. Ships in Luxor dock near the **Karnak Temple,** the most colossal ancient monument in the world.

Begin your visit to Egypt in Cairo. The oldest part of the city, known as **Old Cairo,** has Persian and Roman forts and an Arab mosque. The center of the modern

EMBASSY: *2310 Decatur Place N.W., Washington, DC 20008; (202)232-5400.*

SYSTEM OF GOVERNMENT: Capitalist-socialist industrial republic.

ETHNIC GROUPS: Egyptians, 87%; Arabs; Israelis; Armenians; Greeks.

RELIGIOUS GROUPS: Moslems, 93%; Christians, 7%.

LANGUAGES: Arabic (official); English.

POPULATION: 52 million.

AREA: 386,900 square miles (1.002 million square kilometers).

CAPITAL: Cairo (population 6.205 million in 1986).

TERRAIN: Primarily desert, except in the Nile valley.

CLIMATE: High daytime temperatures fall quickly at night. Very little rain.

TELECOMMUNICATIONS
   Country Code: 20.
   Time Zone: +7 hours Eastern Standard Time.
   Code of Capital: 2.

LOCAL/NATIONAL AIRLINES: **EgyptAir,** *(800)334-6787;* **TWA,** *(800)892-4141;* and **Pakistan International,** *(800)221-2552* or

(212)370-9150 in New York.

U.S. CONSULATE IN COUNTRY: *5 Latin America St., Cairo; tel. (20-2)355-7371; telex 93773.*

CURRENCY: Egyptian pound. Travelers may import 20 Egyptian pounds and export 20 Egyptian pounds, subject to license.

GROSS NATIONAL PRODUCT: $35.8 billion.

WORK FORCE: Agriculture, 37%; services, 27%; industry, 13%; commerce, 12%.

OUR QUALITY OF LIFE RANKING: 31.54.

VISA REQUIREMENTS: A visa and a passport are required. To obtain a visa (good for six months), send your passport and a photo to the consulate in San Francisco, Washington, D.C., New York, Chicago, or Houston. Visas also can be obtained at the Cairo airport; however, because of the possibility of a delay, it is a good idea to obtain your visa before you get to Egypt.

TOURIST OFFICE IN THE UNITED STATES: **Egyptian Tourist Office,** *630 Fifth Ave., New York, NY 10111; (212)246-6960.*

city is **Midan al Tahrir** (Liberation Square), from which roads lead north to the business and shopping areas. Also see **Bulac, Opera Square,** the **Ezbekiya Gardens,** the heart of Cairo at the time of the Napoleonic invasion, and the **Mouski.**

East of the square is the **Bab el Luk** district; beyond that the **Citadel,** the most historic part of the city, filled with great mosques and museums. Here is the great fortress built by Saladin in the 12th century, which contains the beautiful **Mosque of Mohammed Ali,** with its alabaster walls, Kufic inscriptions, and myriad brass lamps under gilded domes and a double minaret.

Westward is the **Al Akhzar University,** the most important in the Islamic world, and the **Road to the Pyramids.**

The pyramids start a mere nine miles west of the city at **Giza,** overlooking the **Nile Valley,** and can be reached by city bus if you don't mind the crowds. The oldest of Cairo's 80 pyramids is the **Great Pyramid of Cheops**, at Giza, which covers 13 acres and is one of the Seven Wonders of the Ancient World. It was built in 2690 B.C. and is the largest stone structure in the world. The Great Pyramid has a museum containing a funeral boat.

The **Sphinx** is nearby and is the site of a nightly sound-and-light show. The monument is slowly disintegrating, so you probably should see it before another great chunk of its shoulder falls off.

Memphis, south of Cairo, the former capital of Egypt, has its own, much smaller Sphinx, made of alabaster. **Thebes,** which offers the **Tomb of Tut-ankh-amen,** is about 450 miles south of Cairo along the Nile, in the heart of Upper Egypt, pyramid country. Here are the greatest, most gigantic ruins of the pharaohs' power and fear of death, at **Luxor,** across the Nile. Here also is the **Valley of the Kings,** the burial grounds of the rulers, and the **Valley of the Nobles,** where somewhat lesser Egyptians are entombed in caves decorated with brightly colored scenes of Egyptian life 4,000 years ago. Other sites include **Denderah,** with a beautifully preserved temple, one of whose chapels is decorated with the theme of the zodiac and a fresco of Queen Cleopatra.

Other sites worth visiting are the **Sinai Peninsula,** the mountain where the Ten Commandments were given to Moses, and the **Red Sea** coast, which offers fabulous marine life, coral reefs, and tropical fish.

For a break from all the ancient sights, consider a side trip to the Mediterranean coast north of Cairo, centered around **Alexandria,** which offers the seaside and beaches.

Food in Egypt is extraordinarily varied. Some dishes to try are *maloukhia,* a soup made with a gelatinous leaf somewhat like spinach that is beloved by Egyptians and known nowhere else; *foul,* a dish made with a type of bean; *mezze,* an overwhelming hors d'oeuvre that comes in dozens of varieties; anything made from lamb; and the country's sweet desserts and sherbets. Be careful about eating raw food and salads—the water used to wash them probably wasn't pure. Don't drink unbottled water; don't even use it from the faucet to brush your teeth. The country's strong, sweet coffee and hot tea are both good—and safe to drink; curiously, they seem to cool you off even when you drink them hot.

Egypt is a great country for shopping. Hit the bazaars of Cairo, which offer everything from clothing to leather goods, anything made of brass, carpets, marble and alabaster, and gold- and silver-inlaid jewelry. Be prepared to bargain.

The people of Egypt are intensely civilized, as might be expected of such an established culture. They are also courteous, patient, and kind at times when even the most saintly American would be shouting or cursing. Try to emulate them. It will make your stay more pleasant. ❦

FINLAND

Finland is a European curiosity. Its people are racially linked to those of Scandinavia, both the tall, blond Nordic folk (a minority of whom actually speak Swedish as their mother tongue) and the short, dark-haired Lapps who have cousins across the border in Sweden, Denmark, and Norway. Finnish, too, is an anomaly, a language linked to Estonian, Turkish, and Hungarian—but not part of the Scandinavian group of Germanic languages. Politically, the Finns are also a curiosity. They are neutral under a system that the Russians have dominated since the end of the 18th century. What this means in practice is that Finland has a democratically elected government that does not bow to the popular will in one major area: it does not cross the Soviet Union in matters of foreign policy.

A Nordic country, Finland is naturally a center of modern architecture. The capital, **Helsinki,** was designated in 1812 to be the government center, and its original early-19th-century neo-classical buildings (including masterpieces by Carl Engel) were added to by such architects as Alvar Aalto and the Saarinens, Gesellius, and Lindgren. View **Finlandi Hall** and the elder Saarinen's train station— which is where Lenin arrived in 1917 en route from Zurich (where he lived before and during World War I) back to Russia to start a Revolution (he was shipped across enemy Germany in a sealed car). The museums stress national history and applied arts, another Finnish specialty. An open-air museum in Helsinki recreates village life.

EMBASSY: *3216 New Mexico Ave. N.W., Washington, DC 20016; (202)363-2430.*

SYSTEM OF GOVERNMENT: Constitutional republic.

ETHNIC GROUPS: Fins; Swedes; Lapps; Gypsies.

RELIGIOUS GROUP: Evangelical Lutherans, 92%.

LANGUAGES: Finnish, 93.5% (official); Swedish, 6.5% (official); Lappish dialect.

POPULATION: 4.9 million (in 1985).

AREA: 130,119 square miles (337,009 square kilometers); slightly smaller than Montana.

CAPITAL: Helsinki (population 484,000).

TERRAIN: Low but hilly in the south; mountainous in the north. More than 70% of the land area is forested. More than 60,000 lakes.

CLIMATE: Temperate.

TELECOMMUNICATIONS
   Country Code: 358.
   Time Zone: +7 hours Eastern Standard Time.

Code of Capital: 0.

LOCAL/NATIONAL AIRLINE: Finnair, *(800)223-5700.*

U.S. CONSULATE IN COUNTRY: *Itainen Puistotie 14, 00140, Helsinki; tel. (358-0)171931;* **Public Affairs** is located at *Kaivokatu 10, Helsinki 10.*

CURRENCY: Finnish markka. No limit on import; travelers may export 10,000 Finnish markkas.

GROSS NATIONAL PRODUCT: $69.2 billion (in 1986).

WORK FORCE: Industry and commerce, 46%; services, 28%; agriculture, 10%.

OUR QUALITY OF LIFE RANKING: 71.20.

VISA REQUIREMENTS: A visa is not required for stays of up to three months (period begins when you enter the Scandinavian area—Sweden, Norway, Denmark, or Iceland).

TOURIST OFFICE IN THE UNITED STATES: Scandinavian Tourist Board, *655 Third Ave., New York, NY 10019; (212)949-2333.*

The former capital, **Turku,** is worth visiting for its castle (now a museum), its handicrafts museum (which is outdoors and features potters and weavers working by the old methods), and its soaring Gothic cathedral.

Offshore is the **Ahvenanmaa** between Finland and Sweden, where Swedish is spoken. A center of Stone Age settlements and archeological digs, this is a good area for island hopping and bicycling. Nature lovers find the relatively deserted Finnish countryside a delight for hiking, canoeing, camping—and music. The Finnish Lake District is the site of the **Savonlinna Opera Festival.**

Northern Finland is another popular travel destination. Head for **Kuusamo,** just south of the Arctic Circle, which has dramatic scenery, rapids, canyons, and the Midnight Sun all summer. You can hike and spend the night for free in trail huts. (Bring mosquito repellent.) Visit **Lapland** (via the Lapp capital of **Rovaniemi,** to which you fly from Helsinki), where you can see curiously dressed natives, herds of reindeer, and more beautiful scenery, including clear-blue lakes and the **Enontekio Mountains.**

Laps eat *poro* (reindeer meat), *lohi* (salmon), *silka* (whitefish), and lots of cloudberries. Finns of other areas are masters of the art of preparing and preserving fish, notably *sill* (herring) and salmon. Fish in Finland is salted, pickled, cured, dried, smoked, or prepared through a combination of these processes, always with a variety of spices and herbs. With the fish, you eat *ruisleipa* (rye bread) and *villi* (a yogurt-like spread). Various berries and mushrooms (many unfamiliar) are also popular. Local 100-proof firewaters are customarily drunk with meals. Other times, Finns drink beer or liqueurs made from the fruits and berries of their country.

Shopping in Finland is much more important than the country's population of less than five million would lead you to expect. One reason is that this is the emporium that keeps Westerners in the Soviet Union supplied. From Helsinki's great department stores, care packages of toilet paper, corn flakes, and canned peaches are shipped to the Soviet Union to keep diplomats and businessmen from suffering from their absence.

Finland is a center for furniture design, fabrics for home decoration (especially wool, cotton, and vinyl), crystal and glass, and carpeting. The country's leading designer, **Marimekko,** has created an entire look with the print and cut of her dresses. Because the Finnish markka is a strong currency, goods tend to be expensive, so it is not worthwhile to buy things that are not unique or exceptional.

Finnair flies to Finland from several U.S. cities. Other options include flying into another Scandinavian entry point then either taking one of the frequent flights to Helsinki or sailing from Stockholm across the Gulf of Bothnia to either Turku or Helsinki. You can get rail and air passes for travel throughout Finland or combination passes for travel throughout Finland and other Nordic countries. ❦

FRANCE

F rance is the travel destination many people dream of; so much so that the French say **Paris** is where good Americans go when they die.

Paris is the fruit of centuries of French centralization. Under Louis XIV, who wanted to keep his courtiers under control, under the Revolution's Jacobins, under Napoleon, under the various Republics, Paris has set the pace for all of France—in government, in finance, in museums and the arts, in fashion, and in food. Yet France is not only Paris; the country has major travel destinations in the provinces, notably the **Bordeaux, Burgundy,** and **Champagne** wine-growing regions; the châteaux country of the **Loire River** and its tributaries; the coasts of **Normandy** and the **Côte d'Azur;** the linguistic-minority regions of **Basque** country and **Brittany; Mont St. Michel** and **Chartres,** two monuments of religious architecture; and inland **Alsace** and **Provence.**

France was ruled by the Bourbon kings, who descended from Charlemagne, until the French Revolution of 1789, which led to the storming of the **Bastille** prison and the eventual execution of King Louis XVI and Queen Marie Antoinette. Amidst the chaos and factionalism and assassinations that followed, a young

---

EMBASSY: *4101 Reservoir Road N.W., Washington, DC 20007; (202)944-6000.*

SYSTEM OF GOVERNMENT: Constitutional republic.

ETHNIC GROUPS: Celtics; Latins; Teutonics, Slavics; North Africans; Vietnamese; Basques; a mixture of Mediterranean groups.

RELIGIOUS GROUP: Roman Catholics, 85%.

LANGUAGES: French; local dialects.

POPULATION: 55.506 million.

AREA: 210,025 square miles (543,965 square kilometers); about four-fifths the size of Texas.

CAPITAL: Paris (population 2.189 million in 1982).

TERRAIN: Varied.

CLIMATE: Oceanic, continental, and Mediterranean.

U.S.-ACCREDITED HOSPITALS: Paris American Hospital.

TELECOMMUNICATIONS
  Country Code: 33.
  Time Zone: +6 hours Eastern Standard Time.
  Code of Capital: 1.

LOCAL/NATIONAL AIRLINES: Air France, *(800)237-2747;* **Continental Airlines,** *(800)231-0856;* **Council**

Charter, *(212)661-0311;* **Delta,** *(800)221-1212;* **Icelandair,** *(800)223-5500;* **Rich Airways,** *(305)871-5113;* **Sabena Airlines,** *(800)645-3700* (East Coast), *(800)632-8050* (New York), *(800)645-3790* (Southeast and Midwest), or *(800)645-1382* (West Coast); and **UTA French Airlines,** *(800)282-4484.*

RAILROAD OFFICE IN THE UNITED STATES: French National Railroads, *610 Fifth Ave., New York, NY 10020; (212)582-2110.*

U.S. CONSULATE IN COUNTRY: *ave. Gabriel 2, Paris 8; tel. (33-14)296-1202.*

CURRENCY: Franc. No limit on import; travelers may export FFr50,000.

GROSS NATIONAL PRODUCT: $710.2 billion (in 1986).

WORK FORCE: Services, 46%; industry and commerce, 45%; agriculture, 9%.

OUR QUALITY OF LIFE RANKING: 76.08.

VISA REQUIREMENTS: A visa is required. A visa valid for five years is $15.

TOURIST OFFICE IN THE UNITED STATES: French Government Tourist Office, *610 Fifth Ave., New York, NY 10020; (212)757-1125.*

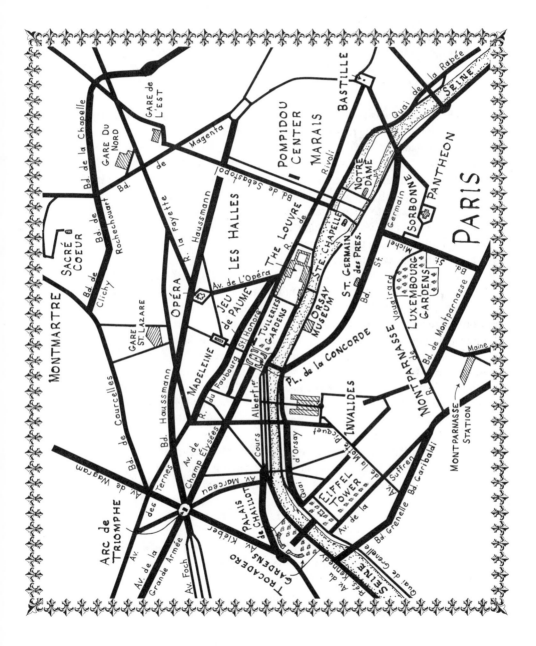

military officer seized power. He was Napoleon, who reigned until his second defeat, in 1815, and was replaced by the restored Bourbons. The 1830 Revolution brought about a switch in Bourbons. A more serious uprising in 1848 brought about another try at republican government, defeated when the empire was restored by Napoleon's nephew, Napoleon III. The reign of Napoleon III ended in 1870, when Germany defeated France in a war, seized Alsace and Lorraine, and imposed reparations on the Third Republic. In 1914-1918, France won back its lost eastern provinces. The Third Republic did not survive the 1940 invasion of France by Germany and the imposition of a dictatorship under the World War I French hero, Marshall Pétain.

The republic was restored (the fourth of the line) in 1945. But Charles de Gaulle, who had led the resistance to Pétain's rule from London, took power when the factionalism and corruption of the Fourth Republic proved too much for the country. De Gaulle instituted a new constitution and the Fifth Republic, which is the country's current system. In 1981, for the first time, a left-wing coalition won power under the Fifth Republic. Since then, François Mitterrand has been president.

Unless you fly to Nice or take a ferry to Calais or drive in from a bordering country, chances are you will begin your French vacation in Paris. This beautiful city is spoiled only by the Parisians, who are impatient and intolerant of anyone who does not speak their language perfectly.

The major Paris sights include churches: **Notre-Dame Cathedral,** *Ile de la Cité,* a Gothic remnant with 19th-century improvements; the perfect tiny church used by the kings of France, located in the middle of the medieval prison of **La Conciergerie,** on the same island; **La Madeleine,** a late-18th-century exercise in Greek Revival that may have inspired much American architecture with its pillars and pediments; and the **Sacré Coeur,** a curious century-old Byzantine church that dominates **Montmartre** hill. Other sights you must see include the **Eiffel Tower,** which was built out of steel in the last century despite the protests of aesthetes of the period (the Eiffel Tower has become the best-loved symbol of the city); and **Les Invalides,** originally a military hospital and considered by Napoleon to be the most perfect building in the world (appropriately, he is buried here).

The great Paris museums include the **Louvre,** home of the *Mona Lisa,* the *Winged Victory of Samothrace,* and more Vermeers than are gathered anywhere else. Other good museums are the **Centre Pompidou**, which looks like an oil refinery (the building is more interesting than its contents); and the recently opened **Picasso** and **Orsay** museums. However, don't limit yourself to these museums; the city has dozens of others.

But Paris is more than its sights. The city's river is graced with quais, and a dozen special parks offer relief from the pace of the city. The best are the **Tuileries Gardens** and the **Luxembourg Gardens,** which give character to the neighborhoods where they are located (the area around the Louvre and the Latin Quarter, respectively). The **Bois de Boulogne**, a former hunting preserve that is now open to the public, acts as the lungs of Paris (at night, this area can be dangerous).

Paris is known as a place to shop. For first-class shopping, visit the **Rue du Faubourg St. Honoré,** the **Place Vendôme,** and the glitzy **Forum des Halles,** a tiered-glass affair built to replace the former wholesale markets smack in the middle of town. For cheaper shopping, head for the **Marché St. Pierre** at the foot of Montmartre or to the **Rue St. Placide** on the Left Bank. The flea market at the **Porte de Clignancourt** draws shoppers on the weekends who are looking for everything from secondhand motorcycle boots to ormolu antiques.

Paris is also home to mouth-watering street markets, an abundance of tiny bakeries where the bakers still get up at 4 a.m. to give their breads a chance to rise before the breakfast customers line up, and little *traiteurs,* where you can stock up on deli food for a picnic. Paris invented the sidewalk café, an admirable institution.

The most important side trip from Paris is to **Versailles,** the château built by Louis XIV to house his court. The place is filled with marvelous rooms, mirrored halls, and fountains (which play on Sundays). You can reach Versailles via the Left Bank RER train—don't bother taking a tour from the city. Relatively easy day trips also can be organized to **Champagne** (you can taste the wine if you visit the *caves* of Epernay), to **Chartres Cathedral,** or to **Giverny,** the Monet museum town.

To really get to know the Paris, you must walk its streets. But its rapid-transit system is a cheap and safe alternative.

Travel throughout France is becoming increasingly fast and easy. The country has not only built new high-speed RER lines to bring Paris suburbs closer to the city, but it also has added new rail lines to bring Lyons and its environs closer to Paris (you now can reach Lyons in two hours). New lines are being built on the east coast as well as to the English Channel. ❦

GREECE

G reece has problems with everything from air pollution to terrorism. None-theless, it is an essential travel destination for anyone who wants to understand the civilization we belong to. It's also very cheap. Most travelers go straight to **Athens** and try to get away as quickly as possible, leaving for the islands after they have made the compulsory stops to see the **Acropolis** (in the course of being restored) and the **Archeological Museum.**

Greece is faithful to something called the Turkish toilet, which really is a hole in the ground with a Niagara-like flushing mechanism that constipates Americans. You can find U.S.-style bathrooms in the more fashionable places, some of which are open to the public. My personal favorite is at the American Express office on Syntagma Square.

The Acropolis is one of the Seven Wonders of the Ancient World. After you've seen it and the Archeological Museum, spend some time trying to learn something about the Byzantine Period as well, visiting museums and some of the city's old churches.

Near Athens are two great sights: **Delphi,** where the Oracle foretold the future (and where her temple bears the profound inscription "Know thyself"); and the **Temple of Poseidon** at Cape Sounion, whose white columns overlook the sea where Lord Byron drowned.

Athens is also a great place to shop. Begin at the base of the Acropolis, an area called the **Plaka,** and work your way to the **Agora,** a market that has operated continuously since classical times. As with restaurants and accommodations,

---

EMBASSY: *2221 Massachusetts Ave. N.W., Washington, DC 20008; (202)667-3168.*

SYSTEM OF GOVERNMENT: Presidential parliamentary republic.

ETHNIC GROUPS: Greeks, 96%; Turks, 1.5%; Slavs; Albanians; Armenians; Bulgarians.

RELIGIOUS GROUPS: Members of the Greek Orthodox Church, 97%; Moslems, 2%; Roman Catholics; Jews; Protestants.

LANGUAGE: Greek.

POPULATION: 10 million.

AREA: 51,182 square miles (132,560 square kilometers); comparable to Alabama.

CAPITAL: Athens (metropolitan population 3.027 million).

TERRAIN: Hilly and rocky. More than 2,000 islands.

CLIMATE: Temperate. Hot, dry summers; cool, wet winters.

TELECOMMUNICATIONS
　Country Code: 30.
　Time Zone: +7 hours Eastern
　　Standard Time.
　Code of Capital: 1.

LOCAL/NATIONAL AIRLINES:
Lufthansa German Airlines,
(800)645-3880; **Olympic Airways,** *(800)223-1226;* **Pan Am,** *(800)221-1111;* **Sabena Airlines,** *(800)645-3700* (East Coast), *(800)632-8050* (New York), *(800)745-3790* (Midwest and Southeast), or *(800)645-1382* (West Coast); **Tower Air,** *(800)221-2500* or *(718)917-8500* in New York; and **Yugoslav Airlines,** *(800)752-6528.*

U.S. CONSULATE IN COUNTRY: *91 Vass Sophias Ave., Athens; tel. (30-1)721-2951.*

CURRENCY: Drachma. Travelers may import and export US$25.

GROSS NATIONAL PRODUCT: $39 billion (in 1986).

WORK FORCE: Services, 42%; industry, 29%; agriculture, 28%.

OUR QUALITY OF LIFE RANKING: 57.23.

VISA REQUIREMENTS: A visa is not required for business or pleasure stays of up to three months. A passport is required.

TOURIST OFFICE IN THE UNITED STATES: Greek National Tourist Organization, *645 Fifth Ave., New York, NY 10022; (212)421-5777.*

shopping in Athens offers something for everyone, from luxury furs and gold (Zolotas and Lalounis, both top-price international jewelry designers, have shops on **Venizelou,** Athens' Fifth Avenue, near Syntagma Square) to bargains along the **Piraeus** waterfront. Among the bargains are Oriental carpets, kilims (flat-woven rugs and covers in Oriental designs), silver peasant jewelry, sheepskins, wool knit sweaters, felt capes, cotton dresses, and shirts. The fashion look the Greeks do best is sophisticated sportswear—but keep your eyes peeled for other goodies as well. My husband once bought a gorgeous gray linen suit from a Plaka market stall for the equivalent of $25.

From Piraeus (which you can get to from Athens via the metro), ferries sail for the Greek islands. The nearest is the island of **Hydra,** which makes a good day trip. However, the most popular travel destinations are in the **Cyclades** group, including **Mykonos,** the windmill island, and **Santorini** (Thira), the volcanic island, one of whose eruptions drowned Atlantis. You can fly to these islands, but you will lose some of the experience of Greece if you do: the boat with lots of people making conversation in a mixture of languages; the dolphins that accompany your ferry through the sea; the understanding of what Thallassa (the sea) meant to the founders of Western civilization; and the excitement of landing in a tiny island port. Ferries also go to **Crete**—and from there to **Rhodes** and the **Dodecanese Islands.**

On the other hand, the newly developed **Sporades** resorts are best reached by air, as is the green and moist northern island of **Corfu,** one of the oldest Greek vacation sites. And if you want to visit the **Pelleponese** (**Mt. Olympus**), you are best off driving.

Crete is different from the other islands, because it is so large. You should rent a car to tour the former capital of Minoan civilization, especially the capital, **Knossos.** Crete also contains the great **Samarian Gorge,** one of the natural wonders of Greece, as well as beaches that are either sophisticated or deserted, depending on how far you get from Iraklion. You should devote an entire trip to seeing Crete.

Unless you insist on a private bathroom or want to go to Mykonos (which is touristy), you should consider following the Columbus system to find your own island. Just set out sailing, without knowing where you will land—and without making reservations. When you do land, touts will meet you at the docks and guide you to a hotel of some sort, usually up a steep street with steps donkeys can handle. If you don't like what you are being shown, go back to the harbor and try again. Most of the Greek islands have deserted beaches and archeological remains, as well as charming citadels and churches. They also often have markets, where you can enjoy the picturesque and look for local crafts.

Even if you never leave Athens, it is in your interest to master the *taverna* system. These are restaurants where you walk into the kitchen and point to the food you want to eat. Begin your meal with *mezze* (variously spelled), which is a collection of hors d'oeuvres. Or have chicken soup thickened with egg and flavored with lemon. After the appetizers, the main dish you chose is served. Good are eggplant casseroles, lentil dishes, stuffed grape leaves, lamb stews, vegetable mixtures, and pasta-cum-tomato dishes. Greek desserts, such as *loukoum, halvah,* and honey-dripping cakes, are very sweet—as is the Turkish coffee.

Wine called retsina (to which pine resin is added, supposedly to help preserve the stuff) is available in white or red. If you can't stand it, order Coke or *nero krio* (cold water). ❦

HONG KONG

Hong Kong, known as the Pearl of the Orient, is a bustling city where a marriage of opposites has produced one of the world's most robust societies. Hong Kong is the gateway between worlds: the East and the West; the ancient and the modern; the communist and the capitalist; and the poverty-stricken and the wealthy.

Hong Kong is unique in the world politically. An island off the coast of China, it is a dependency of the United Kingdom and a Crown Colony. After 1997, it will revert to the People's Republic of China. The Chinese government has pledged to allow Hong Kong to continue the same economic system and way of life until 2047.

Hong Kong, whose wealth originated from the opium trade, is a trade and financial center with a population of five-and-a-half million, most of whom are crammed into tall buildings in an area just a few miles wide and long. Hong Kong has more people and more Mercedes Benz per square inch than any other spot on earth. In 1988, Hong Kong replaced Rotterdam as the largest container port on earth.

Despite its claustrophobic urban crowds, Hong Kong has more open space than cities half its size. You can make your way easily to rural areas, where the dramatic terrain offers fantastic views.

One of the most exciting views in the world is that of **Hong Kong Harbor** from **Victoria Peak.** Guarded by a tall fortress of mountains (behind which is China), the harbor is alive with ships and boats from every corner of the globe, picturesque Chinese junks, Russian cargo ships, hydrofoils, and tiny sampans of those who make their livings from the sea. Some of the boats in Hong Kong's harbor house people who have never set foot on land.

Out in the water beyond the traffic jams of the central harbor rises a large emerald mountain called **Lantau Island**. And if you look hard, or get up very high, you'll see 236 other islands in the nearby **South China Sea.**

Hong Kong is easily accessible. All the world's major international airlines fly

EMBASSY: None. Contact the **British Embassy** (see page 33).

SYSTEM OF GOVERNMENT: Dependency of the United Kingdom, administered by a governor. Will become part of China in 1997.

ETHNIC GROUPS: Chinese (mostly Cantonese), 98%; Vietnamese.

RELIGIOUS GROUPS: Buddhists; Taoists; Christians, 18%.

LANGUAGES: English (official); Chinese (official); Cantonese.

POPULATION: 5.659 million.

AREA: 410 square miles (1,061 square kilometers).

CAPITAL: Victoria (Hong Kong).

TERRAIN: Hilly. Excellent natural harbor. Uncultivable, 78.5%; arable, 13.5%; urban, 8%.

CLIMATE: Tropical, but with seasons: cool, dry, and sunny in the fall; hot and rainy in the spring; hot and humid in the summer.

TELECOMMUNICATIONS
Country Code: 852.
Time Zone: +13 hours Eastern Standard Time.

Code of Capital: 5.

LOCAL/NATIONAL AIRLINES: All of the world's major international airlines.

U.S. CONSULATE IN COUNTRY: *26 Garden Road, Hong Kong; tel. (852-5)239011.*

CURRENCY: Hong Kong dollar. No limit on import or export.

GROSS NATIONAL PRODUCT: $21.5 billion.

WORK FORCE: Commerce and services, 36.2%; manufacturing, 34%; government and utilities, 17.4%; construction 7.4%; agriculture and fishing, 1.6%.

OUR QUALITY OF LIFE RANKING: 63.27.

VISA REQUIREMENTS: A visa is not required if you are staying less than one month and you can show an onward/return ticket.

TOURIST OFFICES IN THE UNITED STATES: Hong Kong Tourist Association, *548 Fifth Ave., New York, NY 10036-5092; (212)869-5008.*

81

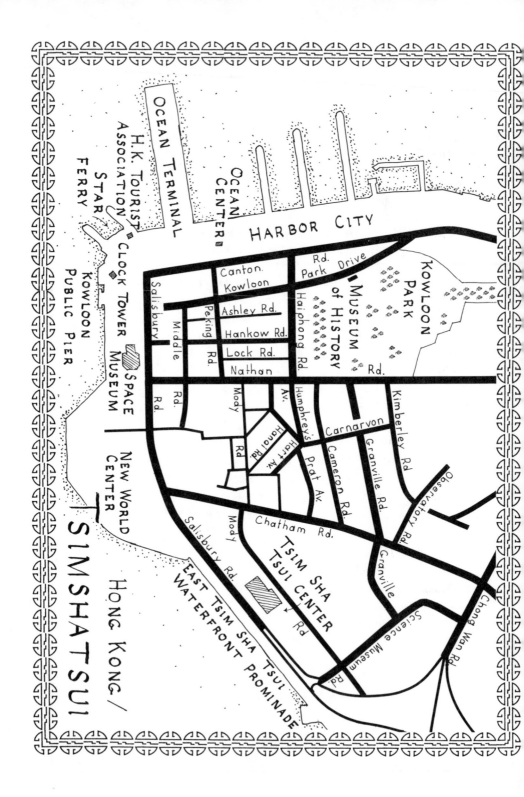

HARBOR CITY

OCEAN TERMINAL
H.K. TOURIST ASSOCIATION
STAR FERRY
KOWLOON PUBLIC PIER
OCEAN CENTER
Clock Tower

Canton Kowloon Rd.
Park Drive Rd.
Salisbury
Peking Rd.
Middle Rd.
Ashley Rd.
Hankow Rd.
Lock Rd.
Nathan
Rd.
Haiphong Rd.
MUSEUM of HISTORY
KOWLOON PARK

SPACE MUSEUM
Mody Rd.
Hanoi Rd.
Hart Av.
Humphrey's Av.
Prat Av.
Cameron Rd.
Carnarvon
Granville Rd.
Kimberley Rd.
Observatory Rd.

NEW WORLD CENTER
SIMSHATSUI
HONG KONG/
Salisbury Rd.
Mody
Chatham Rd.
Granville
TSIM SHA TSUI CENTER
Rd.
EAST TSIM SHA TSUI WATERFRONT PROMENADE
Science Museum Rd.
Chong Wan Rd.

82

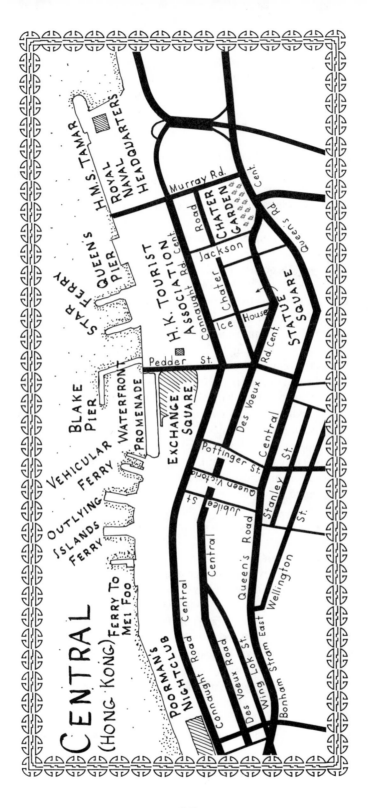

CENTRAL
(HONG-KONG)

FERRY TO Mei Foo

POORMAN'S NIGHTCLUB

OUTLYING ISLANDS FERRY

VEHICULAR FERRY

BLAKE PIER

STAR FERRY

WATERFRONT PROMENADE

QUEEN'S PIER

H.M.S. TAMAR

ROYAL NAVAL HEADQUARTERS

Murray Rd.

CHATER GARDEN

Road

Jackson

H.K. TOURIST ASSOCIATION

Chater

Ice House

Connaught Rd Cent

Pedder St.

EXCHANGE SQUARE

Queen's Rd

Cent.

STATUE SQUARE

Rd. Cent.

Des Voeux Central

Pottinger St.

Queen Victoria

Jubilee St

Stanley St.

St.

Wellington

Queen's Road Central

Wing Stram East

Bonham Stram East

Des Voeux Road Central

Connaught Road Central

into Hong Kong or have offices in the territory. About 1,000 flights go in and out of **Kai Tak International Airport** every week. Hong Kong's domestic airline is Cathay Pacific, a subsidiary of Swire Pacific, descendent of one of Hong Kong's early trading houses.

From Hong Kong you can book tours to China through **China International Travel Service** (CITS). (This is much less expensive than booking the same tours from the United States.) CITS also can arrange visas, usually within a day or two. The main CITS offices are located on Queen's Road Central and on the other side of the harbor in Tsimshatsui.

Hong Kong's **Mandarin** has been named by the bankers who read *Institutional Investor* as the world's best hotel. Service here is excellent.

The best way to see Hong Kong is on foot. Driving is both crazy and unnecessary, because Hong Kong is compact and its transportation systems are good. The **Star Ferry** is the world's cheapest and most scenic ferry ride—it costs about 9 cents for the short ride across the harbor.

Hong Kong has a new metro system. Taxis are metered and inexpensive. Double-decker buses and small mini-buses are routed extensively throughout the country. Trams trundle through the waterfront area on Hong Kong Island. You can take a tram up to Victoria Peak, an unforgettable experience.

Hong Kong is the biggest bazaar in the world. Because you do not pay import taxes on merchandise purchased here (with the exceptions of cigarettes, liquor, automobiles, and makeup), Hong Kong has some of the world's best prices. Clothes, electronic gadgets, watches, cameras, jewelry, and Chinese goods should all be at the top of your shopping list.

Hong Kong's major industry is textiles—this is the place to buy silks, sweaters, furs, and jeans. The country's best-kept secrets are its factory outlets, which carry overruns or rejects of items with well-known labels. Originally manufactured for export to the United States or Europe, these items are sold for fractions of what you'd pay elsewhere.

The best place to shop for camera equipment, watches, and electronic goods is along the **Golden Mile,** Nathan Road in Tsimshatsui. The farther up Nathan Road you go, the cheaper the merchandise.

It is safest to deal only with shops that display the Hong Kong Tourist Association's red junk logo on the window.

For a glimpse of age-old Chinese-style shopping, go to a night market. The largest is set up in the alleyways of the **Temple Street** area on Nathan Road above Jordan Road, in Yaumatei. Hawkers, portable restaurants, fortunetellers, and crowds gather to create a carnival atmosphere.

The famed **Jade Market** is set up on Canton Road, near the waterfront, every morning. If you don't know much about jade, don't expect to get a great bargain. This is the heart of the world's jade trade. You'll be able to pick out the big-time dealers—they're the Chinese holding newspapers over their hands. Traders bargain beneath the papers, tapping each others' hands so competitors can't tell what the bids are.

If you are interested in gambling, visit nearby **Macao.** This Portuguese enclave, only a 50-minute jet-foil ride from Hong Kong, has casinos, nightclubs, and some of the best restaurants in the region. The most advertised game room is the **Casino do Lisboa,** located in the Lisboa Hotel. The **Macao Palace** is more exotic, a red and gilded Chinese boat moored on the inner harbor off the Avenida de Almeida Ribeiro. Games include those familiar to Westerners, as well as Chinese games, such as *fan-tan, silk-po,* and *pai-kao. (*If you're interested in learning how to play these games, obtain a copy of *A Gambling Handbook,* published by Walter K. Hoffman and available in Hong Kong bookstores.)

Hong Kong's quiet coves, beaches, and small villages offer welcome relief from the pace of the big city. They can be reached by ferry from the city center. **Lantau, Lamma,** and **Cheung Chau** islands have beautiful beaches and seafood restaurants.

To see terraced farms, ancient temples and monasteries, mountains, and the sea, take a ride on the **Kowloon-Canton Railway,** which travels through the New Territories to China.

Try to time your visit to coincide with one of Hong Kong's many and colorful festivals: the **Chinese New Year** in January or February; the **birthday of Tin Hau,** goddess of the sea, in May, when fishermen decorate their boats and converge on seaside temples; the **Cheung Chau Island Bun Festival** in May, when special buns are distributed to ensure good luck and prosperity; the **Tuen Ng** (Dragon Boat) **Festival** in June, when dragon-headed boats race to commemorate the death of historic hero Ch'U Yuen; or the **Yuen Lan** (Hungry Ghosts) **Festival** in August, when spirits roam the world and are appeased with food. ❦

HUNGARY

It was a nightmare. There we were, two American women locked in a taxi in the middle of the Hungarian hills. Surrounding us were Russian soldiers, red stars on their hats, guns across their chests. I racked my brain trying to remember the Russian I had learned in college, but no one came to talk to us. My companion Berna worried about her young children.

We had been sightseeing throughout Hungary with a tour sponsored by Ibusz (the state tourist association). This is usually the cheapest and easiest way to see the city. The one drawback is that these tours are usually boring. So we had decided impulsively to go sightseeing on our own. We had abandoned our Ibusz tour group in the Szentendre studio shop of Margit Kovacs, a Hungarian ceramist. We had found an old lady who spoke German in the artist's village and had negotiated with the taxi driver for us. Stefan, the driver, had agreed to take us to see the sights on the Danube Bend. However, he spoke only Magyar—and he had disappeared.

After what seemed an eternity, Stefan returned. He pointed to the road and said, *"Russky Commissar si; Coca-Cola taxi nyet."* We understood. The road to Visegrad was closed because of Soviet army maneuvers. We would have to detour.

Stefan's message was a typical product of the new international *lingua franca* (because we were in Eastern Europe, it probably contained more Russian words than elsewhere). As our Hungarian adventure continued, we managed to buy sandwiches for lunch and two sorts of paprika from a local grocery store. At the end of the sightseeing, we each tipped Stefan with a dollar bill. He thanked us by saying, "Dollar, *merci.*"

Communication is the biggest obstacle to enjoying Hungary. The language is unique. Even simple concepts, such as airport, menu, waiter, hotel railroad station, and the names of foods, are incomprehensible, even if you have studied other

---

EMBASSY: *3910 Shoemaker St. N.W., Washington, DC 20008; (202)362-6730.*

SYSTEM OF GOVERNMENT: Communist unitary state. Part of the Soviet bloc.

ETHNIC GROUPS: Hungarians, 99.3%; Germans; Slovaks; Serbians; Croatians.

RELIGIOUS GROUPS: Roman Catholics, 54%; Calvinists, 20%; Protestants, 22%; members of the Eastern Orthodox Church, .5%; Unitarians; Jews.

LANGUAGE: Hungarian.

POPULATION: 10.624 million.

AREA: 35,900 square miles (930,030 square kilometers); comparable to Indiana.

CAPITAL: Budapest (population 2.1 million).

TERRAIN: Flat plains; low mountain ranges in the north and west.

CLIMATE: Humid, continental climate with seasons of equal length (warm summers and cold winters).

TELECOMMUNICATIONS
  Country Code: 36.
  Time Zone: +6 hours Eastern Standard Time.
  Code of Capital: 1.

LOCAL/NATIONAL AIRLINES: Maled, *(212)757-6480;* Czechoslovak Airlines, *(800)223-2365;* Lufthansa German Airlines, *(800)645-3880;* Pan Am, *(800)221-1111;* and Sabena Airlines, *(800)645-3700* (East Coast), *(800)632-8050* (New York), *(800)645-3790* (Southeast and Midwest), or *(800)645-1382* (West Coast).

U.S. CONSULATE IN COUNTRY: *V. Szabebsag Ter 12, Budapest 1054; tel. (361)126-450.*

CURRENCY: Forint. Travelers may import 100 forints and export 100 forints (in coins).

GROSS NATIONAL PRODUCT: $80.3 billion (in 1984).

WORK FORCE: Industry and commerce, 42%; services, 32%; agriculture, 20%.

Our Quality of Life Ranking: 56.18.

VISA REQUIREMENTS: Passports and visas (valid for six months) are required. To obtain a visa, apply to the embassy in Washington, D.C. or to the consulate in New York, at the Budapest Ferigegy Airport, or at frontier crossing points (this is not possible when traveling by train or boat).

TOURIST OFFICE IN THE UNITED STATES: **Hungarian Travel Bureau** (Ibusz), *630 Fifth Ave., Room 2455, New York, NY 10111; (212)582-7412.*

European languages. *Tej* means milk, not tea. Goulash is *tokany*; *gulyas* is a thick soup. The few words you will recognize are *bank, muzeum, busz, taxi, tram, kastely,* and *templom* (church).

Older Hungarians often speak rusty German. However, younger ones generally studied only Russian in school, and because they didn't like that, they developed a distaste for all foreign-language study. Only in the last decade, since the country began to develop its potential as a tourist site, have students been offered the chance to learn other languages.

Budapest has the most stunning hotels of any city in the world, because the best architectural brains of the past decade were put to work to build them. Near the railroad station is the **Hotel Budapest** (unfairly called "a stone dustbin" by Fodor). The **Hilton** was built into the ruins of an ancient abbey on top of a hill in Buda. The **Duna-Intercontinental, Atrium-Hyatt,** and **Forum** are beautifully designed palaces on the Pest side of the Danube. The Duna has river views but is a bit too big. The Atrium has a glass-covered central court through which glass-sided elevators soar. The Forum, which is a four- rather than a five-star hotel, is moderately cheaper.

Hungary is one of the few East European countries with a flourishing private sector in bed and breakfasts (it also has a private sector in taxis and real estate). You can make arrangements for bed-and-breakfast accommodations through Ibusz.

Hungary's architectural sights are not limited to modern hotel buildings. A main bridge across the Danube (from Buda to Pest, which at one time were two separate cities) was built by two British engineers named William Tierney Clark and Adam Clark. The Hungarian one-party parliament meets in a neo-Gothic building that is an exact replica of the Westminster parliament building in London (except that it is topped with a red star and the members' votes are meaningless).

If you visit Hungary as part of an Ibusz tour, you'll visit **Heroes' Square** at the edge of the city park in Pest. The square is filled with statues built to commemorate a man most Europeans feared but whom Hungarians venerate: Arpad, son of Attila the Hun.

Nearby are the major museums of Budapest. Don't miss the **Szepmuveszeti Muzeum** (Fine Arts Museum), filled with world-scale old masters. Try to visit without Ibusz. Budapest has three Rembrandts and major works by El Greco, Goya, Raphael, Rubens, Franz Hals, Monet, Renoir, and Cézanne. (It may have a Leonardo sculpture as well, depending on whether you listen to the Hungarians or the Italians.)

The **National Museum** on Castle Hill (the site of the former Hapsburg Palace) focuses on ethnography, the history of Hungarian socialism, the history of the city (with labels in Hungarian that the Ibusz guides can translate for you), socialist art, and books in Hungarian. However, the only things worth seeing here are the **Nemzeti Galeria** (National Gallery) and the excavations of the castle itself.

The **Matthias** (Coronation Church) is a magnificent Gothic church with a fine rose window and a treasury graced by an unusual object called an *encolpium* (a casket that contains a miniature copy of the Gospels and is worn around the neck), which belonged to the 12th-century King Bela III. The inside of the cathedral was painted in bright medieval colors as invented by Victorian artists for the coronation of Emperor Franz Joseph of Austria-Hungary.

Outside the cathedral is the lovely **Trinity Column.** If you walk from it toward the promenade down to the river on the weekend, you will stumble upon a lively Gypsy market on your right. In Hungary, Gypsies are a free-enterprise element. They deal in both secondhand goods and crafts. Among the bargains are leather clothes (jackets for men, skirts and tops for ladies), embroidery (clothing and tablecloths), and jewelry. Offer half the price the Gypsies ask for in dollar bills.

After you visit the market, walk through the old town upriver from the cathedral and wander among the restored houses. Peek into courtyards, and visit the unusual museums (a pharmacy museum, a printing museum, and a musical instruments museum). Most have brochures in English that make it possible for you to follow the exhibits without the help of Ibusz. (The Ibusz tour of the old town takes you to a perfectly pointless wax museum.) The city's chic restaurants and bars are concentrated in this area, too.

The Gypsies are better sources of handicrafts than the Hungarian state stores. However, I did find a lovely embroidered felt suit in the **Vaci Utca Handicrafts** shop, which is run by Ibusz, for about $25. It was available in only one color (red) and in only one size (40, about a U.S. 12).

Hungary also has department stores, including one on Vorosmarty Square called **Luxus.** My companion found a beautiful blue suede suit with knee breeches for $35. It was only half-price, because it was soiled. However, even after the cost of dry cleaning, it was a great bargain. You can get to Vorosmathy Square from the Buda hotels via the metro running in the direction of Mexikoi Ut-Deli Palyaudvar. This is a good base for shopping. Walk along the feeble Budapest equivalent of Fifth Avenue, **Vaci Utca,** then have coffee or tea at the smartest café in Budapest, **Gerbeaud,** *Vorosmathy Square.*

In addition to picturesque **Szentendre,** with its artists and restaurants, and the dramatic 14th-century castle of **Visegrad** that controls the river, the sites of the Danube Bend include the **Cathedral of Esztergom.** While the cathedral is a 19th-century marble concoction and not particularly interesting, the Primate's art collection in the attached museum is worth a visit for its Memlings and tapestries.

Also see the yellow stucco **Eszterhazy Palace,** now beautifully restored, where Hayden was concertmaster to the counts, and the nearby restored medieval town of **Sopron,** one of the most picturesque sites in Europe. Sopron is dominated by the **Tuztorony,** a fireman's tower, from which the firemen look out for blazes.

Hungary's **Lake Balaton** is popular among sportsmen, and in the summer East European campers mob the shores here. Lake Balaton produces a fish called *fugas* that is good eating. East of Budapest are **Eger** (from which the famous Bull's Blood wine comes) and **Tokaj,** where the most unusual Hungarian wine, Tokay, is produced.

Food in Hungary is spicy with paprika and accompanied by Gypsy zithers and violins. It is cheap by the standards of Western Europe—but not that cheap; and it is customary to tip 15%. The city's top-drawer places include **Hungaria** (formerly New York), a café-restaurant at Lenin Korut by the train station; **Alabardos** and

Feher Galamb, on Castle Hill; **Matyaspince,** in the new hotel zone, a beerhall with the best Gypsy orchestra in the world; and the **Duna,** in Szentendre. Pastry shops (in addition to Gerbeaud and the Hungaria in Pest) include **Angelika** in Buda.

It is usually cheaper to visit Hungary with a package tour, as we did. But it is because the guided tours are so boring that we were tempted to strike off on our own. 🦃

ICELAND

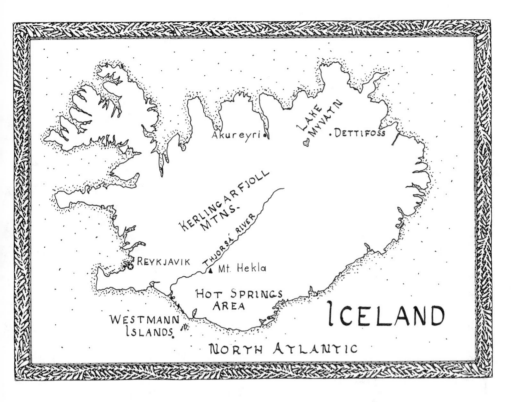

Iceland, a land of icy glaciers and steaming springs, is a world unto itself. It is the part of Europe closest to North America geographically, and experts are almost certain that pre-Columbian explorers starting out from Iceland were the first to discover the North American continent, which they called Vineland.

Inhabitants of Iceland are unusual, a product of their somewhat isolated environment. More books per capita are printed, bought, and read in Iceland than anywhere else in the world—the people have little else to do during the cold winters. Another curious feature of Iceland is its ban on beer. You can legally buy liquor and wine; only beer is outlawed.

You can get to Iceland on Icelandair, which is also a cheap way to get to Europe in general (although less so than in the old days, when the Icelanders first broke the trans-Atlantic price-fixing cartel). Special offers to encourage people to spend at least one night in Iceland en route to Europe are frequently available. It takes about five hours to get from New York to **Reykjavik,** Iceland's capital.

The best time to visit Iceland is from mid-June to the beginning of September, although temperatures are surprisingly mild year-round thanks to the Gulf Stream. The sun never shines for more than a few hours in midwinter, and it never sets at all in the summer.

The problem in Reykjavik is deciding what to see—there is so little. Visit the **National Theater,** the **university,** the **National Museum,** and the **Arbaer Folk Museum.** The view from the observation platform in the steeple of **Hallgrims Church** takes in the entire city, which, despite having been the site of a summit conference between President Reagan and Mikhael Gorbachev, is really only a small town. It is flat and treeless, with pretty little houses. It resembles a village more than the capital of a country.

If you are interested in Icelandic sagas and manuscripts, visit the **Arni Magnusson Manuscript Museum,** *Arnagardi, Sudurgotu.* The sagas being recited, may sound strangely familiar, even though you won't be able to recognize any of the words. The familiarity is thanks to Longfellow, who used the rhythm of Icelandic sagas for his poem *Hiawatha.*

EMBASSY: *2022 Connecticut Ave. N.W., Washington, DC 20008; (202)265-6653.*

SYSTEM OF GOVERNMENT: Constitutional republic.

ETHNIC GROUPS: Homogeneous mixture; descendents of Norwegians and Celts.

RELIGIOUS GROUPS: Evangelical Lutherans, 93%; Lutherans, 3.7%.

LANGUAGE: Icelandic.

POPULATION: 244,000 (in 1986).

AREA: 39,769 square miles (502,845 square kilometers); comparable to Virginia.

CAPITAL: Reykjavik (population 89,000).

TERRAIN: Rugged. Three-quarters of the land area is wasteland: a lava desert, glaciers, lakes, geysers, and hot springs.

CLIMATE: Mild because of the Gulf Stream. The average temperature in January is 30 degrees Fahrenheit; the average temperature in July is 52 degrees Fahrenheit.

TELECOMMUNICATIONS
   Country Code: 354.
   Time Zone: +5 hours Eastern Standard Time.

Code of Capital: 1.

LOCAL/NATIONAL AIRLINES: Icelandair, *(800)223-5500;* **Scandinavian Airlines Systems,** *(800)221-2350;* **Finnair,** *(800)223-5700;* and **Northwest Airlines,** *(800)447-4747.*

U.S. CONSULATE IN COUNTRY: *Laufasvegur 21, 101 Reykjavik; tel. (354-1)29100.*

CURRENCY: Krona. Travelers may import 700 kronur and export 8,000 kronur.

GROSS NATIONAL PRODUCT: $3.4 billion.

WORK FORCE: Industry and commerce, 49%; services and government, 30%; fishing, 14%; agriculture, 7%.

OUR QUALITY OF LIFE RANKING: 70.82.

VISA REQUIREMENTS: A visa is not required for stays of up to three months (period begins when you enter the Scandinavian area—Denmark, Finland, Norway, or Sweden).

TOURIST OFFICE IN THE UNITED STATES: Scandinavian Tourist Board, *655 Third Ave., New York, NY 10019; (212)949-2333.*

Take a dip in Iceland's open-air pools, which are filled with hot water year-round. Pools, like buildings here, are heated by natural hot springs, a feature of Iceland that has made it habitable despite its forbidding winters. Take a side trip to the hot springs of **Krisuvik.** If you take the Golden Circle tour out of Reykjavik, you will see the **Gullfoss waterfall** (Golden Fall), which was named after the double rainbow in its spray. You also will see the **Great Geyser** zone, with bubbling and steaming hot springs, mud pools, and geysers (the most active, **Strokkur,** spouts up to 100 feet). The tour also takes you to **Thingvellir,** the dramatic volcanic home of Iceland's parliament, the oldest democratic legislature in the world.

The **Thjorsardalur Valley** is impressive. **Mt. Hekla,** one of the world's most famous volcanoes, overlooks the area, which includes the Viking Age farm manor at Stong. Farther east is the lovely oasis of **Skaftafjell National Park,** guarded by **Vatnajokull,** Europe's greatest ice cap.

The west of Iceland was where they set out for Jules Verne's *Journey to the Center of the Earth*. The **Westmann Islands** off the coast were created a few years ago with the eruption of **Helgafjell,** near the town of Heimaey.

Iceland's other city, **Akureyri,** is in the north near the head of a fjord. From here you can visit the volcanic landscapes around **Lake Myvatn,** a mecca for bird watchers. **Dettifoss,** to the northeast, is Europe's largest waterfall.

Iceland's vast, uninhabited interior is covered with gravel deserts, lava fields, mountains, and ice caps. Hiking and mountain climbing are popular (expeditions should be undertaken only with a guide), as are salmon and trout fishing, reindeer hunting (in August and September), and wild goose shooting (from Aug. 20 to Nov. 20).

If you like to ride horses, you can rent Icelandic ponies, which are direct descendants of ponies brought to Iceland by the Vikings. Skiers can enjoy the ski resorts near **Akureyri** in the north and (during the summer) in the **Kerlingarfjoll** mountains in the south near the valley of Askard.

Unless you are traveling as part of a tour, the best way to see Iceland is by air. Domestic routes link about a dozen of the island's main towns and villages. You also can travel by bus.

The value of Iceland's currency, the krona, is pegged to a trade-weighted basket of the currencies of Iceland's major trading partners. The effect is to link Iceland's currency to that of other Nordic countries, making Iceland an expensive place to vacation. Hotels, especially, are expensive, but the tourist office may be able to make arrangements for you to stay in a private home.

Iceland is a good place for fish; in fact, it is the source of much of the frozen fish sold throughout the world. But Iceland's fish is better fresh (despite what Bird's Eye will tell you). Like all Scandinavians, the Icelanders offer vast help-yourself buffets, where you can make open-faced sandwiches. Try reindeer; unlike more easterly areas, Iceland was spared the fallout from Chernobyl, and its herds are intact. Reindeer is often served with cloudberries, which, like reindeer, live only in the far north.

The best souvenirs from Iceland are gray, beige, brown, and cream wool sweaters knitted in traditional geometric designs. ❦

INDIA

India is one of the world's most fascinating travel destinations. Allow plenty of time for a visit to this country, where even luxury accommodations are cheap.

India is a land of exotic customs and peoples, of powerful fortresses and delicate palaces, and of huge, lavish temple complexes dedicated to gods in the Hindu pantheon. India boasts the most beautiful tomb in the world (the **Taj Mahal**), the most bloodied house of worship (the **Golden Temple** in Amritsar), the world's highest mountains (the **Himalayas**), and the fertile **Ganges Plain,** one of the places where humans first became civilized.

India, a land of mysticism and spirituality, gave birth to two great religions: Hinduism and Buddhism. In India, two great 20th-century moral leaders have worked against poverty and injustice: Mahatma Gandhi and Mother Teresa. India is a land of terrifying fauna, including man-eating tigers and cobras. It is also a place where many, including Moslems, Hindus, and Sikhs, are prepared to kill for their faiths.

India is a land divided by region and racial type; by a rigid system of castes; by language (Hindi, a language derived from Sanskrit, is spoken in the north; unrelated Dravidian languages are spoken in the south); and by climate, which separates the cool highlands of Kashmir, Simla, and Darjeeling from the sweltering south. Even Indian cuisine is divided to reflect different regions (rice-growing and wheat-

EMBASSY: *2107 Massachusetts Ave. N.W., Washington, DC 20008; (202)939-7000.*

SYSTEM OF GOVERNMENT: Federal republic.

RACIAL AND ETHNIC GROUPS: Indo-Aryans, 72%; Dravidians, 25%; Mongoloids, 3%.

RELIGIOUS GROUPS: Hindus, 84%; Moslems, 10%; Christians, 2.6%; Sikhs; Jains; Buddhists.

LANGUAGES: Hindi; English (14 official languages).

POPULATION: 100 million.

AREA: 1,269 square miles (3,136 square kilometers).

CAPITAL: New Delhi (population 619,417).

TERRAIN: The Himalayan Mountains, the highest in the world, stretch along India's northern borders. The Deccan Peninsula is weathered and eroded. The Ganges Plain is fertile and densely populated.

CLIMATE: Varies from tropical to arctic, depending on the altitude.

TELECOMMUNICATIONS
  Country Code: 91.
  Time Zone: +10.5 hours Eastern

Standard Time.
  Code of Capital: 11.

LOCAL/NATIONAL AIRLINES: AirIndia, *(800)223-7776;* and **Pan Am,** *(800)221-1111.*

U.S. CONSULATE IN COUNTRY: *Shanti Path, Chanakyapuri 21, New Delhi; tel. (91-11)690351.*

CURRENCY: Rupee. Travelers may not import or export currency.

GROSS NATIONAL PRODUCT: $200.5 billion (in 1984).

WORK FORCE: Agriculture and fishing, 64.4%; commerce and services, 12.3%; manufacturing, 11.1%; construction, 1.8%; government, 8.9%.

OUR QUALITY OF LIFE RANKING: 36.44

VISA REQUIREMENTS: Visas (valid for three months) and passports are required. To obtain a visa, contact the embassy in Washington, D.C., or the consulate in New York, San Francisco, or Chicago.

TOURIST OFFICE IN THE UNITED STATES: Government of India Tourist Agency, *30 Rockefeller Plaza, North Mezzanine, Room 15, New York, NY 10112; (212)586-4901.*

growing, for example) and different religious and caste taboos.

India is also divided by class. Its population includes the heirs of fabulously wealthy maharajahs, rajputs, and politicians; a thriving commercial middle class in the cities; exploited and terrorized landless laborers; and the beggars of Calcutta, who may be among the most miserable people in the world. But the specter of widespread famine has been eliminated since the dawn of independence (1948), and the country today is largely self-sufficient in food.

India is a shopping emporium. With the exceptions of government stores, you bargain everywhere, even if the merchant insists that his prices are fixed. Goodies range from hand-knotted Oriental carpets to superb teas, from miniature Rajasthan paintings (antique or faked) to Jaipur or Hyderabad brass bangles, from saris of silk to Madras cotton scarves, from silver filigree or Cochin ivories to sandalwood soap.

Although Indian travel authorities try to encourage year-round tourism, you probably wouldn't enjoy visiting during the pre-monsoon summer heat. The winter season ends with the Hindu festival called **Holi,** which usually takes place in March, and resumes again with **Rama** in the fall. (Because the Indian calendar is lunar, the dates of festivals vary from year to year.)

Most people fly to **New Delhi,** the capital, although international flights also fly to Bombay, Calcutta, and Madras. Air India—which has developed tourist-pampering to an art—offers an excursion fare (14 to 120 days) with a stopover each way to either Delhi/Bombay or Calcutta/Madras.

Options for traveling inside the country include ultra-cheap but packed buses, railroads (including a Palace on Wheels route that covers the most popular Delhi-Agra-Rajasthan-Taj Mahal region), and the domestic airline, Indian Airlines. Both the railroads and Indian Airlines offer various passes that really can save you money. If you're planning your first trip to India, consider a package tour, which will allow you to see a great deal of the country in a short time. Unlike more mundane destinations, India attracts tourists whom you would probably find stimulating and companionable.

Inside a city, the way to get around is yellow-and-black (registered) taxis, which you can hire for the day or the excursion. (This is easier than trying to find a taxi for the return or onward trip.) Taxis are dirt cheap in India but you must set the fare in advance (bargain) since meters tend not to work for tourists. You can only rent cars in some cities and they are usually not air-conditioned; in other cases you will have to employ an Indian to drive you (this is not very expensive after you have paid for the car-rental).

Delhi and its northern neighbor, **New Delhi** are worth a visit. Sights include the **National Museum,** the astronomical observatory of **Jantar Mantar,** the **Red Fort,** and buildings of the Indian government—ranging from the Houses of Parliament and Presidential Palace to the striking U.S. Embassy. Remnants of British rule (the Raj) are worth visiting too.

In the Delhi area, the must-see excursion is to **Agra,** site of the **Taj Mahal,** a 17th-century mausoleum built by the Moghul Shah Jahan, one of the Moslem rulers of India, to commemorate his beloved wife. In Agra too is a Red Fort that is older than Delhi's. It contains Shah Jahan's palace, with its two mosques, bath, and harem.

97

Another logical expedition would be to the arid state of **Rajasthan**, to cities like **Jodphur** and pink-stone Jaipur, which can be reached by air, rail, or bus from the capital. Once in these cities you can travel around by taxi, camel, or elephant. Another Delhi-based excursion could go to the ill-fated city of **Bhopal**, site of the Union Carbide disaster. It was built according to the architectural ideas of powerful ladies, the Begums of the Moghuls. Or visit the Buddhist-founded town of **Sanchi**.

If you head north, **Amritsar** and its Golden Temple and **Chandigarh**, disputed by Hindus and Sikhs, are currently off-limits to travelers. Consider instead the Himalaya foothills; fly into the **Vale of Kashmir** to **Srinagar**, a town of mountain lakes and beautiful water gardens where you can live on a house-boat. Or hop over the Himalayas into **Ladakh**, a Buddhist center and a base for climbing and visiting monasteries (give yourself time to acclimatize to the thin air). Or watch tea grow, see the sun rise, and visit the Tibetan refugees in **Darjeeling.** Or go to **Simla**, where the British wives were sent to escape the heat of summer during the Raj, and where India looks like a cross between Switzerland and Brighton High Street as a result. Stroll wearing your parasol or pith helmet, and then take tea or a Choti Peg (small drink) in honor of the Empire.

Alternative bases for discovering India are Bombay, Madras, and Calcutta. **Calcutta** is as sprawling, as crowded, as appallingly poor as rumored. You can take an air-conditioned train overnight from Delhi to Howrah station in Calcutta, a matter of 18 hours. The port city of nine million people is a magnet for the poor of Bengal and Bihar, who provide bodies to fill its slums, its railroad station (home to thousands), its brothels, and even its sidewalks. The city was the Victorian capital of India and still maintains fine old Victorian houses around Dalhousie Square (still called that in spite of being rechristened to honor B.B.D. Bagh). More 19th-century houses line the Maidan, a grassy mall with a memorial to the Empress of India, other statues, a race course, a zoo, a botanical garden, and the former residence of the Governor of Bengal, now a library. You can visit Mother Teresa's Missionaries of Charity House and the home of Rabindranth Tagore, the writer, who also was from Calcutta.

Madras is the gateway to south India, although the city is not particularly interesting in itself. From here you should go to **Mabhalbalipuram** and **Kan-chipuram**, sites of elaborately-carved monuments, caves, cliffs, and temples of the Pallava dynasty, which ruled the Tamil zone in the tenth century. Other temples are a bit further afield at **Tiruchipalli** and **Chidambaram**. The nearby city of **Pondi-cherry** was formerly a French colony and still boasts Gallic-inspired restaurants. It was the home of yet another person touched by Indian mysticism, the French-born Mother of the Sri Aurobindo movement, whose ashram has been extended by the creation of a new French-designed Unesco-funded city called **Auroville**. You can visit and even spend the night.

Another interesting southern site is **Kerala**, the most Christian Indian state and the most left-wing. Here head for **Cochin**, home of India's largest Jewish community with a 400-year-old synagogue, a 2,000-year-old charter, the tomb of Vasco da Gama, and a Dutch palace.

Bombay is another megalopolis, home to India's version of Hollywood and center of its urban industrial revolution. The city sits on a peninsula where breezes (and storms) waft in from the Arabian Sea. This is a cosmopolitan city, home to India's Parsis (who are of Persian extraction and practice Zoroasterian religion and exposure of the dead) and to its Jains. This city also has Jews. It is famed for its gardens, aquarium, art museum (Prince of Wales Museum), and beaches. Nearby are the **Elephanta Caves**, which you visit by boat across the bay, and slightly further are the **Kanheri Caves** (in **Krishnagari National Park**). They were built by Buddhists starting in the second century. The National Park offers a lion safari in which you view the big cats from a closed vehicle.

Indian food is too complex to summarize here and it certainly goes beyond what we have been taught to call curry. (Indians do not use curry powder.) The food is unbelievably diverse, from *boona ghosht* (lamb stew) and *dal* (lentils or split peas) in the north to *prawn biryani* (risotto) in the south. India offers a myriad of special cuisines: vegetarian, Moslem, Parsi, Jain, Brahmin, and other religions. Foreign-influenced foods range from *selice* (white bread) to *vindaloos* (wine sauces) or peppery beef stew (eaten only by Christians in Goa or Pondicherry), to say nothing of modern foreign food (mainly but not exclusively Persian and Chinese). The hot pepper only became part of Indian cuisine after the discovery of America (it originated in the New World) and many delicate dishes are made without it. You can always ask for mild food.

Do not go native to the extent of drinking the water or eating food that has been washed in it. You will suffer Mohandas's Revenge. Everything should be peeled or cooked. Water should be bottled or have been boiled (to make tea, for example). As a general rule, avoid what Indian mothers try to train their children to avoid, junky bazaar food, sold from stalls and stands all around the country. Restaurants and snack bars are so cheap that the fast food option should be avoided. If you cannot go another inch without liquids or nourishment take *lassi*, a yogurt drink available either salted or sweetened. (Salted is said to be more refreshing in the heat.)

Or, depending on where you are, eat some bread: *chapatis, puris, poppadams, naans, parathas, idlis*. You will probably find Indian deserts too sweet and thirst-inducing, particularly as a snack. Indian ice-cream tastes like the sweetened condensed milk of my childhood and is to be avoided (alas, given the climate).

A word about drink. Much of India still practices prohibition and to get a cold beer, a glass of wine (India produces wine and even champagne), or a Choti Peg you will need a permit. This document certifies that you are an alcoholic, but is easily obtained by foreigners from Tourist Offices. Even the permit will not work in **Gujerat** and on certain days of the week in other places. When you order a drink the information on your permit is copied into a book by hand, which makes the order take a while to come to you. After you have gone through this process a few times you probably will have decided to join AA. ❦

INDONESIA

Indonesia is a country of 13,000 islands stretching across 3,000 miles from the Indian Ocean west of Thailand all the way to the Pacific reef between the Philippines and Australia. These are the Spice Islands, which Columbus set out to find, where cloves and nutmeg, pepper and cinnamon, are grown for the world, as well as premium coffee (the Indonesian island of Java gave its name to the American slang for coffee) and coconuts, rice, cassava, rubber, tin, tea, and oil. Originally settled by Asian and Malay people, Indonesia later drew Arabs (most Indonesians are Moslems—Indonesia has the largest Moslem population of any country in the world), Indians, Chinese, and, during the colonial period, Dutch. Indonesia has the fifth largest population in the world. There are distinct racial differences as you go from island to island, and there is some disaffection among ethnic groups that feel that they are discriminated against, such as the Moluccans, and the Hindus from Bali. The official language is Bahasa, but there are 250 languages and dialects.

Most travelers go to the most populated island, **Java**, where the capital, **Djakarta,** is located, and to the neighboring small island of **Bali**. But intrepid travelers can fly with Garuda or sail with the state-owned PELNI shipping line from island to island using bed and breakfast and pension facilities which exist in **Sumatra, Ambon, Molucca,** (best for snorkeling in coral seas), and **Sulawesi/Celebes.**

Once on shore you can travel on anything with wheels: bemos, opelets, and colts (which are types of van), ojeks (motorcycle taxis), or conventional taxis.

While Djakarta can be extremely hot, polluted, and smelly, it is worth a brief visit. The city's best sights include **Merdeka Square**, dominated by the Freedom Monument (400 feet high), and **Banteng Square**, with the statue of Indonesian

Independence. At **Glodok** waterfront, you can see gabled 17th-century Dutch houses with diamond-paned windows and massive wooden shutters, and the 17th-century Zion church, built by the Portuguese (who were displaced by the Dutch), with its immense pump organ. The cannon in the Glodok museum is visited by infertile Indonesians who hope it will help them bear children. Djakarta also offers picturesque markets and sophisticated nightlife. Lost-wax prints and tie-dyed cloths are among the specialties of Indonesia.

Outside Djakarta, Java island offers vistas from its two active volcanos, batik and silver markets, and the temple of **Borodudur**, the largest Buddhist temple in the world, one of the seven wonders of Asia. A mass of carved stone and rock built in nine concentric circles, it is a must see. (There are almost no practicing Buddhists left in Indonesia.)

Indonesian nights feature shadow puppets performing scenes from the Ramay-

---

EMBASSY: *2020 Massachusetts Ave. N.W., Washington, DC 20036; (202)775-5200.*

SYSTEM OF GOVERNMENT: Independent republic.

ETHNIC GROUPS: Malays; Chinese; Irianese.

RELIGIOUS GROUPS: Moslems, 90%; Christians, 5%; Hindus, 3%.

LANGUAGES: Bahasa Indonesian (official); 250 local tongues.

POPULATION: 176.764 million (in 1986).

AREA: 741,091 square miles (1.919 million square kilometers); slightly smaller than Alaska and California combined.

CAPITAL: Djakarta (population 7.585 million in 1984).

TERRAIN: More than 13,500 islands; the larger ones are coastal plains with mountainous interiors.

CLIMATE: Tropical.

TELECOMMUNICATIONS
　Country Code: 62.
　Time Zone: +12 hours Eastern
　　Standard Time (Djakarta).

Code of Capital: 21.

LOCAL/NATIONAL AIRLINES:
Garuda Indonesian, *(800)248-2829;* and **Japan Airlines,** *(800)525-3663.*

U.S. CONSULATE IN COUNTRY:
Jallan Merdeka Selatan 4, Djakarta Pusat; tel. (62-211)360-360.

CURRENCY: Rupiah. No limit on import or export.

GROSS NATIONAL PRODUCT: $84.8 billion (in 1984).

WORK FORCE: Agriculture and fishing, 54.7%; services and commerce, 18.2%; government, 12.3%; manufacturing, 10.4%; construction, 3.7%.

OUR QUALITY OF LIFE RANKING: 35.39.

VISA REQUIREMENTS: A visa is not required for stays of up to two months. You must have a valid passport and be able to show a return ticket when you enter the country.

TOURIST OFFICE IN THE UNITED STATES: Indonesian Consulate General and Information, *5 E. 68th St., New York, NY 10021; (212)879-0600.*

ana, a sacred Hindu religious text. The puppet shows are loved even by the 90 percent of the population that is Moslem. In **Bali,** where the population is largely Hindu, you must see the sinuous long-nailed dancers who, in gorgeous costumes and headdresses, are among the most graceful and charming in the world. Bali offers dozens of colorful religious ceremonies with feasting and dancing to cover all the deities of the Hindu canon, so there almost always is something to see. Balinese are graceful also in art, and sell metalwork (including gold and silver), and intricately woven sarongs and cloths. The artists' colony of **Ubud** (near Den Pasar) is worth a visit. The oldest temple on the island is **Pura Beskih**, on the slopes of **Mount Agung**, which Balinese consider to be the Navel of the World. At **Giangjar,** which is a center of cockfighting (legal in Indonesia), you will find the statue of the Garuda, the Hindu Phoenix, after which the national airline is named. It spouts water by the Bangli Beach.

Indonesia offers foods as varied as its population. Most Moslems will not eat pork, which is a feature of the cuisine of Hindu Bali, where the people do not eat beef. Whichever meat is allowed, a great dish you can safely eat from food stalls is *saté,* skewers of barbecued meat served with a peanut and chile-pepper sauce. *Nasigoreng* and *bamigoreng* (rice and noodle dishes with sauce) are good snacks; for finer fare, try curries. One thing the Indonesians have re-introduced is a dish originally put together by their Dutch colonial masters called Rijstafel, which simply is about 20 or 30 different dishes served in small quantities so you can taste a lot of different things. The accompaniments include chutneys and raisins, hot pepper sauce, ketchup (invented in Indonesia; but theirs is more like a soy sauce than a tomato concoction), coconut, peanuts, and fruits. Indonesian Chinese food is highly appreciated by non-Chinese Indonesians. In some areas the Chinese restaurants do not use pork out of respect for their customers' religion. ❦

IRELAND

ATLANTIC
OCEAN

NORTHERN
IRELAND

Sligo

CONNEMARA MTS.

IRELAND

IRISH
SEA

Galway

DUBLIN

Wicklow

Ennis

Limerick

Kilkenny

Wexford

Tralee

Waterford

Killarney

Cork

Ireland has castles, the Blarney Stone, deserted abbeys, moors broken by prehistoric burial sites, whitewashed cottages, and elegant Georgian townhouses. The Irish have the gift of the gab. Great writers who hailed from Ireland include: James Joyce, Jonathan Swift, William Butler Yeats, Samuel Beckett, Oscar Wilde, George Bernard Shaw, Edna O'Brien.

Ireland is small—295 miles from north to south, 171 miles from east to west.

In a day's drive, you can travel from the Gothic city of **Galway** through stone white **Connemara** into the violet red forests and mountains of Yeats' **Sligo**. The sea is never more than 70 miles away.

Ireland, for centuries the mysterious Western fringe of the world, is rich in prehistoric remains. Differing from its British neighbor in religion, ethnic background, history, and character, Ireland has always been a country of rebels, adventurers, and hermits. An independent Irish State came officially into being as late as 1922, after nearly 300 years of British occupation. The conflict in Northern Ireland today is confined to the six counties in Ulster that are still governed by the British.

Aer Lingus, Ireland's official airline, flies from New York and Boston and lands at Shannon and Dublin. You can also fly to London and then cross over on Aer Lingus or British Airways. This route is sometimes cheaper.

EMBASSY: *2234 Massachusetts Ave. N.W., Washington, DC 20008; (202)462-3939.*

SYSTEM OF GOVERNMENT: Parliamentary republic.

ETHNIC GROUPS: Celts; an English minority.

RELIGIOUS GROUPS: Roman Catholics, 94%; Anglicans, 4%.

LANGUAGES: English; Irish (Gaelic).

POPULATION: 3.624 million (in 1986).

AREA: 27,137 square miles (70,282 square kilometers); slightly larger than West Virginia.

CAPITAL: Dublin (population 502,000).

TERRAIN: Limestone plateau rimmed by coastal highlands. Many lakes, bogs, and low ridges in central plain area.

CLIMATE: Temperate maritime.

TELECOMMUNICATIONS
   Country Code: 353.
   Time Zone: +5 hours Eastern
   Standard Time.
   Code of Capital: 21.

LOCAL/NATIONAL AIRLINES: British Airways, *(800)247-9297;* **Aer Lingus,** *(800)223-6537;* **Northwest Airlines,** *(800)447-4747;* and **Sabena Airlines,**
(800)632-8050 (New York), *(800)645-3700* (East Coast), *(800)645-3790* (Southeast and Midwest), or *(800)645-1382* (West Coast).

U.S. CONSULATE IN COUNTRY: *42 Elgin Road, Ballsbridge, Dublin 4, Ireland; tel. (35-341)688-777.*

CURRENCY: Irish punt. No limit on import; travelers may export 100 Irish punts.

GROSS NATIONAL PRODUCT: $21.3 billion (in 1986).

WORK FORCE: Services, 31%; industry and commerce, 30%; agriculture, 16%.

OUR QUALITY OF LIFE RANKING: 66.13.

VISA REQUIREMENTS: A valid passport is required. A visa is not required for tourist stays of up to 90 days. You may be asked to show an onward/return ticket, necessary travel documents, or sufficient funds for your stay when you enter the country.

TOURIST OFFICE IN THE UNITED STATES: Irish Tourist Board, *757 Third Ave., 19th Floor, New York, NY 10017; (212)418-0800 or (800)223-6470.*

Touring by car is the most popular way to travel. But many of the well-maintained thoroughfares are one-lane, twisty roads bordered by stone walls. Along the curves you meet other cars, farm machinery, cyclists, runners, sheep, cows, and ponies, as well as the proverbial Irishman walking his pig (to feed it on public grass). For car rentals, you only need your U.S. license. Like the English, the Irish drive on the left side of the road.

Accommodations range from castles to manor houses, farmhouses to bed and breakfasts. The Hotel Central Reservation Service in Dublin can be reached at (353)1-735-209. All hotels include a service charge of 15 percent.

The best way to explore Ireland is to circle around its coast: Dublin, Wicklow, Wexford, Kilkenny, Waterford, Cork, Killarney, Limerick, Burren, Galway, County Mayo, and Sligo.

Centuries ago, the Normans fortified **Dublin** with a system of walls and castles known as The Pale (west of the fortification was a wild land known as "beyond the Pale"). The city then became the seat of the Anglo-Irish ruling class, which set Georgian houses among the wide boulevards and designed lovely squares and parks. The city is divided by the River Liffey. The jewel of Dublin's treasures is the "Book of Kells," over 1,000 years old, the most beautiful illuminated manuscript in the world, located in the library of Trinity College.

Dublin sights include its castle, with its handsome State Apartments and Heraldic Museum, where family trees are traced; the Martello Tower at Sandycove, where Joyce once lived; the Guinness Brewery, which offers a tour ending in the Tasting Room; the General Post Office on O'Connell Street, scene of the 1916 uprising; the National Museum; the National Gallery; the former residence of Percy Shelley at 1 Grafton St.; and Phoenix Park, one of Europe's finest, with a race course and zoo.

Visit **Enniskerry**, Ireland's prettiest village; **Wexford**, where the Vikings founded a seaside town; **Kilkenny**, which has medieval buildings and a grand castle; **County Kerry**, with its beautiful 100-mile drive hugging the coast of the **Inveragh Peninsula**; **County Galway,** where Gaelic is still an official language and where the **Cliffs of Moher** rise a spectacular 700 feet from the ocean; and **Sligo**, the dramatic countryside where the poet Yeats spent his childhood and asked to be buried.

The old market town of **Ennis** is a good base for exploring the west of Ireland, from which so many Americans stem. Visit **Bunratty House** (15th century, restored in the 20th), which shows how the ascendancy lordlings lived, and then the folk park behind the manor, which shows how lesser Irishmen survived. Nearby sights include **Gregans Castle** in **Ballyvaughan**, the stalactite-filled **Aillwee Caves,** and the **Craggorowan Ring Fort.**

The town has escaped the inflow of tourists that ruined the zone around Shannon Airport, now turned into a theme park for Americans with colleens serving Irish stew at fake banquets in **Bunratty Castle** each night, and antique stores selling junk for the U.S. market. But Ennis is unspoiled, with genuine antiques (pricey), crafts, and a beautiful monastery, as well as an old coaching Inn (The Old Ground) where you can stay. From here visit **Tralee** and the **Dingle**

Peninsula, notably **Conor Pass** and **Sybil Head**, cliffs with thatched cottages and the rolling Atlantic surf below. The **Cliffs of Moher** are a spectacular spot north of Ennis, 700-foot black crags with the rush of the sea and spectacular sunsets.

Shopping in Ireland should be focused on antiques (cheaper than in England and this country), crystal from Waterford, woolens knitted or woven, and, of course, Irish linen.

Meat, game, dairy products, and seafood are of high quality and reasonable cost. Lamb really is good; and the potatoes too have a rich taste. All those myths about Irish stew being better in Ireland are true. A fine broth of a dish is Dublin Bay prawns, which are a kind of shrimp. Vegetables are always fresh but limited in variety. Fruit is limited and expensive. From these good ingredients the Irish make simple but tasty food. 🐚

ISRAEL

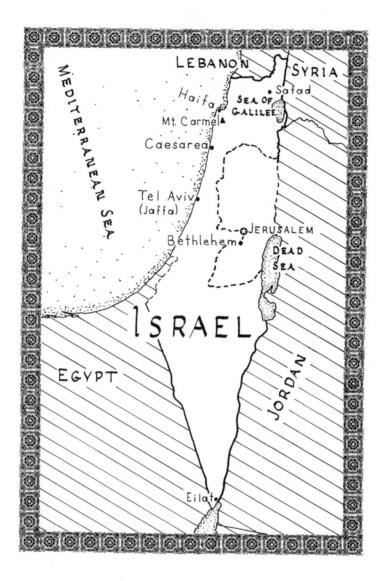

Israel is (alas) theologically too significant. The restored historic home of the Jews, it is also the country where Jesus was born, preached, and was crucified, and the place from which Moslems believe Mohammed ascended bodily to heaven. The resulting squabble between monotheistic religions has resulted in interminable wars and constant misunderstanding. At the Bethlehem Church of the Nativity of the Prince of Peace, monks and priests of different Christian sects battle with cudgels for the right to turn on a light or open a door. In **Jerusalem**, the **Dome of the Rock** sacred to Moslems is near the **Wailing Wall**, the sole remains of the **Biblical Temple**, sacred to Jews, and just down the road from the **Garden of Gethsemane** where Jesus spent the night before his capture and trial. All this religion brings out the savage worst in people and the country is periodically torn by strikes, usually by Arabs against their Jewish rulers, and by terrorist incidents.

Israel is also a geological wonder, being at the joining place of three continents (Europe, Africa, and Asia), and the northern extension of the Great Rift Valley, which runs through Africa. The **Dead Sea** is the lowest point on earth, its waters so

---

EMBASSY: *3514 International Drive N.W., Washington, DC 20008; (202)364-5500.*

SYSTEM OF GOVERNMENT: Democratic republic with no written constitution.

ETHNIC GROUPS: Jews, 85%; Arabs, 15%.

RELIGIOUS GROUPS: Jews; Moslems; Christians; Druses.

LANGUAGES: Hebrew; Arabic; English; Yiddish.

POPULATION: 4.331 million.

AREA: 8,302 square miles (21,501 square kilometers).

CAPITAL: Jerusalem (population 431,000).

TERRAIN: Mountains, desert, and fertile Mediterranean coastal plains.

CLIMATE: Temperate, except in the desert areas.

U.S.-ACCREDITED HOSPITALS: Herzliya Medical Center.

TELECOMMUNICATIONS
 Country Code: 972.
 Time Zone: +7 hours Eastern Standard Time.
 Code of Capital: 2.
LOCAL/NATIONAL AIRLINES: TWA, *(800)892-4141;* and **El Al Israel**

Airlines, *(800)223-6700.*

U.S. CONSULATE IN COUNTRY: *71 Rehov Hayarkon St., 63903 Tel Aviv; tel. (972-2)03-654338.*

CURRENCY: Shekels. No limit on import; travelers may export 500 shekels. American dollars are used in stores and restaurants. Change is given in shekels.

GROSS NATIONAL PRODUCT: $21 billion (in 1984).

WORK FORCE: Services, 60%; industry and commerce, 34%; agriculture, 6%.

OUR QUALITY OF LIFE RANKING: 53.75.

VISA REQUIREMENTS: Passports are required. Tourist visas are not required for stays of up to three months (apply to the Ministry of the Interior for extensions). Holders of official/diplomatic passports must obtain visas before entering the country. To obtain a visa, contact the consulate in Washington, D.C., Boston, New York, Atlanta, Chicago, Houston, Los Angeles, Miami, Philadelphia, or San Francisco.

TOURIST OFFICE IN THE UNITED STATES: Israel Government Tourist Office, *350 Fifth Ave., New York, NY 10118; (212)560-0650.*

salty and mineral-laden that you cannot drown but can only float; if you have a scratch or a cut, you will be in agony. The **Red Sea** is full of unique plant life and corals, and tropical fish found nowhere else. Haifa is one of the world's most beautiful natural harbors, a bowl sloping down to the water from Mount Carmel.

Israel is also where the desert was made to bloom. At the start of this century, when Israel was called Palestine and was ruled first by the Turks and then by the British, the early Zionist settlers came here motivated by Biblical prophecy and a desire to escape the narrow anti-Semitic ways of Europe. They drained the swamps and developed sophisticated irrigation techniques making Israel one of the most important food exporting countries (particularly of citrus fruits). They developed the only successful form of collective agriculture, the Kibbutz, as well as more free-enterprise farming structures. This pioneer group gave birth to the first *sabras* (native-born Israelis), who are still an elite. (A *sabra* is a cactus plant with nasty spikes outside and a sweet fruit inside.)

As Hitler's horrors led European Jews to a search for a refuge, Israel's population grew, and along with it increased pressure on Britain from its Arab allies to stop the exodus. Massive immigration by survivors of the Holocaust, and terrorism by both Jews and Arabs, marked the period after World War II. In the middle of this turmoil, the British gave the country its independence in 1948. Immigration of Jews from countries such as Yemen, Iran, the Soviet Union, and Ethiopia has kept the population growing.

Obviously the most important things to see in Israel are old: **Bethlehem, The Wailing Wall, Capernaum** (Tiberias) on the **Sea of Galilee,** the ruins of the **Masada,** where the Hebrew resistance to the Romans culminated in mass suicide, the **Via Dolorosa,** the hill town of **Safad,** which was a center of medieval Jewish mysticism and **Kabbala** (an occult theosophy based on Hebrew scriptures), and the old Crusader port of **Jaffa,** or the Roman port of **Caesarea.**

But the Jewish State builds and builds. Major modern sights in **Jerusalem** include the **Yad Vashem** museum and archive, devoted to documenting the Holocaust, and the Chagall stained glass windows at the **Hadassah Hospital Synagogue.** In **Tel Aviv** you have the **Knesset** (Parliament) buildings and boulevards such as Dizengoff Street and Allenby Road lined with sidewalk cafés. You also have fine museums of art and history, good shops, and a beach. In **Haifa** you have the gold-domed **Bahai Temple** and its magnificent gardens—holy spot of yet another religion, and the old **Technion** (technical institute) campus in the Turkish style. This city even has a cable car railroad and it has excellent art and archeology museums.

Israeli food is not confined to chicken soup with matzo balls. The country has adopted several meatless Arab dishes and given them an Israeli twist, notably *hummous bi tahina* (a garbanzo bean and sesame seed mixture) and *falafel* (garbanzo bean "meatballs" with salad and dressing served in a pita bread). But traditional European Jewish food is available from corn beef brisket to *cholent* (a meat, white bean, and vegetable stew), from *challah* (Sabbath bread) to *gefilte* fish (carp and whitefish quenelles). So are Viennese- and Danish-style pastries and cakes. And Israeli wine is much better than Manischevitz.

109

Shopping goodies include colored stones and diamonds (which are an international Orthodox Jewish monopoly), and Yemenite jewelry in silver filigree. Intricate embroidered garments and accessories, often with metal threadwork, are also produced by Yemenite Jews. And "Persian" miniatures can be of very high quality. The usual copper and brass items, leather goods (such as huaraches and handbags), and olivewood carvings are sold in Israeli markets. *Hondle* (bargain). An awful lot of poor-quality goods are being mass produced; let your taste be your guide.

Israeli internal travel can be done by air, by Eged bus, or by hitchhiking, which is safe and standard in this country of youthful population and compulsory military service. The country's tourism business has not yet become a target of terrorists, but visitors should take precautions if they go to the Occupied West Bank or areas near the Lebanese frontier.

In addition, travelers may prefer not to have Israeli visas stamped in their passports on arrival (to avoid a future travel ban when trying to go into an Arab country). As a Jewish State, Israel gives its nationality to anyone born of a Jewish mother who does not adhere to any other religion.

Although several airlines fly to Israel, the safest may be El Al, which has had the most severe problems with Arab terrorists—and therefore has the experience of having overcome them. 🍂

ITALY

Italy was the favorite destination of the earliest recreational travelers, British gentlemen and German intellectuals of the early 18th century. And they have left their mark on the way we view Italy. In no other country has a set of place names in English been imposed to the same degree as in Italy. We insist on saying Rome (for

111

Roma), Florence (Firenze), Milan (Milano), Genoa (Genova), Leghorn (Livorno), Venice (Venezia), Turin (Torino), Sicily (Sicilia), Naples (Napoli), etc. The proliferation of foreign names reflects the late political unification of Italy, which as a country with a single government is 90 years younger than the United States. Before that time, Italy was a geographical figure of speech, where people were unsure of the pronunciation and spelling of their language—which left room for foreign imperialist nomenclature.

We will start with **Rome**, the center of Italian political life, the Roman Empire, and the Papacy. Roman remains include the **Forum** and the **Colosseum**, temples

---

EMBASSY: *1601 Fuller St. N.W., Washington, DC 20009; (202)328-5500.*

SYSTEM OF GOVERNMENT: Republic.

ETHNIC GROUPS: Italians (the majority); Germans; French; Slovenes; Albanian Italians.

RELIGIOUS GROUPS: Predominantly Roman Catholics.

LANGUAGE: Italian.

POPULATION: 57.226 million.

AREA: 116,308 square miles (301,233 square kilometers).

CAPITAL: Rome (population 2.834 million).

TERRAIN: Primarily rugged and mountainous, with some coastal plains.

CLIMATE: Generally mild Mediterranean. Varies with the region and altitude.

TELECOMMUNICATIONS
 Country Code: 39.
 Time Zone: +6 hours Eastern Standard Time.
 Code of Capital: 6.

LOCAL/NATIONAL AIRLINE: Alitalia, *(800)223-5730;* and **Council Charter,** *(212)661-0311.*

RAILROAD OFFICE IN THE UNITED STATES: Italian State Railroads, *666*

Fifth Ave., New York, NY 10019; (212)757-5944.

U.S. CONSULATE IN COUNTRY: *via Vittorio Veneto 119A, 00817 Rome; tel. (39-6)4674.*

CURRENCY: Lira. No limit on import; travelers may export 5 million lira.

GROSS NATIONAL PRODUCT: $368 billion.

WORK FORCE: Services and government, 46%; industry and commerce, 30%; agriculture, 10%.

OUR QUALITY OF LIFE RANKING: 78.90.

VISA REQUIREMENTS: Passports are required. Visas are not required for stays of up to three months. For longer stays, obtain a visa before departure from the embassy in Washington, D.C., or the consulate in New York, Chicago, Boston, New Orleans, Los Angeles, Philadelphia, San Francisco, Detroit, or Newark. Visa extensions can be obtained from the Italian police.

TOURIST OFFICE IN UNITED STATES: Italian Government Travel Office, *630 Fifth Ave., New York, NY 10111; (212)245-4822.*

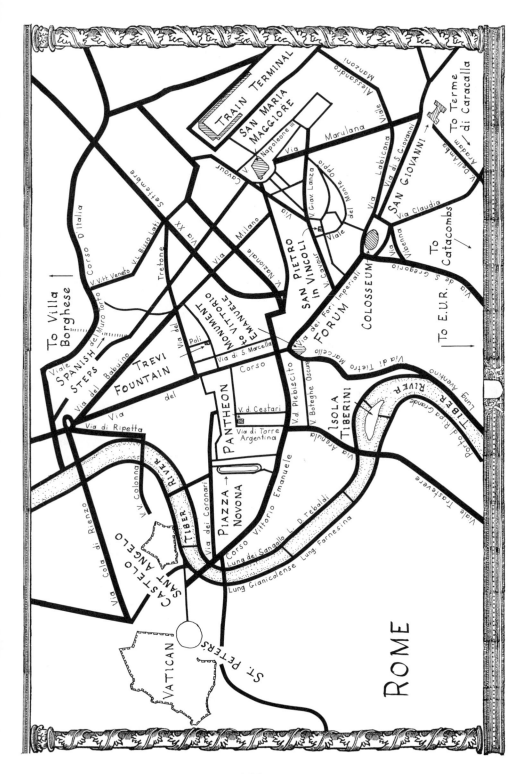

ROME

TRAIN TERMINAL

SAN MARIA MAGGIORE

V. Napoleone III

V. Cavour

To Villa Borghese

Corso D'Italia

V. Vitt. Veneto

V.le Bisso Latio

Tretone

Via XX Settembre

Via Milano

V. Nazionale

Via del Muro Torto

SPANISH STEPS

TREVI FOUNTAIN

Viale

Via del Babbuino

Via di Ripetta

Via del Corso

MONUMENT to VITTORIO EMANUELE

Via del

Poli

Via di S. Marcella

Via di Torre Argentina

V. d. Cestari

PANTHEON

PIAZZA NAVONA

Via dei Coronari

V.V. Colonna

TIBER RIVER

CASTELO SANT ANGELO

Via Cola di Rienzo

VATICAN

St. PETER'S

Via del Monte Oppio

SAN PIETRO in VINCOLI

Via dei Fori Imperiali

FORUM

COLOSSEUM

V. Giov. Lanza

Viale

Via Marulana

Via Labicana

Via di S. Giovanni

SAN GIOVANNI

Via Claudia

Viale Manzoni

Viale Alessandro

To Terme di Caracalla

Via dell'Amba Aradam

Via de S. Gregorio

To Catacombs

To E.U.R.

Corso

Corso Vittorio Emanuele

V. d. Botteghe Oscure

Via Arenula

V.d Plebiscito

Lung Gianicolense

Lung. Farnesina

Lung dei Sangallo L. D. Tebaldi

ISOLA TIBERINI

Via di Tietro Marcello

TIBER RIVER

Lung Aventino

Porto di Ripa Grande

Viale Trastevere

and baths, arches and the **Pantheon**, several roads and the catacombs that line them. Inside some of the catacombs are the symbols of the new Christian religion, which flourished as the Roman Empire declined—not a cross, but a fish. The tomb of the most important early martyr to the the faith, St. Peter, is underneath the main altar of the **Vatican.**

The papal power in the middle ages ruled the spiritual life of Europe. But even in its period of decadence (under not very spiritual popes), the popes had the wealth and good taste to bring in the best artists of the Renaissance. Their works make the **Vatican** a must-see for people of all faiths. Here is the **Sistine Chapel** ceiling by Michelangelo, here is his Pietà, here are great murals by Raphael. And here too is the Laocoön—a Greek statue that was a major influence on Renaissance sculpture.

Outside the Vatican are other important Medieval and Renaissance works of art: Filippo Lippi and Holbein works in the **National Gallery**; Titian paintings and Bernini sculptures in the **Villa Borghese Gallery;** Michelangelo's Moses in **San Pietro in Vincolo church.**

Walk along the Tiber and visit the city's squares, notably the **Piazza Navona** with its great fountains and the **Trinita dei Monti** with its **Trevi Fountain** and **Spanish Steps**; here lived Shelley and Keats. Window shop along the **via del Corso** below, or take in the gardens of the Villa Borghese above the steps.

Florence, which was ruled by the powerful and corrupt Medici clan during the Renaissance, is an even more magnificent monument to patrons of art. Here is a lovely cathedral whose baptistery contains the most beautiful bronze doors ever cast, by Lorenzo Ghiberti. At the **Signoria**, from which the city was ruled, stand copies of Michelangelo's David and Donatello's Judith; the originals are in the **Accademia** gallery. The **Uffizi** off the Piazza dei Signori used to be the city hall; now an art gallery, it contains masterpieces by Botticelli, Leonardo, Raphael, Piero della Francesca, Dürer, Holbein, and Rubens.

But almost any old church in Florence is worth visiting because almost every one contains one great work of art or another. The Tuscan countryside around Florence also is full of art and wonders: **Siena,** with its medieval town and striped cathedral; **Pisa** with its leaning tower; **Bologna** with the oldest university in the world.

Milan is home to **La Scala,** a great opera house, and to The Last Supper by Leonardo, which is located in the rectory of a suburban convent. Here is the **Duomo,** a curious squat church with hundreds of pinnacles, and here is the **Galleria Vittorio Emmanuele II**—the most beautiful shopping mall in the world.

Then there is **Venice**, which is itself an architectural masterpiece, a city built on piles along a lagoon, with canals instead of streets. Visit **St. Mark's Basilica,** a Byzantine masterpiece, and watch the pigeons and the strollers from the cafés outside it (have a refreshing Italian ice). Sigh on the **Bridge of Sighs** and then visit the **Doge's Palace,** where the autocratic rulers of the Adriatic accepted denunciations. And above all, walk to see the vistas of this floating city, its great domed church and its **Accademia** gallery, its **Ghetto** (the first) and its markets, its tiny streets and its boat-filled canals.

Other sights in Italy include the beautiful **Lake District** and the **Isle of Capri,** the great excavations of **Herculaneum** and **Pompeii** (both suburbs of Naples), the **Dolomite Alps,** the **Riviera** coast, and the fishing port and yacht basin of **Portofino.** Offbeat tourists are heading for undeveloped regions such as **Sicily** and **Sardinia.**

Italy's art, created over thousands of years (at least since the Etruscans), is scattered all over the country. This can be blamed on the nation's late centralization. You can spend a lifetime exploring Italy; I would love to.

Italy is also a good place for shopping, with relatively cheap prices by European standards. Things to look for: shoes and leather goods, silk and imitation silk clothing, cameos, coral, marble, fake "designer-label" luggage, and belts. Beware fake antiques, which are mass-produced here. Cotton shirts and silk ties are of very good quality for the price; women's clothing is often overpriced, in contrast.

Italian food is not confined to pasta and pizza. In fact, outside Naples, there is not much pizza in Italy. In the north people eat rice and in the south they eat polenta—not just spaghetti and macaroni. This country has one of the healthiest diets in the world, based on good fresh salads and vegetables, and food cooked in low-cholesterol olive oil. The country's veal is wonderful—nothing like the travesty of veal sold in America. Italian ices (a sort of water-based ice cream) are excellent, but most meals end in fruit, which Italians eat with knife and fork. The wine is good and cheap. ❦

JAMAICA

"**C**arry me ackee go Linstead market, not a quatie would sell." This is the refrain of a Jamaican calypso song about the problems of making a market in *ackee* (breadfruit), which is the foundation of Jamaican cuisine. But for a few years the song also reflected the doldrums of the tourist market in Jamaica, as tourism also didn't sell. Travelers were discouraged from visiting the country, because of a brutal golf course murder of an American tourist, political unrest, and a wave of nationalizations. The situation is improving, and tourism is picking up—which is just as well because Jamaica needs the money.

Jamaica (see map on page 17) is an island 90 miles south of Cuba. It is about the size of Connecticut. Its highest point is Blue Mountain (7,400 feet), which is the home of one of the world's best coffees; the island also is a major source for bauxite, from which aluminum is made. The volcanic mountains and hills make this an interesting island to look at, and there are rivers and waterfalls as well.

Jamaica, discovered by Columbus, was used for growing sugar after the British captured it in 1655. The natives (Arawak Indians) died off, and African slaves were brought in to do the work. A number of escaped slaves, called Marroons, survived and established villages in the mountains. The slaves were freed in 1833. In 1865 there was an uprising related to the low price of sugar at the time, and this resulted in Jamaica becoming a colony.

Jamaica was granted independence in the West Indies Federation in 1958 but this attempt to unify the former British Caribbean colonies failed and the country became independent in 1961.

The island has long suffered from underemployment and became a source for emigration to Britain and other Caribbean countries, as well as to the United States Under Michael Manley's left-wing government, U.S. aluminum companies on the island were nationalized. His successor, Edward Seaga, has been more pro-American, as a result of which Jamaica has again been the beneficiary of U.S. aid. Curiously, although the overwhelming majority of the island's population of 2 1/4 million is black, both Manley and Seaga are fair-skinned.

Jamaica is the home of one of the great musical cultures of the world, called reggae—which is closely linked to two other Jamaican traditions, *ganja* (marijuana) and the peculiar Jamaican cult of Rastafarianism, which involves wearing unshorn hair (dreadlocks), rebellion or revolution (according to Manley), and idolizing the late Haile Selassie of Ethiopia. The late Bob Marley was the most important reggae performer (his Kingston home has become a museum), but there are flourishing groups and stars both on the island and among the Jamaican diaspora in the United States and in Britain. Reggae, one of the island's attractions, is closely linked to some of the things that discourage tourists. Other talents of the population include calypso music and limbo dancing (which involves getting under or over a bar by the most incredible acrobatic feats).

Kingston, on the south coast, has many slums and a high crime rate. Americans should take precautions when visiting the great reggae bars of Kingston. Among them is **Junkanoo Lounge.**

Instead of going to Kingston, which is a lively and exotic city, most travelers head for the north coast, which runs from **Negril** (which has a nude beach) in the west past **Montego Bay** (also called Mobay), still the most aristocratic travel destination here, although there has been overbuilding), and on toward **Ocho Rios.** The new tourist zone beyond it takes in **Oracabessa** (where Noel Coward had his house) and **Port Antonio** and the island in the middle of its harbor (once owned by Errol Flynn). These areas are the center of private homes and lack entertainment.

Along this coast are beaches, golf resorts, scuba diving, sailing, tennis, and horseback riding. Many fine old colonial houses and former sugar plantations still stand, now used as hotels. Furnished with antiques, with an extensive Jamaican staff, they create an aristocratic ambience where travelers feel pampered. Then, to make Americans happy, there usually are swimming pools, jacuzzis, and air condi-

---

EMBASSY: *1850 K St. N.W., Suite 355, Washington, DC 20006; (202)452-0660.*

SYSTEM OF GOVERNMENT: Constitutional monarchy.

ETHNIC GROUPS: Blacks, 90%; East Indians, Europeans, and Chinese, 10%.

RELIGIOUS GROUPS: Protestants, 70%; Rastafarians.

LANGUAGES: English; Jamaican Creole.

POPULATION: 2.288 million.

AREA: 4,244 square miles (10,991 square kilometers).

CAPITAL: Kingston (population 100,000).

TERRAIN: Mountainous. Coastal plains on the southern coast.

CLIMATE: Tropical at sea level. Temperate in the uplands.

TELECOMMUNICATIONS
Country Code: 809.
Time Zone: +0 hours Eastern Standard Time.

LOCAL/NATIONAL AIRLINE: Air Jamaica, *(800)622-3009;* **American,** *(800)433-7300;* **Eastern,** *(800)327-8376;* and **Northwest Airlines,** *(800)444-4747.*

U.S. CONSULATE IN COUNTRY: *Jamaica Mutual Life Center, 2 Oxford Road, Third Floor, Kingston 5; tel. (809)929-4850.*

CURRENCY: Jamaican dollar. No limit on import or export.

GROSS NATIONAL PRODUCT: $2.4 billion (in 1984).

WORK FORCE: Agriculture, 35%; services, 19%; manufacturing, 13%.

OUR QUALITY OF LIFE RANKING: 45.83.

VISA REQUIREMENTS: Passports and onward/return tickets are required. Visas are not required for travelers.

TOURIST OFFICE IN THE UNITED STATES: Jamaica Tourist Board, *866 Second Ave., 10th Floor, New York, NY 10017; (212)688-7650.*

---

tioning. High season in Jamaica is midwinter, when the tropics are most alluring. (There are bargains to be found in the off-season.) The most popular time to visit is *Junkanoo* (Christmas).

Apart from *ackee*, Jamaican food features the *plantain*, which looks like a banana but isn't, fruit (including coconuts and *ugli*), jerk pork, peanuts, and wonderful fresh lobster and fish. Jamaicans make soup out of pumpkins. The best drinks include rum and Rose's lime juice, fresh orange juice, and Blue Mountain coffee.

Shopping goodies include baskets, straw hats, and beads. And of course, reggae records. ❦

JAPAN

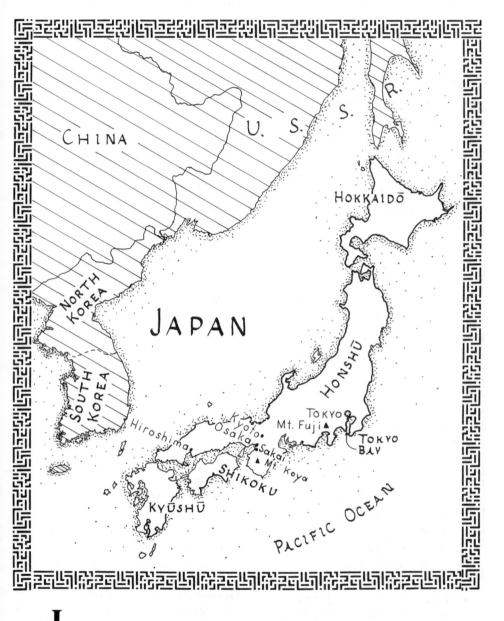

J apanese are among the most ambitious tourists in the world, and one way to get even with them is to head for Japan as a tourist yourself. The Japanese taste for tourism began in their own islands and they developed a beautiful style of country inn, called the *ryokan*, which is one of the charms of the nation. Surrounded by gardens, these inns feature typical Japanese architecture: simple wood frames with paper-filled windows, sliding walls, *futons* (roll-up beds), and baths. You are expected to leave your shoes at the door and to wear kimonos provided by the *ryokan*.

The population of Japan is 121 million and it is spread over nearly 4,000 Japanese islands. The volcanic islands stretch across 1,700 nautical miles. Some are subject to volcanic eruption. Most of the people live in greater **Tokyo** and other cities. The climate is very damp and rainy.

EMBASSY: *2520 Massachusetts Ave. N.W., Washington, DC 20008; (202)234-2266.*

SYSTEM OF GOVERNMENT: Parliamentary democracy.

ETHNIC GROUPS: Japanese, 99.4%; Koreans, 0.5%.

RELIGIOUS GROUPS: Shintoists; Buddhists; Christians.

LANGUAGES: Japanese (official); English.

POPULATION: 121 million (in 1986).

AREA: 145,841 square miles (377,728 square kilometers); comparable to California.

CAPITAL: Tokyo (population 8.514 million).

TERRAIN: Hilly, with narrow coastal plains.

CLIMATE: Varied. Cold in the winter in the north, subtropical in the south.

TELECOMMUNICATIONS
   Country Code: 81.
   Time Zone: +14 hours Eastern Standard Time.
   Code of Capital: 423.

LOCAL/NATIONAL AIRLINES: China Airlines, *(800)227-5118;* **Japan Airlines,** *(800)525-3663;* **Northwest Airlines,** *(800)447-4747;* **Pan Am,** *(800)221-1111;* and **Varig Airlines,** *(800)327-2604.*

U.S. CONSULATE IN COUNTRY: *1-10-5, Akasaka, Minato-Ku 107, Tokyo; tel. (81-423)583-7141; telex 2422118;* **U.S. Consulates General,** *Naha, Okinawa; Osaka-Kobe.*

CURRENCY: Yen. No limit on import (subject to declaration); travelers may export ¥5 million.

GROSS NATIONAL PRODUCT: $1.994 trillion (in 1986).

WORK FORCE: Commerce and services, 53.1%; manufacturing, 25%; construction, 9.1%; agriculture and fishing, 8.5%; government, 3.4%.

OUR QUALITY OF LIFE RANKING: 76.00.

VISA REQUIREMENTS: Passports and visas (available at no charge) are required. Transit visas are valid for 15 days; short-stay visas, with entry up to 90 days, are valid for 5 years; business visas are determined according to your period of stay, with multiple entries within 48 months of issue. You must show an onward/return ticket when entering the country.

TOURIST OFFICE IN THE UNITED STATES: Japan National Tourist Organization, *630 Fifth Ave., New York, NY 10111; (212)757-5640.*

Tokyo is both expensive, for those spending dollars, and unpleasant, because of the teeming population and the city's sprawl (partly due to the fear of building high in an area subject to earthquakes). It became the capital of the country as part of the Meiji restoration (1868), which began the modernization of Japan and its opening to the West. The palace of the former Edo dynasty is now incorporated into the Imperial Palace, although most of the Palace was built in the 1960s. Its gardens are a main park in downtown Tokyo (with flower gardens, fountains, and jogging paths). The northern part of the gardens, Kitanomaru Park, holds the Science and Modern Art Museums (worth visiting) as well as a concert hall. Part of the palace is the private residence of the emperor, and open to the public only on his imperial birthday.

The newness of the **Imperial Palace** is typical of Tokyo, which was destroyed twice in this century, first by an earthquake and then by wartime bombing. Much of the city is new and noisy—with the exception of some tranquil parks. Southeast of the Palace is the **Ginza**—the business, entertainment, and shopping heart of Tokyo. The department stores stretch along **Chuo Dori** (except for the Daimaru store near the railroad station). Even apart from the steep prices and shoving crowd, this area is one which travelers should avoid in their search for the real Japan. Instead, you should try to participate in a tea ceremony, or visit a shrine, a Japanese garden, or an art museum.

The main shrine in central Tokyo is called **Meiji-jingu** (in the Shibuya-Harajuku district, a western part of downtown). It is the destination of pilgrimages from all over Japan. About 70 years old, it was built to honor the Meiji emperor, and was rebuilt after World War II. It has lovely gardens and a typical *torii* gate, the largest in Japan. The gardens feature irises and chrysanthemums. On November 15, an endearing pilgrimage for children aged 3, 5, and 7 is held. A torii gate is typical of the Shinto religion (Japan's minority religion, whose rites even Japanese Buddhists sometimes observe); it is shaped like a bridge with the top section extended outward and slightly upward. The fact that Japanese can be both Shinto and Buddhist is typical of a certain pragmatism in religious matters that makes them inscrutable to Westerners.

Another day, visit **Ueno. Ueno Park,** northeast of the Palace, holds the **Ben-zaiten Temple,** the **Zoo** (with pandas from China), the **National Museum of Western Art,** other museums of art, science, and history, a monorail, temples, shrines, and a monument to Ulysses S. Grant (who visited it). The **Yasukuni Shrine** to the Japanese war dead, a somewhat sober place, is liked by some. **Asakusa Kannon** (also called Sensoji) is the oldest Buddhist temple in Tokyo, founded in the first century. However, most of the buildings were reconstructed after the War. (This neighborhood, called Akasuka, offers the cheapest Tokyo shopping.)

Tokyo's most beautiful gardens are called **Rikugien** and date to the 18th century, located just outside the downtown area. But even central Tokyo has a typical Japanese garden (called **Kiyosumi**), which looks exactly like what you want a Japanese garden to look like. Downtown also offers bird-watching and nature-study facilities right on Tokyo Bay.

Kanda, north of the palace, is the Japanese Latin Quarter, with book stores, a Russian orthodox cathedral, and two shrines. One of the shrines, the **Yushima**, is where you pray for good results on your exams by writing your hoped-for grade on a special wooden slat under the plum trees.

The major hotels offer tea ceremonies—sometimes combined with flower-arrangement lessons—open to foreigners. If you want to be a bit more adventurous, go to Sakura-kai 3-2-25, near the Meiji-ro subway stop. It costs half of what a hotel tea ceremony runs. Or you can take a Japanese bath (for example at **Tokyo Onsen,** *6 Ginza*).

But to see the real Japan, you have to leave Tokyo. The easiest side trip is to take a bus to **Mount Fuji** (under two hours), and climb the beautiful snow-covered mountain. Here you can benefit from the medicinal hot springs and visit plantations growing cacti, bananas (using the steam from the springs), or bonsai plants. Mount Fuji, 12,365 feet high, is the tallest mountain in Japan. Sometimes (smog permitting) it can be seen from the top of high hotels and department stores in Tokyo. You only can climb the mountain in the summer. Cheat by spending the night at the fifth station the previous night, then rising at 4 a.m. for the last climb to see the sunrise from the mountaintop. The climb is possible along a half dozen different routes and while strenuous, does not require mountaineering skills. You will, however, need raincoats some days and warm clothing every day.

North of the mountain is the **Japanese Five Lake District,** a major site for Japanese tourists, with amusement parks, a sex show (second floor of the Fuji Museum, only open to adults), and temples and shrines. The mixture of sacred and sex is typically Japanese.

Kyoto is for history buffs. Here you can see the Rashomon gate and the To-ji temple, rebuilt after the 15th-century civil wars, and the early 17th-century moated and fortified **Nijo Castle.** There are dozens of museums, shrines, temples, and a university, plus several palaces (some of which are closed to the public). Here is **Kinkaku-ji,** the Temple of the Golden Pavilion, reconstructed from the 14th-century model after being burned down by a mad monk (you can read all about it in the Mishima novel). It started out as the Shogun's personal home. There also is a **Silver Pavilion,** now a Zen monastery, and a half dozen major temples and gardens. **Sanjusangendo** temple is a National Treasure.

The last holdout of the Shoguns against imperial centralization was at **Osaka,** an industrial city today. This port was the entry point where Chinese and other mainland influences, including the Buddhist religion, entered Japan. When Tokyo was a barely inhabited swamp, this was Japan's capital. Not far from downtown is **Shitennoji Temple,** the oldest Buddhist site in the country, with a five-story pagoda and famous wall paintings. **Sumiyoushi Taisha,** a shrine, is supposed to date to the 3rd century, and is very simple and tranquil with its wood-and-thatch buildings and an arched bridge over the pond. Lanterns are left by worshipers along the walks. From here you can visit the tourist and religious center of **Mount Koya.** Here is the center of **Singon,** a Buddhist sect, a complex of monasteries, temples, and shrines. The **Emperor Nintoku's Cemetery** in Sakai, near Osaka, is the largest in the world. The **Osaka Castle,** also called the Brocade Castle, is a veritable walled city (the walls are over seven miles around). It burned in the 19th century, but its turrets and watchtowers are still worth a visit. The site is now a museum of history.

Autumn is the time to go to **Nikko,** which has a festival on October 17 at its Toshugu shrine, the burial place of the Shoguns of Tokugawa. The other attraction is to see the leaves turning in this area of magnificent scenery.

Make a pilgrimage to **Hiroshima** to see the **Peace Park,** the memorial to the victims of the atom bomb attack, and the carillons of the Memorial Hall. The day for pilgrimages is Aug. 6, the date the bomb dropped, when an international peace congress convenes.

Japanese food is extraordinary and during your trip you should try out the Buddhist vegetarian *shojin ryori* restaurants. Here you will be served a seven-course menu full of interesting dishes with curious flavors—all of which have been made from vegetarian ingredients. The amount of labor involved makes these *shojin ryori* meals among the most expensive in Japan. Some well-known dishes are sukiyaki, sushi (pickled fish and rice rolls), tempura (breaded fried meat, fish, shrimp, and vegetables, which the Japanese learned to cook from the Portuguese), and *sashimi* (raw fish served with daikon or horseradish), all of which you eat at the counter of special restaurants. The brave may want to try *fugu*, a fish whose innards may be poisonous if not carefully removed, but which is supposed to be delicious. *O-bento* are prepared lunches sold in containers; each compartment contains a different beautifully-presented dish, usually rice, fish, shrimp, and vegetables. These are cheap. Even cheaper are *yaki*—pancakes that you cook yourself in a restaurant after having selected the fillings, which include noodles, fish, or meat. With Japanese meals you drink beer or *sake*, a very alcoholic rice brew, usually served warm, and usually too sweet for Western tastes (ask for krakuchi or dry sake if you agree).

Shopping in Japan combines the defects of East and West. On the one hand, in most of Japan you cannot bargain about prices as you can in other Oriental countries. On the other hand, the multi-tiered distribution system makes goods expensive and the wonderful potteries and kimonos, lacquerware and pearls, are often very expensive. Wealthy Japanese are prepared to spend unheard of sums for beautiful goods. Even duty-free is not really cheap, and as a result, many Japanese spend their vacations in the United States stocking up on typical Japanese exports which turn out to be cheaper here: VCRs, cameras, make-up. ❧

KENYA

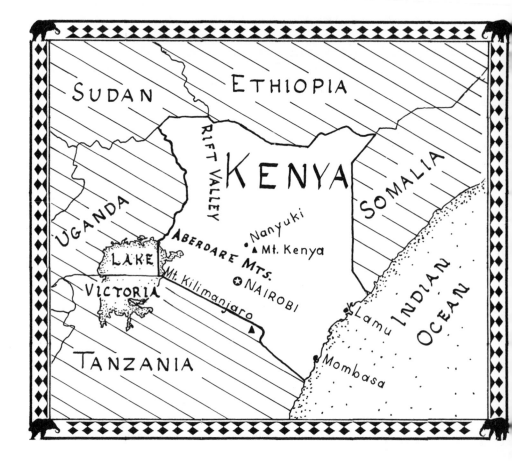

Kenya is the land of wildlife safaris. Today, hunting is done with cameras, as big game killing has been banned. Most of the educated population speak English and practice Christianity—both heritages of British colonial rule (ended in 1963 after the Mau Mau uprising against the British). Because of its attractive climate, Kenya was a place of British settlement, not just colonial rule, most of it in the so-called White Highlands around Nairobi (where Isak Dinesen's farm of *Out of Africa* fame was located). But apart from the somewhat dissolute European settlers and white hunters, Kenya is also home of extraordinary African tribes, notably the tall and noble Masai warriors and herdsmen of legend, wild camel-herding Somali tribesmen in the northern deserts (the Northern Frontier, now closed to travelers), and so-called Arabs.

The groups all are minorities in Kenya; the dominant tribe is the Kikuyu (who

124

were most involved in the Mau Mau uprising, and whose leader, Jomo Kenyatta, became the first president). Daniel arap Moi, the current president, is a Luo, one of several farming tribes. The coastal Arabs are the most economically important minority. They dominate Kenya's second largest city, **Mombasa,** and first developed the East African *lingua franca*, Swahili (which with English and Kikuyu is an

EMBASSY: *2249 R St. N.W., Washington, DC 20008; (202)387-6101.*

SYSTEM OF GOVERNMENT: Centralized one-party republic.

ETHNIC GROUPS: African tribes, 98%; non-African (Asians, Europeans, and Arabs), 2%.

RELIGIOUS GROUPS: Protestants, 38%; Roman Catholics, 28%; Moslems, 6%; tribal religions, 19%.

LANGUAGES: Swahili (official); English; tribal languages.

POPULATION: 21.044 million (in 1986).

AREA: 224,960 square miles (582,488 square kilometers); slightly smaller than Texas.

CAPITAL: Nairobi (population 1.1 million).

TERRAIN: Varied. Low-lying, fertile coastal region. The northern three-fifths are desert-like; the southwest has high plateaus. Bisected from the north to south by the Great Rift Valley.

CLIMATE: Varies from tropical to arid. Nairobi has a mean annual temperature of 66 degrees Fahrenheit.

NECESSARY INNOCULATIONS OR MEDICATIONS: Typhoid and hepatitis immunizations are recommended before visiting remote areas. Anti-malaria pills are also recommended.

TELECOMMUNICATIONS
  Country Code: 254.

Time Zone: +8 hours Eastern Standard Time.
Code of Capital: 2.

LOCAL/NATIONAL AIRLINES: Kenya Airways, *(212)832-8810;* **Pan Am,** *(800)221-1111;* **Air France,** *(800)237-2747;* **Alitalia,** *(800)223-5730;* **British Airways,** *(800)247-9297;* **Lufthansa,** *(800)645-3880;* and **Swissair,** *(800)225-3569.*

U.S. CONSULATE IN COUNTRY: *Cotts House, Wabera Street, P.O. Box 30137, Nairobi; tel. (254-2)334141.*

CURRENCY: Shilling. Travelers may not import or export currency.

GROSS NATIONAL PRODUCT: $5.8 billion (in 1984).

WORK FORCE: Agriculture and forestry, 23%; industry, manufacturing, and communications, 23%; services, 13%.

OUR QUALITY OF LIFE RANKING: 28.53.

VISA REQUIREMENTS: A visa (valid for six months) is required. You also must have two photos and an onward/return ticket. Obtain your visa before departure from the embassy in Washington, D.C., or the consulate in New York.

TOURIST OFFICE IN THE UNITED STATES: *Kenya Tourist Office, 424 Madison Ave., New York, NY 10017; (212)486-1300.*

official language here). The Arabs—who are largely black by race but Moslem in religion—dominated the trade between Africa and the Persian Gulf in spices like cinnamon, in coffee, in ivory—and in slaves. Their coastal cities, notably **Lamu,** are exotic, with shuttered stucco houses and veiled women. *Souks* are lined with stalls that sell carpets, pearls, and Islamic amulets. *Dhows* bob in the harbor.

Nairobi is a modern city with an exotic touch, notably the flowers and the clothing of its people. The city boasts world-class museums. The **National Museum of Nairobi,** has the collection of fossils discovered by the Leakey family of anthropologists in the Kenyan Rift Valley. Here, too, are paintings by Joy Adamson (author of the lion book, *Born Free*). You can visit the Dinesen (Blixen) house. The Nairobi Bomas, seven miles out of town, are dioramas in miniature or full-size of the different types of tribal village in Kenya. In some, you can see tribal dancing and buy crafts.

If you can, rent a car to sightsee. Drive three hours north of Nairobi to **Nanyuki,** stopping en route to see the grave of Lord Baden-Powell who founded the Scout Movement. On his tomb is a circle with a dot in it, the scout symbol for "gone home." Nanyuki is 8,000 feet high, on the slope of **Mount Kenya,** the snow-topped mountain that sits smack on the Equator. In Nanyuki you can enjoy the White Highland experience, staying at an old colonial relic and drinking gin under the circling fan, or betting on a horse race; alternatively you can stay at William Holden's game lodge. You can climb monkey-filled Mount Kenya from Naro Moru River Lodge. If you can, head north to Archer's Point, a spring in the middle of the desert (the last point in the Northern Frontier you can visit independently). The spring attracts game. If it is possible to join a group going farther, go to an even more remote spring, **Marsabit**, a tree-covered mountain in the Kaisul Desert. It attracts animals in the dry season.

Back in Nanyuki, take the Nakuru road, which runs along the edge of the **Rift Valley.** Huge cliffs drop on either side of the deep valley, which runs right down Africa. This geological phenomenon enabled archeologists to sift sediment that covered traces of the earliest ancestors of humans. You will see beautiful mountains and the dusty plain. About halfway to Nakuru is Kyahururu Waterfall (formerly Thomson's Fall), an olde-English site where you can take tea on the lawn. Here is the courthouse where Kenyatta was tried. When you get to Nakuru go to the lake, a National Park and a sanctuary for birds, particularly pink flamingos.

For game animals—which is after all the point—you want to go to a game lodge, which is easier and cheaper than a full safari, but still an expensive option. **Treetops,** in the Aberdare Mountains at Nyeri, became world famous because then-Princess Elizabeth was staying there when she became Queen upon the death of her father. She was viewing elephant, black leopard, lion, and antelope. Other lodges are the Ark, quite nearby but cheaper. You can even stay at **Nairobi National Park,** a mere five miles from the city. Contact the Kenya Tourist office for information.

Take the train from Nairobi to **Mombasa,** another colonial experience. Upon waking, you will be served a full English breakfast. Enjoy the beautiful bird-laden beaches of the Indian Ocean coast, too often neglected by travelers.

126

Kenya is one of the world's leading producers of both coffee and tea, which are of exceptional quality. The beer is good and served cold, not lukewarm as in Britain. The basic food is dull: *ugali* (corn meal and beans), *mandazi* (fried dough), and *ino* (a mixture of seeds). Luckily, food is influenced by the hunters and colonialists. You can taste the meat of exotic animals from antelope to zebra at the Carnivore Restaurant in Nairobi. And all over the country you can have *samosas* (Indian ravioli) or Kenya curry, local meat (lamb or beef) with an Indian touch, served with chutneys, bananas, mango, coconut, hot pepper, peanuts, and soy sauce. The British left their tradition in desserts, which are very good. (Jomo Kenyatta was known for his sweet tooth.)

Good buys in Kenya include wood carvings, batiks, and colorful woven baskets. Or try to find an antique: perhaps a sword with an Amharic inscription, or a tribal chief's stool carved out of a solid piece of wood and decorated with beads hammered into the wood; or a chain loaded with silver coins and amber, or a hammered tray in the Arab tradition.

Be sure to contact your doctor before traveling to Kenya. Anti-malarial medication should be taken before, during, and after your stay.

Safaris are expensive, particularly if booked through the United States, with the largest chunk of money going for the air fare. To cut down on this cost, if you have time, fly via London and use a British bucket shop to get a round-trip ticket— you will save nearly half the direct flight cost. ❦

LUXEMBOURG

Nestled in the heart of central Europe, the Grand Duchy of Luxembourg—smaller than the state of Rhode Island—retains a romantic, old-world charm. Castles and fortresses dot its landscape. The northern third of the country is virgin forest, the hilly Ardennes, while the south is filled with fertile farmlands and vineyards. Perched on the edge of two steep gorges formed by the Petrusse and Alzette Rivers, **Luxembourg City** (the capital) overlooks the Alzette River valley.

Luxembourg has maintained its independence and national identity despite being buffeted by the European power politics of the last millenium. At various times in its history, it has been ruled by Burgundy, Spain, Austria, and France. It severed its ties to the German Confederation in 1866 only to be occupied by Germany during the two World Wars.

Still a constitutional monarchy, Luxembourg is the smallest country in the European Common Market. Perhaps because of its centrality—Belgium to the northwest, France to the south and west, and the Federal Republic of Germany to the north and east—Luxembourg is the seat of the European Court of Justice and various other EEC administrative offices. This centrality has also led to a multiplic-

---

EMBASSY: *2200 Massachusetts Ave. N.W., Washington, DC 20008; (202)265-4171.*

SYSTEM OF GOVERNMENT: Constitutional monarchy.

ETHNIC GROUPS: Frenchmen; Germans; Portuguese; Italians; other Europeans.

RELIGIOUS GROUPS: Roman Catholics, 96.9%; Protestants; Jews.

LANGUAGES: Luxembourgian (Letzeburgesch); French; German.

POPULATION: 367,000.

AREA: 998 square miles (2,586 square kilometers); slightly smaller than Rhode Island.

CAPITAL: Luxembourg (population 80,000).

TERRAIN: Heavily forested and mountainous. Continuation of the Belgian Ardennes in the north; extension of France's Lorraine Plateau in the south, with open, rolling countryside.

CLIMATE: Cool and rainy; comparable to the Pacific northwest in the United States.

TELECOMMUNICATIONS
Country Code: 352.
Time Zone: +6 hours Eastern Standard Time.

LOCAL/NATIONAL AIRLINE: Icelandair, *(800)223-5500.*

U.S. CONSULATE IN COUNTRY: *blvd. Emmanuel Servais 22, Luxembourg City, 2535; tel. (352)40123/6.*

CURRENCY: Luxembourg franc (Belgian and French francs are also used.) No limit on import or export.

GROSS NATIONAL PRODUCT: $5.2 billion (in 1986).

WORK FORCE: Services and government, 48%; industry and commerce, 42%; agriculture, 1%.

OUR QUALITY OF LIFE RANKING: 72.31.

VISA REQUIREMENTS: Passports are required. Visas are not required for stays of up to three months. For longer stays, send $10 plus return postage and four photos to the embassy in Washington. You also must have sufficient funds for your stay and an onward/return ticket when you enter the country.

TOURIST OFFICE IN THE UNITED STATES: Luxembourg National Tourist Office, *801 Second Ave., New York, NY 10017; (212)370-9850.*

ity of tongues. Although French is the official language, Luxembourgian is spoken most often, and German continues to be used. Furthermore (a solace to most Americans), English is required in high school where, remarkably enough, there is a 100% attendance rate.

Sigefroid, the youngest son of the House of Ardennes, built the castle that was to become the center of **Luxembourg City**—officially founded in 963. The capital was once one of Europe's largest fortresses, protected by 16 miles of tunnels and casemates hewn from solid rock. During World War II, 13 miles of underground fortifications were transformed into bomb shelters that could protect up to 35,000 people. Today, you can wander through underground byways called the **Bock Casemates** that run underneath the Promenade de la Corniche. Enter at rue Sigefroi or Place de la Constitution.

The capital is a walking city. The **Promenade de la Corniche** follows roughly the lines of the old medieval ramparts. Nearly 100 bridges span the ravines. Be sure to explore the old town where you will find the 15th-century cathedral and the 16th-century **Grand-Ducal Palace** built in grand Spanish Renaissance style. Other attractions include the **State Museum,** with its art and natural history wings, and the **Place d'Armes,** where you can relax with a locally brewed beer at an outdoor café and listen to a brass band. Three miles east of Luxembourg City is the **United States Military Cemetery** where 5,000 American soldiers who died during World War II, including General George S. Patton, Jr., are buried.

The countryside is also accessible by foot. The government has marked in yellow a system of walking paths that pass by the main castle towns. Hilly cycling routes and narrow cobblestone lanes also run from town to town. **Echternach** on the German border is particularly intriguing both for its charming setting and rich history. Built in the 14th century, it was originally a focal point of European Christianity. Its Benedictine Abbey, founded by St. Willibord in the 7th century, contains many bejewelled relics as well as St. Willibord's own remains. **St. Peter and Paul Church,** the oldest Christian sanctuary in Luxembourg, is located in the center of town. Try to visit Echternach between mid-June and mid-July during its annual festival of music, art, and dance. Oenophiles are encouraged to travel to any of the 17 villages in the **Moselle Valley,** which is known for its light, fresh wine.

Unlike the country as a whole, Luxembourg cuisine lacks any particular national identity. It most nearly resembles French cooking, although it is distinguished by German and Belgian touches. Some specialities include quiche Ardennaise, Ardennes ham, *écrevisses* (crayfish) *à la Luxembourgeoise,* and other fresh seafood dishes. Be sure to sample any of the four locally brewed beers as well as the various Moselle wines.

After its initial stop in Reykjavik, Icelandair flies directly to Luxembourg. Centrally located, Luxembourg is an ideal point of departure and/or return for Europe. 🍎

MEXICO

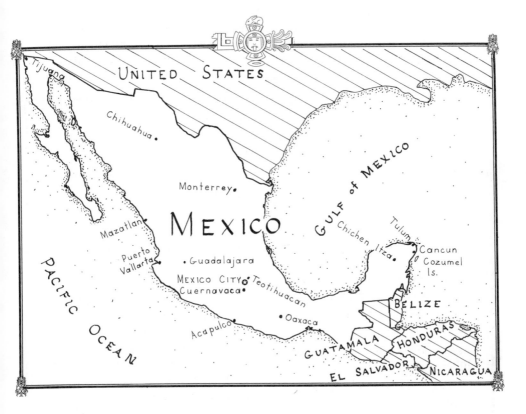

Mexico is the most exotic country easily reached from the United States. As such, it is the most familiar country where people speak a foreign language and are part of an alien culture. Bad trips in Mexico are a source of many of our ideas and misconceptions about foreign travel. Most of us know what is wrong with Mexico. Mexican water, by and large, is unsafe to drink; Mexican nationalism is tinged with anti-gringo sentiments; Mexico's poverty is inescapable and appalling; Mexican politics are confusing and corrupt; Mexican history is marked by a series of rhetorically bold revolutions, which culminated in an oligarchy.

Most U.S. tourists go to Mexico for its cheap beach resorts, on both east and west coasts, the destinations of bargain package tours. If you want to take this kind of trip, shop around using newspaper ads, the yellow pages, and a good travel agent. Packages put together by the Mexicans are available from 11 U.S. gateways, and are usually the cheapest. For this kind of travel, there is no need for a guide-book. As a general rule, the older beach resorts offer all the comfort you need and far more cachet; furthermore, unlike the newer beaches, prices tend to be lower, and you are less likely to run into your neighbors. My own favorite is Acapulco, the Mexican attempt to create the stylishness of Monte Carlo.

In Mexico, you can either lounge lazily in the sun, or participate in a variety of sports, including surfing, scuba diving, golf, tennis, horseback riding, and deep-sea fishing. Mexico also appeals to mountaineers, bird-watchers, and hunters.

But even for non-sportsmen, this is a country worth visiting, mainly for its vast pre-Columbian ruins. Of the descendants of the Mongolian tribes that crossed the Bering Straits from Asia 30,000 years ago, the early inhabitants of Mexico developed some of the most advanced civilizations. The most intriguing pre-Columbian

---

EMBASSY: *2829 16th St. N.W., Washington, DC 20009; (202)234-6000.*

SYSTEM OF GOVERNMENT: Federal republic.

ETHNIC GROUPS: Mestizos, 60%; American Indians, 30%; Caucasians, 9%.

RELIGIOUS GROUP: Roman Catholics, 97%.

LANGUAGES: Spanish, 97%; indigenous languages and dialects, 3%.

POPULATION: 81.709 million (in 1986).

AREA: 756,053 square miles (1.958-million square kilometers).

CAPITAL: Mexico City (population 15 million).

TERRAIN: Varies from coastal lowlands to high mountains.

CLIMATE: Varies from tropical to desert, depending on the altitude.

TELECOMMUNICATIONS
　Country Code: 011.
　Time Zone: +2 hours Eastern Standard Time.
　Code of Capital: 5.

LOCAL/NATIONAL AIRLINES: Pan Am, *(800)221-1111;* **Mexicana,** *(800)531-7921* or *(213)646-9500* in California; **Eastern,** *(800)327-8376;* and **American,** *(800)433-7300.*

U.S. CONSULATE IN COUNTRY: *Paseo de la Reforma 305, Mexico 5,*

D.F.; tel. (011-5)25-211-0042.

CURRENCY: Peso. No limit on import or export.

GROSS NATIONAL PRODUCT: $158 billion (in 1984).

WORK FORCE: Agriculture, 41%; industry and commerce, 25%.

OUR QUALITY OF LIFE RANKING: 43.52.

VISA REQUIREMENTS: Passports and visas are not required of U.S. citizens visiting as tourists for less than 90 days. Tourist cards (available at no charge and valid for three months) are required. You can not renew or extend tourist cards in Mexico. To obtain a tourist card, contact the embassy, consulate, tourist office, or immigration office at ports of entry or airlines serving Mexico; four photos are required.

If children enter Mexico with their parents, they must depart the country with them as well, unless prior arrangements were made with the Mexican Department of Immigration. Travelers entering Mexico for reasons other than tourism should inquire at the consulate regarding the necessary documentation.

TOURIST OFFICE IN THE UNITED STATES: *Mexican Tourism Office, 405 Park Ave., Suite 1002, New York, NY 10022; (212)755-7261.*

group is the Maya, who reached the peak of their culture around A.D. 900. The Mayas were masters of abstract knowledge and developed an accurate calendar long before the Europeans. They also developed an alphabet (still not deciphered) and sophisticated mathematics. Maya culture centered on the Yucatán Peninsula, Guatemala, and sites such as Chiapas and Tabasco. Long before the arrival of Europeans, the Maya civilization mysteriously disappeared.

The Mayas were preceded by the Olmecs (500 B.C. to A.D. 1150), who may have built Teotihuacán, the grandest pre-Columbian ruin in the Western hemisphere. It can be visited outside Mexico City.

Around A.D. 1000, a new culture arose, the Toltecs. The first people who were able to smelt metals, they established their power in the cities of Tula and Teotihuacán. And they expanded and embellished the Maya City, Chichén Itza.

In the 14th century, yet another culture arose, that of the Aztecs, centered around what is now Mexico City. These were the people who worshipped the plumed serpent, were masters of mathematics and astronomy, and practiced human sacrifice.

The Aztecs were destroyed, however, upon the arrival of Hernán Cortéz. Their civilization collapsed when Montezuma, the Aztec King, surrendered to the Spanish Conquistadores in 1521.

Almost from the first, the Mexicans were tempted to win their independence from Spain. While our Pilgrims were keeping loyal to the King of England, the Mexicans began to rebel already under Hernán Cortéz's son. After the first rebels were defeated by the Spaniards, independence was finally granted to Mexico in 1821. Two years later, after an initial try at monarchy, the country patterned its government after the U.S. Constitution. In its first decades, the new Republic of Mexico had to battle its expansionary northern neighbor over control of Texas, California, Arizona, and New Mexico. Both countries invaded each other. The military leader who had run the Mexican campaign, starting with the battle of the Alamo in 1836, wound up as the head of state—only to be deposed in 1860 by Benito Juarez, the first post-Montezuma Indian to rule the country (and nearly the last). He was anticlerical and in favor of public schooling. Juarez was temporarily displaced during a ridiculous and tragic interval when the French army (of Napoleon III) attempted to preserve the power of the Catholic church in Mexico and run the country through a proxy Emperor, Maximilian of Hapsburg. Juarez (secretly backed by the Americans) returned in 1867 and had Maximilian shot. He himself died in 1872. The subsequent dictatorship, which opened the country to American industrial investment, was opposed by the legendary Pancho Villa and Emiliano Zapata. In the course of the rebellion, the United States invaded again and Mexico acquired a new constitution in 1917. Since then it has been ruled by the Institutional Revolutionaries (PRI), whose platform includes anticlericalism and varying levels of anti-Americanism. Both from the left and the right, clean-up parties opposing PRI corruption are gaining in strength.

People will spend a fortune to travel to far-off Asian jungles and deserts, to war-ridden Cambodia, to the Nile, or to the edge of the Sahara to see fascinating archeological remains. Yet many of them miss seeing the far more accessible (and

133

cheap) wonders of the pre-Columbians south of our border. Just because package tours go to a place does not mean it is over-developed or without interest. Even **Cancún,** the purpose-built brand-new resort zone on the **Yucatán Peninsula,** is worth heading for—if only because it is easy to reach the Maya ruins at **Chichén Itzá,** the curious walled seaside city of **Tulum, Uxmal**, and **Cobá** (where excavations have only begun).

Mexico City's Aztec ruins (which are still being excavated) can be visited just steps from the **Zócalo** (the central square of the city). The site, discovered in 1978 when a new power line was being laid, has been made accessible to the public by the construction of stairs and ramps. When the Metro was being built, the excavators of **Pino Suarez** station stumbled upon another Aztec ruin, now the center of the ultramodern subway station. About 30 miles from town, you can visit **Teotihuacán**, and climb the steps of the tallest pyramid in the Americas. The Olmec site of **Chalcatzingo,** the Toltec capital of **Tula**, the church-topped pyramid of **Cholula** are within reach of the adventurous from the capital. But much of the most splendid art from these Indian sites and others has been carted off to the **Archeological Museum** in Mexico City, which is probably the best (and easiest) way to learn about the Indians.

Mexico City's other sites include the **National Palace** (with Diego Rivera murals) and the **Metropolitan Cathedral,** with its neighboring 18th-century chapel, both on the **Zócalo**; the **Hospital de Jesus,** the oldest in America, founded by Cortez; the city park (**Chapultepec**), with a tendentious historical museum (more Rivera frescoes) in what once was Maximilian's castle, and a good museum of modern art (formerly Rivera's house; he exchanged works with most of his contemporaries giving Mexico stunning works of modern art).

Those who like muralists will want to visit **Coyoacan** for the **Frida Kahlo Museum** (the crippled Kahlo, an artist in her own right, was married to Rivera) and **San Angel** for the **Gil Museum**. Rivera's own collection of Columbian art is housed in **Anahuacalli**. These three museums are south of the city, as is the house where Leon Trotsky was killed, and the ultra-modern university (which nonetheless is the oldest college in the New World).

North of Mexico City, besides Teotihuacán, is the shrine of the **Virgin of Guadalupe**; the original shrine, next door had to be closed because it makes the leaning tower of Pisa look straight. Views about the modern basilica vary; it reminds me of an airport, complete with a people-mover to rush pilgrims (many of whom have crawled in on their knees) past the cloak where the Virgin's image miraculously appeared in 1531.

From Mexico City it is possible to take trains to the artists' colony town of **San Miguel de Allende** or to the silversmiths' center of **Taxco**.

Because it is sometimes smoggy, and because it is high enough to trouble some people (7,000 feet above sea level), and because it is a huge city with vast social differences, many tourists are put off by Mexico City. But despite its bad image, it is quite pleasant (its altitude means it never gets really hot in the summer), with lovely broad boulevards and tidy green parks, surprisingly few beggars (they cluster in the Zona Rosa luxury shopping and restaurant area), and lots of shopping bargains.

In Mexico, bargains include clothing (both ordinary clothes and specialities such as dressy, white *guayabera* shirts with ruffles), *rebozos* (shawls), *sarapes,* hats, leather goods, onyx, silver (buy only from shops and make sure that it is hallmarked .925), ceramics, embroidery, and handicrafts. Mexico is developing a handknotted carpet industry. **Toluca,** about 37 miles west of Mexico City, is famous for its Friday Indian market (*tianguis*). You should bargain unless you are in a luxury shop or one run by the government. Mexicans even bargain in department stores. Offer half what the salesman asks for and be prepared to spend time before settling (roughly) at 75 percent.

Mexico gave the world chocolate, chili pepper, turkeys, sweet and regular potatoes, tomatoes, many pumpkins and squashes, and above all, corn. Except for a region in the north, most of Mexico still survives on variations of the Indian corn flatbread or tortilla, stacked, rolled, topped, steamed, dipped, chipped, or made into ravioli or pizza-like pies, or refried. In the north they do the same thing with burritos made of wheat. Mexicans still eat a lot of *mole* made with chili (sometimes with chili pepper and chocolate), and still eat a lot of poultry. Almost everything is accompanied by mashed refried beans, which are very wholesome, and topped by melted cheese. Mexican additives, which give variety to this diet, include *cilantro* (the green herb grown from coriander seeds, which looks like parsley but is not); pine nuts, tomatoes, and *epazote* (stinkweed to us). Fish is very good and rarely frozen; try *ceviche* (raw fish salad), *camarones* (shrimp), *robalo* (sea bass), or *huachinango* (red snapper). Another famous dish is guacamole, mashed avocados. Desserts are oversweet and boring. The beer is good and the wine is improving. *La turista* (diarrhea) is a common problem for travelers. To avoid it, never drink water that hasn't been bottled or boiled; never eat produce that hasn't been cooked or peeled. If you get it, drink a lot of liquid (*agua mineral sin gas*) and let nature take its course. ❦

135

Monaco

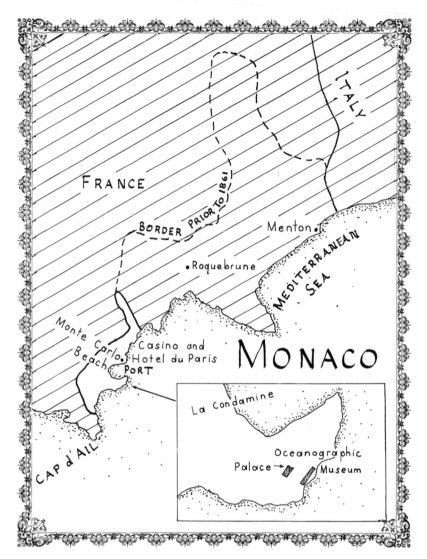

$\mathbf{M}$onaco is a Ruritanian mini-state that has managed to survive as an independent country (and tax haven) thanks to the public relations savvy, sound business sense, and shrewd marriage policy of its ruling family, the Grimaldis. They are descendants of Francesco Grimaldi, a monk who entered the gates of Monaco in 1297 by subterfuge, pulling a sword from under his habit to overwhelm the guards. Prince Rainier Grimaldi, the current ruler, by marrying the former Grace Kelly, was following in an old family tradition of marrying into wealthy

American familes. In the 19th century, the prince of Monaco married the former Miss Heine of Chicago. (The first American Princess of Monaco was a cousin and patron of the German poet Heinrich Heine.) But even this advantageous marriage was not enough to keep the Grimaldis out of the poor house. And in 1861 Napoleon III of France annexed two townships that had been part of Monaco since 1297, Roquebrune and Menton, stripping the principality of three-quarters of its territory. The Grimaldis were reduced to a little rock topped by a pretty little palace. Something had to be done.

Health resorts were drawing rich Europeans to take the waters at this time, none more successfully than Bad Homburg in Germany, which offered an extra attraction: gambling. Prince Charles Grimaldi decided to give a casino concession in Monaco to the man who had made Bad Homburg a success, François Blanc. The entrepreneur connected Monaco with the French railroad system at Nice and built the **Hôtel de Paris**—still the best place to stay in Monaco—in 1864. A new city sprang up around the casino, named after Prince Charles—called **Monte Carlo.** Blanc made a profit of 800,000 francs in the first year, and when he retired his fortune topped $14 million.

Blanc's hotel and casino, now property of the Société des Bains de Mer, are effectively under the control of the Grimaldis today. Loans from Aristotle Onassis,

---

EMBASSY: None. Contact the **French Embassy,** *4101 Reservoir Road N.W., Washington, DC 20007; (202)944-6000.*

SYSTEM OF GOVERNMENT: Constitutional monarchy.

ETHNIC GROUPS: Expatriates, 85% (Frenchmen, 47%; Italians, 16%); Monégasques, 17%.

RELIGIOUS GROUPS: Roman Catholics, 80%.

LANGUAGES: French; Monégasque.

POPULATION: 28,000 (in 1986).

AREA: 0.73 square miles (465 acres).

CAPITAL: Monte Carlo.

TERRAIN: Hilly.

CLIMATE: Mediterranean. Temperature rarely falls below 32 degrees Fahrenheit.

TELECOMMUNICATIONS
Country Code: 33.

Time Zone: +6 hours Eastern Standard Time.
Code of Capital: 93.

LOCAL/NATIONAL AIRLINE: No direct U.S. flights; you must take a connecting flight from Paris or another European capital.

CURRENCY: French franc or Monégasque franc. No limit on import or export (subject to declaration).

OUR QUALITY OF LIFE RANKING: 66.90.

VISA REQUIREMENTS: Visas are not required for stays of less than three months. Passports are required.

TOURIST OFFICE IN THE UNITED STATES: Monaco Government Tourist and Convention Bureau, *845 Third Ave., New York, NY 10022; (212)759-5227.*

who liked to berth his yacht in Monaco harbor, and from the Kellys of Philadelphia, enabled Prince Rainier to win control of the money-making business. For those who want a turn-of-the-century experience, the Hôtel de Paris, and the casino (Le Sporting d'Hiver), located on top of the hill, are the best places to go. From here, the main shopping drag runs along the hill and down to the edge of the harbor, which is lined at street level with lovely shade trees and flowerbeds. Like all public services, the landscaped harbor is financed by the casino profits. Along the boulevards and avenues are a series of high-rise apartment buildings, thrusting their way in front of last year's high rise apartments—your view is not likely to last.

The palace is the center of old Monaco, called **Le Rocher**, or The Rock. A perilous hilltop area, it juts out to sea on the other side of the port from the casino. Le Rocher has 18th-century stucco houses, wrought-iron balconies, narrow streets, and palm-shaded squares. This zone resembles Italian villages with one exception: everyone who lives in it is prosperous. You can view the changing of the guard just before noon and visit the throne room weekdays except Monday. In the Old Town is the **Oceanographic Museum** featuring Jacques Cousteau's bathysphere. Cousteau is based in Monaco and from here is leading a valiant (and vain) attempt to clean up the Mediterranean. Uphill is the zoo, another attraction, with natural-looking settings for the animals. It is right on the border with France.

Opposite the Hôtel Blanc is **Loew's Monte Carlo**, built on pillars over the sea. This is the place for modern gambling. Instead of roulette, you have one-armed bandits and blackjack—and instead of rococo gilded game rooms with murals of voluptuous nudes looking down on gamblers in dinner jackets, you have high-rollers wearing Hawaiian shirts. Frankly, for my taste, I would rather be in Las Vegas.

Beneath the casino is the Monaco beach, around the **Sporting d'Eté**, which was the center of international pigeon-shooting contests until Princess Grace banned the sport. Most of the beach is private, owned by the Hôtel de Paris (which also has a pool) and other hotels; you need a pass and, given the Monte Carlo dress code, access to a coveted beach hut. The sand has to be brought in by barge and persuaded to cling to the rock. Dogs are banned and noisy children frowned upon. The public beach is along the Quai Albert I, which is a rather noisy congested road. Walk eastward along it to reach the yacht basin, **La Condamine,** where you can walk the waterfront and stare at the jet-setters.

Monaco is not a place for bargains, but the country does have a few products: Lancaster cosmetics (which have a lovely lily of the valley perfume, and which were patronized by the late Princess Grace), beachware and sports clothes made locally, and curious Monégasque pottery incorporating gold leaf. Most boutiques feature French and Italian products; similarly, most of the food in Monaco is based on (expensive) versions of what comes from its neighbors. Most of the best food is over the border in Eze or La Turbie, France, although the Hôtel de Paris and Mirabeau Hotel restaurants each have a coveted Michelin star.

French currency is used in Monaco. You can get to Monaco by train from Nice, by car, or by yacht if you have one. ❦

MOROCCO

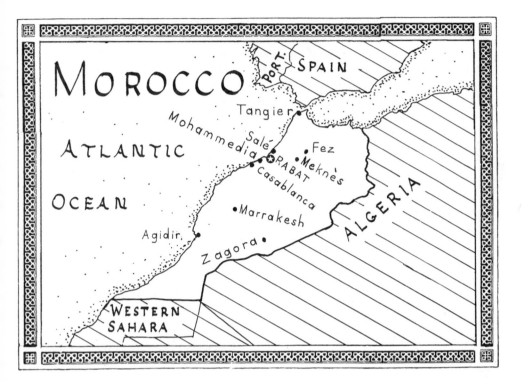

Morocco is the gateway to Africa with port cities on both the Mediterranean and Atlantic coasts. It runs from the Straits of Gibraltar in the north, across the snow-capped Atlas and Rif Mountains, to the arid Sahara Desert, in the southwest. The inland is hot and dry all year round except for mid-winter. The coastal and mountain areas are pleasantly warm most of the year. Many hotels do not have central heating, so winter travel to these areas is not advised. Also, avoid visiting during Ramadan, the ninth month of the lunar calendar, during which Moslems may not eat or drink from sunrise to sunset.

Morocco is a geographical and cultural bridge between Europe and Africa. Originally inhabited by Berber tribes over 3,000 years ago, Morocco was first colonized by the Phoenicians who, in turn, were conquered by the Carthaginians around 700 B.C. In A.D. 44, the Romans annexed northern Morocco. The Arabs invaded in the seventh century, bringing Islam to Morocco. Various Moslem dynasties fought over Morocco until the French gained control in 1912. Now a constitutional monarchy, Morocco achieved its independence from France in 1956. Morocco's linguistic history parallels its political history. Although Arabic is the official language, French is spoken in most urban areas. A footnote of interest to Americans: in 1787, Morocco under Emperor Mohammed III signed the Treaty of Marrakesh—thereby becoming the first foreign government to recognize the new United States.

Most international flights fly to and from Casablanca. In Hollywood's "Casablanca," you might recall, Victor and Ilse had to pass through—via the fictional Rick's Café to pick up letters of transport—to regain their freedom in the West. From Casablanca, you can travel to the rest of Morocco on regularly scheduled planes, buses, and trains. If you buy a second-class train ticket, be careful to avoid riding third or fourth class unless you prefer to be surrounded by clucking chickens and wafting clouds of hashish. For maximum convenience and flexibility, rental cars are suggested. Gas prices can be steep.

EMBASSY: *1601 21st St. N.W., Washington, DC 20009; (202)462-7979.*

SYSTEM OF GOVERNMENT: Constitutional monarchy.

ETHNIC GROUPS: Arabs, 65%; Berbers, 35%.

RELIGIOUS GROUPS: Sunni Moslems, 99%; Christians and Jews, 1%.

LANGUAGES: Arabic; Berber dialects; Maghribi Arabic; French; Spanish.

POPULATION: 23.667 million (in 1986).

AREA: 172,414 square miles (446,550 square kilometers).

CAPITAL: Rabat (population 556,000 in 1984).

TERRAIN: The Atlas Mountains cover most of Morocco. The north is filled with fertile lowlands; the Sahara is in the south and west.

CLIMATE: Hot, desert. The western slopes are cooled and watered by the Atlantic Ocean. The average temperature in Casablanca in January is 51 degrees Fahrenheit; the average temperature in July is 71 degrees Fahrenheit.

TELECOMMUNICATIONS
Country Code: 212.

Time Zone: +5 hours Eastern Standard Time.
Code of Capital: 7.

LOCAL/NATIONAL AIRLINE: Royal Air Maroc, *(800)223-5858.*

U.S. EMBASSY IN COUNTRY: *2 ave. De Marrakaech, Rabat; tel. (212-7)622-62;* **U.S. Consulates General,** *8 blvd. Moulay Youssef, Casablanca, (212)267-716.*

CURRENCY: Dirham. Travelers can import and export small amounts.

GROSS NATIONAL PRODUCT: $14.3 billion (in 1984).

WORK FORCE: Agriculture, 50%; services, 26%.

OUR QUALITY OF LIFE RANKING: 27.73.

VISA REQUIREMENTS: Valid passports are required. Visas are not required for U.S. citizens staying less than three months. For longer stays, apply to the local authorities.

TOURIST OFFICE IN THE UNITED STATES: Moroccan National Tourist Office, *20 E. 46th St., New York, NY 10017; (212)557-2520.*

An Atlantic port, **Casablanca** is Morocco's most modern city, and its least interesting. Its population has grown from less than 30,000 in 1900 to over 2.5 million. The downtown area resembles a western city with luxury hotels, restaurants, and fashion boutiques. An array of parks and pedestrian-only areas enhances the fun of urban strolling. The only site not to be missed is the musical fountain on **United Nations Square,** which splashes a whole spectrum of colors to the tune of everything from Strauss to Andalusian music. Like all Moroccan cities, Casablanca also has its *medina,* or old town. Past the Moroccan houses, with their whitewashed patios, is a market with handicrafts on display. They are, in fact, imported from other Moroccan cities. Postpone any purchases until you reach the interior. Casablanca does have its own beaches, but the most intriguing resort in the area is **Mohammedia**, 20 miles north. Centering around a two-mile craggy beach lined with fine sand, Mohammedia combines modern convenience and romantic charm. It has luxury hotels, a casino, an 18-hole golf course, a seaside promenade surrounded by gardens and villas, and the **Fedala Kasbah,** the remains of a Portuguese fortress. The resort also boasts a fish market and fine seafood restaurants.

What Casablanca is to international air travel, **Tangier** is to international sea travel. On the north Atlantic coast, this is a ferry port. Even before you step on land, you fall prey to the notorious Moroccan hustlers. Many ad hoc "deals" are simply cleverly-disguised rip-offs. Tangier is best known for its medina composed of the **Grand Socco** and **Petit Socco**. The narrow streets are steep; Tangier is in the heart of the Rif Valley. The main marketplace, the Grand Socco, is dotted by cafés scented with mint tea. Shops sell everything from spices and fabrics to exotic jewels and handicrafts. The Petit Socco features a variety of old hotels and cafés. The city's most compelling historic site is the Kasbah at the edge of the medina. Tourists can explore the **Sultan's Palace,** complete with mosque and courtyard. Two museums have been carved out of the palace: one featuring Moroccan handicrafts and the other featuring Tangier's prehistoric and Roman past.

The urban centers of most interest are the four so-called "imperial cities," each of which at one time or another was the Moroccan capital. Located on the Atlantic coast about 60 miles north of Casablanca, **Rabat** has been the capital since 1912. Apart from its modern administrative buildings, Rabat features a bustling medina. The local craftsmen specialize in slippers and leather goods. The **Oudayas Kasbah** sits on the outskirts of the medina, a mighty fortress with a panoramic view of the city. Nearby is the serene **Oudayas Garden,** laid out in the 19th century in the then-popular El Andalu style. Also worth exploring are the five surviving gateways, the most intricately designed of which is the **Bab er Rouah**. Visit the **Royal Palace** and the **Mohammed V Mausoleum,** dedicated to the nation's founder. Adjacent to the mausoleum is the **Hassan Tower**, the remains of a 12th-century structure. Two fascinating historic sites border Rabat. **Chellah,** a 14th-century walled village, is remarkable for its Roman and Arab remains. **Salé,** located across the Hassan II bridge from Rabat, has its own medina where weavers, cabinetmakers, stone carvers, brass workers, potters, and blacksmiths sell their wares. Salé's rich past is reflected in its **Grand Mosque** and 14th-century *medersa* (Islamic university).

The intellectual and spiritual heart of Morocco, **Fez** dates from the ninth century, when the monumental **Qaraouyine Mosque** was built. This mosque, which can hold over 20,000 worshippers, soon developed into the world's first university—predating even the Universities of Bologna and Oxford. With the rise to power of the Merinides (a Moroccan tribe) in the 13th century, Fez reached its imperial peak.

Three new *medersas* were added to the Qaraouyine, and a royal palace was constructed. The **Medersa Bou Anania** is known for its famous clock. The medina in Fez (the second largest in the world) also includes a vast *souk* (market) so labyrinthine that it is advisable to hire a guide. Local craftsmen ply their trades here just as they have for a millennium. You will find everything from jewelry to brass and silk goods, but Fez is almost synonymous with leather. Bargaining is part of the shopping experience. With some patience and skill (try to tap your guide's savvy), items can be purchased for one half, if not one third, of the asking price.

Roughly 40 miles southwest of Fez, **Meknès** was the imperial capital in the late 17th and early 18th century under Sultan Moulay Ismail, who built a spectacular royal palace and mosque. An architectural masterpiece, the **Moulay Ismail Mausoleum** is also one of the few mosques that non-Moslems are permitted to visit. Meknès also has some 12th-century gates and vast gardens. Just to the north of Meknès are **Moulay Idriss,** a holy city named after the founder of the Morocco dynasty, and **Volubilis**, the Roman capital of Mauritania.

In the heart of Morocco, **Marrakesh** casts an almost unparalleled hypnotic spell on travelers. The highlight of the city, or perhaps of Morocco itself, is the legendary **Jemaa El Fna Square**—the center of an almost non-stop cultural extravaganza. During the day you will find a complex network of *souks*, but things really take off in the late afternoon when the daily carnival moves in. You'll be entertained by folklorists, snake charmers, acrobats, and dancers. A dentist sets up shop bandying about his instrument (a pair of pliers) and displaying samples of previously pulled teeth. A water seller also appears on the scene, ringing bells fastened to various garments draped over him and pouring water into brass bowls from his goat-skin sack.

Other sites to explore include the city's 11th-century ramparts, which, according to legend, were built by Christian slaves and with Christian bones, and the **Koutoubya Mosque,** with its magnificent minarets. Marrakesh is also known for its **Madrassa Ben Youssef,** the **Saadian Tombs,** and the 19th-century **Bahia Palace,** the only palace in Morocco open to the public. Of special interest is the National Folklore Festival, which takes place in early June.

Two smaller cities are also worthy of note. **Agidir**, some 325 miles south of Casablanca, on the Atlantic Coast, is an inviting resort. Warm, with a light breeze blowing from the nearby Atlas Mountains all year round, it mixes modern amenities with historic charm. Its 16th-century kasbah has a splendid view of the region. **Zagora,** the gateway to the Sahara, was built in the 11th century to guard the caravan trails. Situated on a hill, it offers a view of the desert landscape punctuated by clusters of sand dunes.

Moroccan cuisine offers more than just the national dish, *couscous*—spiced semolina with meat sauce. Another common dish is *tajine*—a stew mixed in bouillon and steamed for hours in a claypot, the local equivalent of the modern pressure cooker. It can be made with lamb, chicken, or veal. Traditional fare also includes *mechoui*—roasted lamb basted with butter and cumin. A local delicacy to try is pigeon or chicken *bastilla*—a pie whose flaky dough is laced with various spices such as saffron, coriander, ginger, and cinnamon. You will also find an endless variety of fresh fish dishes along the coast. The major urban hotels and restaurants offer not only standard international dishes, but often internationally acclaimed French cuisine. Morocco produces its own wines and beers, which are inexpensive. The national drink—mint tea—is served everywhere (even as you are bargaining at a souk) and consumed at all times of the day and night. ❦

NETHERLANDS

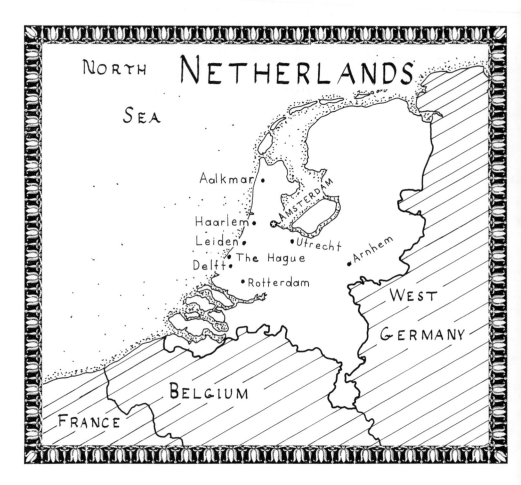

The Netherlands (popularly known as Holland) are often unfairly over-looked by international travelers. Holland is not as exotic sounding as most European destinations—but it doesn't sound reassuringly English-speaking either. However, almost all Dutch people do speak English well, and Dutch children begin studying English in elementary school. Holland lacks spectacular scenery, being flat except for a few hills in the eastern border region. But its canals and fields, its walled towns and harbors, its vistas broken only by a church tower or a windmill, offer a loveliness that grows on you.

Amsterdam is one of the most beautiful cities in the world, but not because of its monuments. It is the 40-some tree-lined canals (Herengracht, Keizersgracht, and Prinsengracht are the busiest) in concentric arcs that are crossed by hundreds of bridges. The canals are lined with banks of solid gabled 17th- and 18th-century burghers' townhouses with huge windows and narrow staircases. The city looks the way it does because the town fathers imposed a tax on windows (so homeowners decided to get the most window for their money) and on the width of facades (which led to tall narrow houses with tall narrow staircases). It is also a wonderful museum city, with the Rembrandts of the **Rijksmuseum**, the Van Goghs of the **Van Gogh Museum,** the **Stedelijk** (modern art) **Museum,** as well as fascinating exhibits on the history of the city. You can visit **Rembrandt's House, Anne Frank's House,** and the **Paleis Op De Dam,** built in 1662 as the Town Hall, but later used as a royal palace. Just off the Spui and the Kalverstraat shopping area is the **Begijnhof,** with 17th-century houses and the church where the Pilgrim Fathers worshipped before they set sail for the New World. Classical music buffs will love

EMBASSY: *4200 Linnean Ave. N.W., Washington, DC 20008; (202)244-5300.*

SYSTEM OF GOVERNMENT: Parliamentary democracy under a constitutional monarch.

ETHNIC GROUPS: Dutch; Indonesians; Surinamese; Turks; Moroccans.

RELIGIOUS GROUPS: Roman Catholics, 42%; Protestants, 42%; Moslems; Jews; Hindus.

LANGUAGES: Dutch, 97%; Frisian (in Friesland).

POPULATION: 14.537 million (in 1986).

AREA: 15,892 square miles (41,160 square kilometers).

CAPITAL: Amsterdam (population 679,400).

TERRAIN: Coastal lowlands. The average altitude is 37 feet above sea level.

CLIMATE: Northern maritime. Cool summers and mild winters.

TELECOMMUNICATIONS
   Country Code: 31.
   Time Zone: +6 hours Eastern
    Standard Time.
   Code of Capital: 20.

LOCAL/NATIONAL AIRLINES: KLM **Royal Dutch Airlines,** *(800)777-5553;* and **Royal Jordanian Airlines,** *(800)223-0470.*

U.S. CONSULATE IN COUNTRY: *102 Lange Voorhout, The Hague, The Netherlands; tel. (31-70)624-911;* **U.S. Consulates General,** *Museumplein 19, Amsterdam, The Netherlands.*

CURRENCY: Dutch guilder. No limit on import or export.

GROSS NATIONAL PRODUCT: $122.4 billion (in 1984).

WORK FORCE: Industry and commerce, 36%; services, 34%; government, 15%; agriculture, 6%.

OUR QUALITY OF LIFE RANKING: 76.63.

VISA REQUIREMENTS: Passports are required. Visas are not required for pleasure or business trips of less than 90 days. You may be asked to show an onward/return ticket, necessary travel documents, and sufficient funds for your stay.

TOURIST OFFICE IN THE UNITED STATES: Netherlands Board of Tourism, *355 Lexington Ave., 21st Floor, New York, NY 10017; (212)370-7360.*

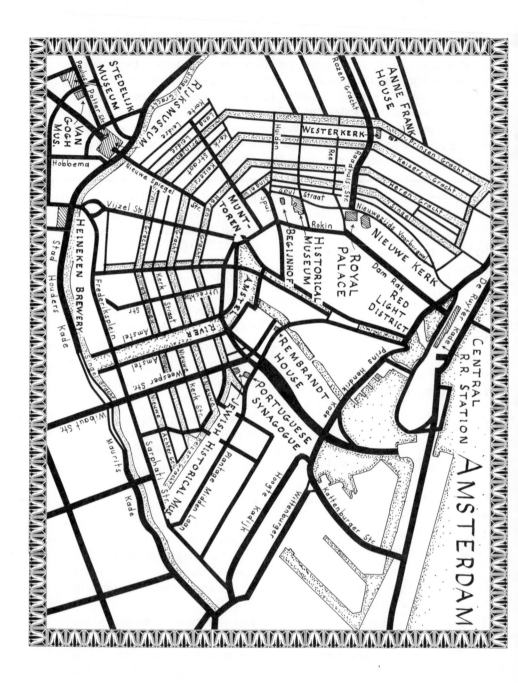

the offerings of the renowned **Concertgebouw**; beer drinkers will visit the **Heineken Brewery** for a tour and tasting; cyclists will love the bike paths through this city, and in the country as well; children will love the miniature version of the Netherlands in **Muiden**, a suburb of Amsterdam; sinners will like the genuine **Red Light District** (complete with red lights in the windows where the prostitutes sit) south of the railroad station.

The capital of the Netherlands, **The Hague,** offers an ancient parliament building (the **Binnenhof**), the palace of the House of Orange (**Huis ten Bosch**), the seat of the **World Court of Justice,** and two more great museums, the **Mauritshuis** and the **Witte Huis.**

Nearby **Delft** offers two great churches, **Oude Kerk,** subject of the famous Vermeer painting, and **Nieuwe Kerk,** site of the tomb of William of Orange (who founded the Dutch monarchy after leading the successful Protestant rebellion against Spanish rule in the 17th century). His home, the **Prinsenhof**, is another great museum, featuring tapestries as well as paintings.

Other interesting cities include **Haarlem**, which has a well-preserved old quarter and the house of Frans Hals, now, needless to say, a museum. Another house in Harlem, the **Goldene Eeuwe,** features scientific instruments going back to Spinoza's work on optics and the navigational tools used during the period of Dutch colonial expansion. **Utrecht**, another charming old town with canals, has an immense number of spaced-out drug-addicted local teenage hippies around its theater. But it also boasts shops, cafés, and a museum with a ninth-century Viking ship. **Leiden**, a university town, has museums of Indonesian and oriental art, and of ethnography, as well as one of the oldest botanical gardens in the world. Other Dutch cities include **Rotterdam**, which has been rebuilt into Europe's busiest port after being virtually flattened during the early days of World War II. It has attractive pedestrian malls and a harbor tower with a revolving view.

But Holland is not just cities. South of Haarlem are the tulip fields, worth a visit when they bloom in the springtime. Other flower fields keep the area interesting all year round. North of Amsterdam is **Alkmaar,** with its famous cheese market and curiously dressed local peasants, who still wear wooden shoes and pagoda-shaped hats. Even more picturesque villagers live on the islands of the **North Sea** coast, many of them belonging to strict religious sects. Some of the ferries don't run on Sunday and some of the islanders will break cameras because photographs are believed to violate the commandment against graven images.

Hoge Veluwe National Park, in the region of Arnhem, is for nature-lovers and for those who want more Van Gogh. In the middle of the park is the **Kroller-Muller Museum,** which has works by the painter, whose canvases now command even higher prices than those of his countryman Rembrandt.

Dutch food is mediocre, with the exception of *Uitsmijter* ("bouncer"), which is ham and eggs; the name refers to its origin as the dish served in bars just before the clientele were thrown out in the morning. Also edible are Dutch cheeses and fresh fish and shellfish. The best way to survive in the Netherlands is by eating Indonesian food, which is widely available: *loemphia* and *satays* make good snacks, and *Rijstafel* (a colonial Dutch invention brought to Holland from Indonesia) the best dinner. In the spring, the fresh herring is sold from pushcarts in Amsterdam and other cities: you get it on a buttered roll with onions to go, and it helps make up for the rest of the year in Holland. Drink beer with the herring, preferably Heineken. Dutch coffee is also quite good, particularly if served with pastries or bread and cheese.

Shopping goodies include Delft tiles (both antique and modern), old prints (the Dutch were big on printing books with vistas and/or maps, which are now being ripped apart by dealers), antiques in general (visit the **Spiegelstraat** in Amsterdam, where antiques are surprisingly well-priced by European standards), puppets, English-language second-hand books, and Droste chocolates. And Amsterdam is supposed to be where cheap diamonds can be procured—to the extent that diamonds ever are cheap. ❦

NEW ZEALAND

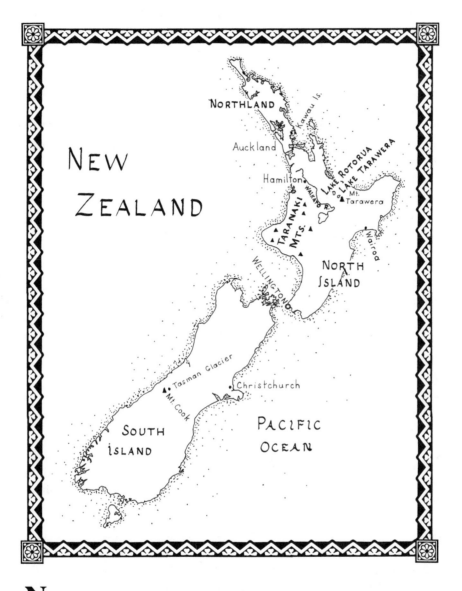

New Zealand is very far away and expensive to get to, but it is gorgeous. This is the destination for those who appreciate scenery—fjords, falls, and forests; beaches with deserted coves and isolated islands; volcanoes and views. New Zealand appeals also to those who like strenuous travel—white-water rafting, mountaineering, summer skiing, fishing—and those who are intrigued by traditional Polynesian Maori tribes. Those who want civilization—nightlife, good restaurants, historic sights more than 150 years old, great art and music—had better find fields closer to home.

New Zealand, like Australia, Canada, and the United States, is a land settled by English-speaking folk from the British Isles. The native Maoris, like our own Comanches, made an attempt to halt the flood of pioneers, but were defeated. On the scale of the globe, this is another one of those large countries with relatively small populations and even smaller historic records—and lots of world-class scenery. You should only go to New Zealand if you have already visited the Grand Canyon, Yosemite, the Hawaiian out islands, the Outer Banks, plus Vancouver and

EMBASSY: *37 Observatory Circle N.W., Washington, DC 20008; (202)328-4800.*

SYSTEM OF GOVERNMENT: Parliamentary.

ETHNIC GROUPS: Europeans, 89.7%; New Zealand Maoris, 8.8%; Polynesians, 2%.

RELIGIOUS GROUPS: Anglicans, 29%; Presbyterians, 18%; Roman Catholics, 15%.

LANGUAGES: English; Maori.

POPULATION: 3.305 million (in 1986).

AREA: 103,787 square miles (268,808 square kilometers); comparable to Colorado.

CAPITAL: Wellington (population 342,000).

TERRAIN: Varied, from snow-capped mountains to expansive plains. Geysers and hot springs.

CLIMATE: Oceanic.

TELECOMMUNICATIONS
   Country Code: 64.
   Time Zone: +17 hours Eastern Standard Time.
   Code of Capital: 4.

LOCAL/NATIONAL AIRLINES: **Air New Zealand,** *(800)262-1234;* **Pan Am,** *(800)221-1111;* **Qantas Airways Ltd.,** *(800)227-4500* or *(800)622-0850*

in California; **UTA French Airlines,** *(800)282-4484;* and **Continental Airlines,** *(800)525-0280.*

U.S. CONSULATE IN COUNTRY: *29 Fitzherbert Terrace, Thorndon, Wellington; tel. (64)4-722-068.*

CURRENCY: New Zealand dollar. No limit on import or export.

GROSS NATIONAL PRODUCT: $24.6 billion (in 1986).

WORK FORCE: Commerce and services, 33.8%; manufacturing, 22.9%; government, 20.7%; agriculture and fishing, 10.5%; construction, 6.1%.

OUR QUALITY OF LIFE RANKING: 80.78.

VISA REQUIREMENTS: Visas are not required for stays of less than three months; however, you must show an onward/return ticket. Visas (which are free) are valid for 48 months with multiple entries. The maximum stay is usually three months. You must hold a passport valid for three months beyond your estimated departure from New Zealand. To obtain a visa, contact the embassy in Washington, D.C., or the consulate in Los Angeles or New York.

TOURIST OFFICE IN THE UNITED STATES: **New Zealand Consulate,** *Suite 530, 630 Fifth Ave., New York, NY 10111; (212)698-4650.*

the Canadian Rockies. I am not being nationalistic; it is just that those American sights are closer to home, and will enable you to get the natural wonders of New Zealand in perspective.

New Zealand is in fact made up of two large islands, imaginatively named North and South. Discovered first by the Dutchman Abel Tasman in 1642, New Zealand was largely left alone (unlike America and Australia) until an Australian missionary decided to convert the Maoris in 1814. A dedicated evangelist, Samuel Marsden was known in Port Jackson, Australia as "the flogging parson." In the course of converting the Maoris, he introduced the plow, wheat, horses and cattle, and the *Muu-muu* (to cover up the native women's bare breasts). This became more necessary as his settlement in Kororarika Bay drew more missionaries and traders. The Bible was translated into Maori and printed.

The settlers were a mixed bunch from the beginning, and since the nomadic Maori lacked any notion of the ownership of land, many poor settlers bought Manhattan-sized tracts from the natives. By 1840, settlement schemes by land speculators were being organized from England to the area around Wellington.

It was not long before the Maoris rebelled, in the 1858-1881 land wars. Naturally, they lost. Settlement schemes grew apace (in one case aided by loans from the London Rothschilds), and new immigrants from the Scandinavian countries and Germany began to arrive.

New Zealand has 3.3 million people now; more than 2 million of them live in cities or suburbs, despite the myth to the contrary. With the influx of new foreign immigrants after World War II, 90 percent of the population is of European origin. Race laws banning non-European immigration have been struck from the books, and New Zealand currently appeals to boat people and Hong Kong Chinese seeking a haven, as well as to Polynesians and Melanesians aiming to improve their lot.

Auckland is the big city, preoccupied with beaches, boats, and barbecues. It has beautiful harbors (there are two, **Waitemata** and **Manukau**) and two dozen secluded offshore islands to give sailors a destination. **King's Wharf** is where the city fathers first hoisted the Union Jack—but the city has sprawled (it reminds one of Los Angeles that way) along 50 miles of coast. The local Valley Girls shop at **Lower Queen Street.** Near the capital is **Kawau Island,** a four-hour boat ride, site of the 19th-century **Mansion House** and the only extant group of parma wallabies (the Australian native animal is extinct in its homeland). North of the metropolis is **Northland** (centered around **Waitangi**), the site of the 1840 treaty that gave the Maoris a reservation. Offshore are the capes and islands where isolated farms used to stand. Even today you can take a cream trip around the isles in the old dairy boats. The climate here is perfect for cows: damp and even, to help the grass grow.

South of Auckland on the west coast is **Waikato** and the volcanic snow-capped mountains of **Taranaki** . Here, too, grass flourishes; the average rainfall is 44 inches per year. Down the Waikato River from the city of **Hamilton,** is the center of the Maori cultural revival at **Turangawaemae Marae**. Nearby is **Mount Taupiri,** where you will find the sacred cemetery of the Waikato tribes and famous caves (one of which, Waikato, is lit by glowworms.)

A less peaceable area inland is **Rotorua,** a volcanic region with bubbling mud

151

pools, great geysers, wasted vegetation burned by hot water and sulphur gas, healing springs, and hot pools. This region has the largest Maori population. George Bernard Shaw said he was pleased "to get so close to Hades and return."

Not everyone did as well as Shaw. Travelers in the last century admired **Lake Rotomahana,** which had pink and white terraces along its shores, formed by silica deposits from the boiling pools. The whole business was destroyed in a few hours in 1886 when **Mount Tarawera** erupted. South of here are more lakes and a red-wood grove. Nearby is **Te Wairoa** (on Lake Tarawera), site of a buried group of Maori villages hit by a volcanic eruption a century ago (now studied by archeologists).

Wellington, on the southwest coast of North Island is the capital of the country. If Auckland is Los Angeles, this is San Francisco, complete with cable cars, wharves, Victorian houses, and a population given to good causes (like stopping the construction of the highway, gentrification, and French restaurants). The yuppie area of Wellington is called **Thorndon.** The equivalent of Bohemian Grove is **Hutt Valley,** where the rich have estates; the equivalent of Stanford is the **Gold Coast.** For hippies, as in San Francisco, you have to cross the water, in this case to **Nelson** on South Island. This is the home of holistic living, alternative lifestyle communes, and cheap digs. Wellington is also the place where immigrants settled. There are flourishing ethnic neighborhoods with Italian, Vietnamese and Greek restaurants, and Polish churches.

The most stirring sight in New Zealand (according to Rudyard Kipling), is **Milford Sound,** on the west coast of South Island. Here are snow-covered crags slicing down toward the sea, aquamarine fjords, dramatic waterfalls, mountain lakes amidst virgin pine groves, and pastures of peace. And bordering the sound are New Zealand's ski slopes and Fjordland National Park. If you go to the **South Island,** this must be your destination: by ship, plane, helicopter, horse, jeep, car, or backpack. This is fjord country—three million acres, part of which has never been explored. There even is a myth that a lost Maori tribe lives in the middle of the wilds, the **Te Anau.** (Te Anau is also the name of the region's tourist boomtown, which is a good base for exploring the southern fjord country. It is also the name of another glowworm-illuminated cave, known to the Maoris and rediscovered in 1948—you can hike to it from the lakeside town.)

In the middle of the east coast of South Island is the New Zealand equivalent of Vancouver, called **Christchurch,** which feels very English. The tallest building is the pseudo-Gothic Anglican Church, which is surrounded by what New Zealanders imagine is a replica of the City of London. Christchurch is full of neo-gothic architecture, snobbism, and—unlike London—smog. Christ's College here is a very posh British-style boarding school. It is the place to send your New Zealand son to if you can't get him into Eton.

The highest Alps in New Zealand are due west of here, and clear skies are one of the things that makes them different from those of Switzerland (all the muck stays at Christchurch). These Alps are good bases for satellite and astronomical observatories, for example. Here is the great **Tasman Glacier,** and the highest point in New Zealand, **Mount Cook.**

There are two cuisines in New Zealand. Maoris eat lightly-steamed vegetables, fish, and shellfish *kina* (sea eggs), eel, and dried shark; meat such as *titi* (mutton bird to ornithologists) and pigeon; and *rewena* (a risen bread) or a doughnut-like bread. And they drink fermented corn juice. Apart from ethnic food, the white population favors lamb (served abundantly, if not well), beef, and pork; fish such as snapper, grouper, John Dory (St. Pierre), oysters, crab, crayfish, and scallops; and the native sweet potato, called *kumara*. For dessert, try the kiwi fruit (if you haven't already) or the country's best-known cake, a meringue-cum-fruit-cum whipped cream concoction called pavlova (usually made with strawberries). New Zealanders drink beer, but the country also has good wine. The best is from Corbans, a vineyard owned by a family of that name, which emigrated from Lebanon. Restaurants with "B.Y.O." after their listing do not have alcohol licenses, but you can bring your own.

Shopping options range from Maori woodcarvings to sheepskins, from pottery to patchwork, from knitware to jade-like greenstone. ❦

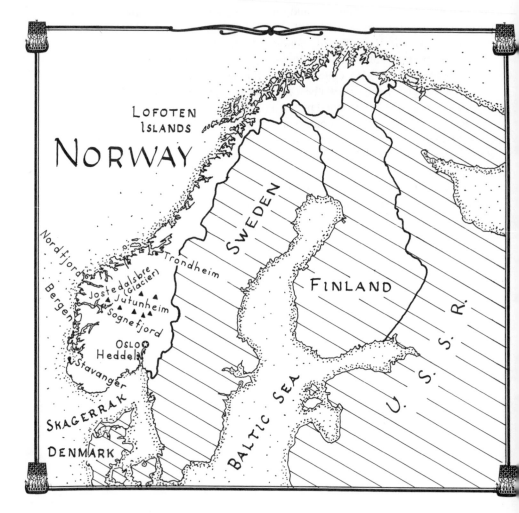

Norway is the land of Norwegians—but there aren't very many of them, so much of their land remains pristine wilderness. Although they are few, the Norwegians are very fine, talented people (Edvard Grieg, Henrik Ibsen, Edvard Munch, Liv Ullmann, and Walter Mondale's parents were, or are, Norwegians).

Furthermore, the Norwegians are largely fluent in English. But because of Norway's low population, this land of rugged coastlines and dramatic scenery has the lowest population density of any continental European country, 33 people per square mile.

Most Norwegians live in **Oslo**, which is the capital. Located in the southeastern corner of the country on the Oslofjord, which gives onto the Skagerrak, Oslo is worth a visit. It is a well-planned modern city surrounding a fjord-harbor. Oslo's sights include **Ibsen's National Theater,** the **Nobel Institute** (where the Swedish Academy meets to decide who gets the prizes), the **Edvard Munch Museum,** the **Kon Tiki** raft, the **Royal Palace,** and **Akershus Castle** on the Oslofjord. The palace and the theater (as well as the railroad station and the tourist office) all are on the Karl Johans Gate, which is also the center of café nightlife in Oslo. Other sights include the **Parliament House** or **Storting,** the **Holmenkollen** and **Slottsparken** parks, **Frogner Park** with the Kon Tiki raft in its museum, the

---

EMBASSY: *2720 34th St. N.W., Washington, DC 20008; (202)333-6000.*

SYSTEM OF GOVERNMENT: Hereditary constitutional monarchy.

ETHNIC GROUPS: Norwegians; 20,000 Lapps.

RELIGIOUS GROUPS: Evangelical Lutherans (state church), 88%; Roman Catholics; Baptists; members of the Greek Orthodox Church.

LANGUAGES: Norwegian (official); Lappish dialect.

POPULATION: 4.2 billion.

AREA: 125,056 square miles (323,895 square kilometers); slightly larger than New Mexico.

CAPITAL: Oslo (population 447,000 in 1986).

TERRAIN: The land area is 70% uninhabitable, with mountains, hundreds of fjords, glaciers, moors, and rivers.

CLIMATE: Temperate summers, cold winters; white nights from the middle of May to the end of July.

TELECOMMUNICATIONS

Country Code: 47.
Time Zone: +6 hours Eastern Standard Time.
Code of Capital: 2.

LOCAL/NATIONAL AIRLINES: Icelandair, *(800)223-5500;* **Northwest**

Airlines, *(800)447-4747;* **Pan Am,** *(800)221-1111;* **Sabena Airlines,** *(800)632-8050* (New York), *(800)645-3700* (East Coast), *(800)645-3790* (Southeast and Midwest), or *(800)645-1382* (West Coast); **Scanair,** *(305)665-8109;* and **Scandanavian Airlines Systems,** *(800)221-2350.*

U.S. CONSULATE IN COUNTRY: *Drammensveien 18, Oslo 2; tel. (47-2)44-85-50.*

CURRENCY: Norwegian krone. No limit on import; travelers can export 2,000 Norwegian kroner.

GROSS NATIONAL PRODUCT: $67.4 billion (in 1986).

WORK FORCE: Industry, banking, and commerce, 47%; government, 26%; services, 18%; agriculture, 7%.

OUR QUALITY OF LIFE RANKING: 76.05.

VISA REQUIREMENTS: Visas are not required for stays of up to three months (the period begins when you enter the Scandinavian area—Finland, Sweden, Denmark, or Iceland).

TOURIST OFFICE IN THE UNITED STATES: Scandinavian Tourist Board, *655 Third Ave., New York, NY 10019; (212)949-2333.*

Viking Museum in Bygdøy (a suburb), with three excavated eighth-century vessels, and the city hall (built in 1950 to commemorate the 900th anniversary of Oslo). Southwest of Oslo is **Heddal,** worth a visit to see the stave church at **Telemark.** Only a few dozen of these 900-year-old timber churches survive.

A more interesting city (if less populated) is on the Norwegian Sea (known elsewhere in the world as the Atlantic) at the same latitude: **Bergen.** Take the train from Oslo; it is one of the most beautiful rides outside of Switzerland. Norway's herring port and second city has picturesque old Hanseatic houses and docks. Most are found in a neighborhood called the **Bryggen.** Much of the Bryggen's beauty is a result of a restoration project undertaken as long ago as 1702—after a fire destroyed the medieval city. A 12th-century church here is covered with a carvings and boasts a gorgeous altar—all gifts of the herring merchants' guilds.

On the west coast, fjords are closer in; a mere 45 miles north of Bergen is the longest and deepest of all, called **Sognefjord.** A bit further is **Nordfjord.** Like Sognefjord, it is fed by glacial streams of the **Jostedalbre,** the largest icefield in Europe. Eastward are the **Jotunheim Mountains,** popular for hiking or skiing, where Jotuns (giants) are said to hang around. South of Bergen is **Stavanger,** another city, founded by the Vikings in the eighth century. Now the center of the North Sea oil industry, it has a huge open market featuring fish. As the night falls, the fishermen stop repairing their nets and start to sing (mostly religious music).

Trondheim is also on the Atlantic, and counts as the gateway to the Norwegian north. Take a steamer cruise, rent a car (and take or rent camping equipment), or join a tour with hotel accommodation and head north from Trondheim. Go to the **North Cape,** the Arctic Ocean coast of Norway, where the sun never sets in summer and never rises in winter. Your route will pass through beautiful scenery and the land of the mysterious Norwegian Lapps, reindeer herders who are racially closer to American Indians and Eskimos than to Scandinavians. You can get right up against the Russian border. (Norway is a member of NATO and some of the busiest Western Alliance electronic and radar stations are in this remote zone. Offshore, the line between Norway and Russia is disputed and there are places where the border is unsafe to visit.) If possible, cross to the **Lofoten Islands.** Go to **Henningsvaer Harbor** to see the fishing boats come in—as many as 1,000 at a time.

Norway used to be cheap for Scandinavia—but thanks to the inflationary effect of North Sea oil, it is no longer. Shoppers go for traditional Norwegian knits, the usual Scandinavian modern glass, linens and other houseware, modern silver jewelry, and sporting gear.

Norwegians are the only people in Europe who eat lunch (*middag*) at noon and supper at 5 p.m., a custom that shortens the day and probably arose out of boredom during the long sunless winter. The noon meal is usually the main one and at night people satisfy their hunger with open-face sandwiches, *smørbrød* in Norwegian. The best features of Norwegian cuisine are *sild,* the humble herring and *laks*, the nobler salmon in all their variety: smoked, pickled, salted, curried, doused in cream sauce, cured or poached. Also good are *poølse* (sausage), *ost* (cheese), and *ägge* (egg). Many prefer the supper menu even at lunch; alternatives are gravy-doused versions of meatloaf (*kjøttkaker*), hash (*lapskaus*), and stew, usually made with pork (*svine*) or chicken (*kylling*). If you get a chance to try reindeer (*rensdyr*), either cooked or treated by the methods described for fish, grab it. (Right after Chernobyl, reindeer meat was withdrawn from the market for health reasons, but now it is becoming available again.) Dessert goodies include *stikkelsabaer* (gooseberries), *jordbaer* (strawberries), *bringebaer* (raspberries), *tyttebaer* (whortleberries), or *kirsebaer* (cherries). The best way to eat them is to mash the best of them with whipped cream to make a lovely pink froth. If you must follow your diet, have Danish pastries instead (which are eaten in Norway, too). 🍒

PERU

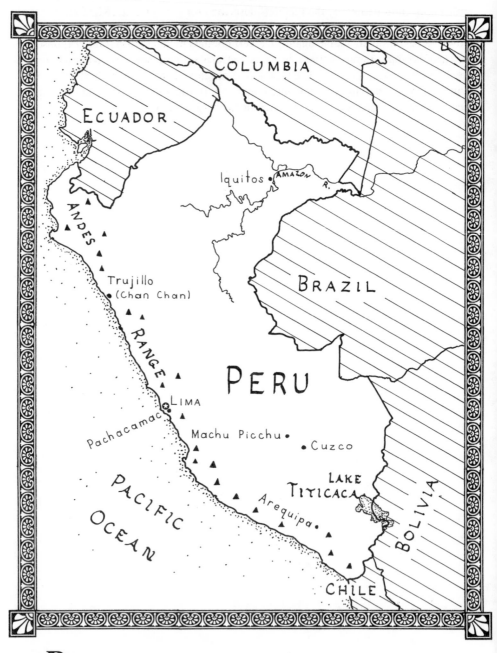

Peru is physically spectacular, caught between the Pacific and the stupendous Andes Mountains. If you take a car from the capital, Lima, into the mountains, you will climb 16,000 feet in a matter of only 85 miles. Peru is among those countries (like Mexico) that one visits for pre-Columbian wonders. The Incas ruled much of South America from Cuzco, a Peruvian valley 11,400 feet up in the Andes. Discovered in 1911, the ruins of Machu Picchu are another impressive Inca site.

The Spanish, too, left impressive monuments in Peru. **Lima,** one of the most fascinating cities in the world, is filled with 17th-century Spanish colonial buildings. The most beautiful is the cathedral, on the Plaza de Armas. Its cornerstone was laid by the famous conquistador, Francisco Pizarro, in 1535. (Besides his cornerstone, the cathedral also contains Pizarro's mummified remains, which were placed here after being found in an unmarked grave in 1891.)

Lima's **Torre Tagle Palace** is a beautiful baroque building with a central

---

EMBASSY: *1700 Massachusetts Ave. N.W., Washington, DC 20036; (202)833-9860.*

SYSTEM OF GOVERNMENT: In transition from military to constitutional democracy.

ETHNIC GROUPS: American Indians, 45%; Mestizos, 37%; Caucasians, 15%; Negroes and Asians, 3%.

RELIGIOUS GROUPS: Roman Catholic, 90%.

LANGUAGES: Spanish (official); Quechua (official); Aymara.

POPULATION: 20.21 million (in 1986).

AREA: 496,222 square miles (1.3 million square kilometers); three times the size of California.

CAPITAL: Lima (population 4.17 million).

TERRAIN: Coastal plains in the west; Andes in the central region; tropical jungle forests in the eastern lowlands.

CLIMATE: Coastal area arid and mild; Andes temperate to frigid; eastern lowlands tropically warm and humid.

TELECOMMUNICATIONS
   Country Code: 51.
   Time Zone: 0 hours Eastern Standard Time.

Code of Capital: 14.

LOCAL/NATIONAL AIRLINES: Aerolinas Argentinas, *(800)327-0276;* **Braniff,** *(800)272-6433;* **Faucett Peruvian Airlines,** *(800)334-3356;* and **Lufthansa,** *(800)645-3880.*

U.S. CONSULATE IN COUNTRY: *av. Wilson 1400, Lima; tel. (51-14)286000.*

CURRENCY: Inti. Travelers may import $300 and export $300.

GROSS NATIONAL PRODUCT: $20.3 billion (in 1984).

WORK FORCE: Services and government, 41%; agriculture, 40%; industry and mining, 19%.

OUR QUALITY OF LIFE RANKING: 34.70.

VISA REQUIREMENTS: Valid passports are required. Visas are not required for U.S. tourists who are staying less than 90 days and who can show return tickets.

TOURIST OFFICE IN THE UNITED STATES: Peruvian Commercial Office, *747 Third Ave., 28th Floor, New York, NY 10017; (212)688-9110.*

---

courtyard, balconies, and stone arches. **San Francisco** (a huge church with 15 chapels, cloisters, and an ancient library) and **San Pedro** (with its dome modeled on that of St. Peter's in Rome) also date from the early years of the Spanish conquest. **San Marcello** is another important 16th-century religious building.

A stone bridge built by the Spanish in the 17th century still spans the **Rimac River**. Almost as old are some of the buildings of **San Marcos University,** which was established in 1551.

Besides Catholicism and architecture, Spanish leftovers in Peru include bullfights, flamenco, cockfights, and parks. Rather endearingly, the conquistadors planted trees to shield the Spanish viceroys from the sun.

From Lima's Plaza de Armas, Spanish viceroys ruled not only Peru, but much of South America. In general, the Spanish conquistadors were vicious and greedy, torturing Indians to find their gold and to achieve religious conformity. (The Inquisition for the New World was set up in Lima in 1569; many of the city's religious buildings were destroyed when the Inquisition finally was abolished in 1813.)

Today, Lima is the capital of Peru, which won its independence from Spain in 1821. It is dotted with government buildings, palaces, museums, and churches that share a Spanish air.

In a Lima suburb called **Monterrico** (rich mount), you can see the gold the Spaniards missed, 13,000 precious objects, including a gold funeral mask with emerald teardrops. These are in the **Mujica Gallo**, which began as the private collection of a Liman determined to preserve his country's heritage. (Most of the pre-Columbian gold the Spaniards found was melted for bullion.)

Just outside Lima is **Pachacamac**, which was a great Inca pilgrimage city before the Spaniards came on the scene. You can visit the ruins of the **Temple of the Sun** and the **House of the Virgins of the Sun**. (As is also the case in Mexico, nobody really knows what mysterious rites the Peruvian Indians engaged in, because the Spanish set out to eliminate this pagan culture. As a result, when naming buildings, archeologists let their imaginations be their guide.) **Puruchuco,** home of an Inca chief 1,000 years ago, has been reconstructed and has a museum. Other nearby ruins include **Cantamarco**, which could be a fortress, a town, or a temple; no one is sure. It is a hard climb of about two hours to reach a stone structure with low doors; inside is a central pillar with a fireplace. Wooden beams hold up a sod roof. The building is 1,000 years old and has a splendid view.

But the archeologically inclined will probably head for the mountains to **Machu Picchu,** a hidden city on the top of the plateau (now reachable by railroad from Cuzco, or by a five-day strenuous hike). This may have been the last refuge of the Inca Emperor Atahualpa, who fled from Pizarro in 1532, and of the Virgins of the Sun. (When the Spanish finally lured the Inca army into Cuzco, down the valley, they massacred the Indians.)

Cuzco itself is worth visiting, with its fine Renaissance cathedral, some say the finest church in America (built on the site of an Inca temple to the god of creation, Viracocha). Also recommended are **El Triumfo** and **Sagrada Familia** churches, which are part of the cathedral complex, and Cuzco's 328 shrines—marvels of masonry built by Indian craftsmen. The 328 shrines correspond to former Inca religious sites (their calendar had 328 days). Because of earthquakes, the Inca sites have held up better than those of the Spaniards. On the feast of Corpus Christi-Inti Raymi (June 21-24, which combines the Catholic feast with the Inca celebration of the summer solstice, the shortest day of the year in the Southern Hemisphere), thousands of colorfully clothed Indians in braid-trimmed ponchos, hats with flaps, or bowlers, come down from their towns in the hilltops to parade with images of the 12 apostles and the Host. The 12 apostles, whose images are laden with silver and often weigh a ton, correspond to the 12 deities of the Inca religion. At the end of the three-day ceremony, which is marked by dances—a llama is sacrificed.

Trujillo, the sunny city filled with Spanish-style houses and ironwork grills, has the largest **Plaza de Armas** in the country, and a most beautiful ecclesiastical sight, the **Convento de Carmen**. In nearby **Chan Chan** are impressive tombs of the Chimus, a people who ruled before the Incas. The nearby **Pyramid of the Sun,** built by the Mochica people, is an enormous structure made of adobe bricks; nearby are the **Pyramid of the Moon** and *huacas* (sacred places) dedicated to dragons and emeralds.

Arequipa, in the valley of the **El Misti** volcano, is the southernmost city in Peru. It is full of white buildings made of sillar, a white volcanic stone not found anywhere else. The **Church of San Augustin,** built in the 17th century, is elaborately carved with shells and pillars. The church chapels are open to the square. (The Jesuits, who built the church, had difficulty persuading the Indians to come into the building, since the Incas had carried out their religious observances in open places.) In the nearby **Valley of the Volcanoes** is **Colca**, the deepest canyon in the world, twice as deep as the Grand Canyon.

The Amazon basin, to the east of the Andes, covers 60 percent of Peru—and very little is known about it. This is home to natives who still hunt monkeys (monkey is said to taste like turkey) with blowguns. Several dozen other Indian tribes who live here are almost wholly without contact with the modern world. The jungle swallows up roads and paths, so the river is the way to get around, by motorboat, canoe, or raft. The former missionary town of **Iquitos** is the gateway to the 700 miles of the Amazon basin accessible from Peru. Here you can see wildlife found nowhere else: rare monkeys, tree frogs, toucans, and 4,300 species of bird. And here you can see rain forest tribes (no longer headhunters, we are assured).

Apart from monkey, Peruvian food features spicy barbecue cuisine and a tea made from coca leaves (which help you bear the high altitude).

If you were born to shop, Peru is for you. You can find good buys in handicrafts ranging from llama and alpaca weavings (rugs, ponchos, blankets) to gold and silver jewelry, from leather goods to pottery. Multicolored braid is used to trim or make up unusual garments; the Indians who do the plaiting can be bargained with in the squares of Lima and major cities. Prices are low and negotiable. Dollar bills are particularly useful to bargain with (the inflation rate in inti, the Peruvian currency, is horrendous). ❦

POLAND

In Poland, you can ski the Carpathian Alps or visit the Chopin birthplace at Zelazowa Wola. You can explore the perfect medieval walled city where Copernicus taught (Cracow) or see the miraculous and mysterious Black Madonna at Czestochowa. You can see the Gdansk shipyards where Lech Walesa started *solidarnosc* or visit the site of Auschwitz (Os'wiecim).

Apart from its southern border with Czechoslovakia, most of Poland is a flat plain—which is one reason why its has been so easily invaded throughout history. In the 12th century, the first invaders arrived: Mongols from the east and Teutonic knights from the west. The Teutons were defeated at Tannenberg in 1410 and became vassals of the Polish king. Poland rose to great power in the 14th century and controlled Lithuania and a huge chunk of eastern Europe. But Polish power ended with the 16th century. In 1683 the Polish monarch, Jan Sobieski, turned back the invading Turks outside the gates of Vienna.

After that it was all downhill. The Polish nobility sucked the wealth of the country and made it ungovernable. In the Seym, or parliament, every third-rate lordling had the right of veto, so nothing could be voted on. Invaders from the east and west periodically chopped off a bit of Poland. There were three partitions between 1772 and 1796, with the result that all of 19th-century Poland was ruled by Russia, Austria-Hungary, and Prussia. Only in 1918 was the country declared to exist again, with Jan Paderewski, the famous pianist and Polish nationalist, as the first president. He was deposed by a dictatorship in 1926. In 1939 Hitler and Stalin reverted to historic example and divided up Poland between them, which had the

---

EMBASSY: *2640 16th St. N.W., Washington, DC 20009; (202)234-3800.*

SYSTEM OF GOVERNMENT: Communist.

ETHNIC GROUPS: Poles, 97%; Ukrainians, Byelorussians, Germans, and Gypsies, 3%.

RELIGIOUS GROUP: Roman Catholics.

LANGUAGE: Polish.

POPULATION: 37.546 million.

AREA: 120,727 square miles (312,683 square kilometers); comparable to New Mexico.

CAPITAL: Warsaw (population 1.625 million).

TERRAIN: Flat plains; mountainous along southern border.

CLIMATE: Continental climate. Southern humid areas. Cold winters, cool summers.

TELECOMMUNICATIONS
  Country Code: 48.
  Time Zone: +6 hours Eastern Standard Time.
  Code of Capital: 22.

LOCAL/NATIONAL AIRLINES: Air France, *(800)237-2747;* **Czechoslovak Airlines CSA,** *(800)223-2365;* **LOT**

Polish Airlines, *(800)223-0593;* **Lufthansa German Airlines,** *(800)645-3880;* and **Pan Am,** *(800)221-1111.*

U.S. CONSULATE IN COUNTRY: *Aleje Ujazdowskle 29/31, Warsaw; tel. (48-22)283041.*

CURRENCY: Zloty. Travelers may not import or export currency.

GROSS NATIONAL PRODUCT: $110 billion (in 1984).

WORK FORCE: Industry and commerce, 41%; agriculture, 30%; government and services, 11%.

OUR QUALITY OF LIFE RANKING: 42.50.

VISA REQUIREMENTS: Valid passports are required. Transit visas are valid 48 hours; regular visas, for business, cultural, educational, scientific, and tourist purposes, are valid up to 90 days. Contact the embassy in Washington, D.C., or the consulate in Chicago or New York.

TOURIST OFFICE IN THE UNITED STATES: Orbis, *500 Fifth Ave., New York, NY 10110; (212)391-0844.*

---

incidental effect of starting World War II. The Germans sited concentration camps in Poland, wiping out Poland's large pre-war Jewish population, and destroying the Warsaw Ghetto as well as much of the rest of the city (which was rebuilt after the war). The Russians concentrated on eliminating the Polish army and the country's upper and middle classes.

After the war, the Polish borders were redrawn to add to Russian territory at the expense of Polish, and to add to Polish territory at the expense of defeated Germany. Rubbing it in, the Russians made Poland the center of their system of controlling Eastern Europe, the Warsaw Pact. **Warsaw** was rebuilt—but there were no Jews or gentry to replace those who had been killed. The **Old Town** was rebuilt from prints and photographs and is now closed to traffic. The subject is covered in a free documentary film that you can see at the **Warsaw Historical Museum** (which also has chamber music concerts).

Warsaw's 14th-century **St. John's Cathedral,** where Polish kings were crowned, has been rebuilt. The **Dziekanis Arcaded Gallery,** which once connected to the royal castle, can also be visited. So can the early 17th-century **Jesuit Church.**

A little-known Warsaw sight is a manhole cover at the intersection of Dluga and Miodawa streets. Here, 5,300 insurgents exited the sewer canal through which they escaped from the old town during the Warsaw Uprising against the Nazis in September 1944. At Ul. Freta 16 is the **Marie Curie Museum**. Visit the walls of the old town, and the reconstructed **Barbican**, a 16th-century tower now used as an outdoor art gallery. Also interesting is the **Radziwill Palace,** where Chopin made his debut; the senior Radziwill prince used to be married to Jacqueline Kennedy's sister.

The **Wilanow Palace,** now a museum, has a sound and light show. Also near Warsaw is the **Chopin Home**, 30 miles down the Vistula. Here, concerts are held on Sunday during the summer months. Other sights include the home of **Casimir Pulaski** at **Warka.** Pulaski, a Polish veteran, took his skills and fervor to help George Washington's troops. At **Bialowieza** you can see the last primeval forest in Europe, home of rare animals such as European bison, lynx, and tarpan ponies (ancestors of the modern horse).

Polish drinkers share a culinary taste with the Bialowieza bison. In Poland, you can get a special green-tinted vodka flavored with bison grass, normally eaten by the huge animals. This gives the vodka a flavor, making it a good accompaniment to food, rather than the basis for mixed drinks. Polish food combines the Baltic tradition (lots of herring) with inland goodies such as wild mushrooms, cabbage, and beet soups. A dollop of sour cream is added to everything.

The best bargains in Poland include pretty wooden boxes either painted or burned by a hot poker. Other good buys are crystal (decanters and glassware) and amber, which is found on the Baltic coast and made into jewelry. Poland is the source of a lot of Western European fake antiques, so be sharp about things that look too cheap to be true; they aren't. Although the Polish market system for consumer goods is the most mismanaged of all those in Eastern Europe (if they are not out of diapers, they are out of toilet paper), the black market works very well.

Unlike other places, in Poland it is legal for the locals to sell goods for hard currency (like dollars), and the Poles actually will give you home-made "change," slips of paper representing fractions of a dollar, which you can spend. Clothing tends to be available in an erratic way, but you can get good buys when some factory has dumped its over-production on the local market. We bought ski parkas for the whole family at a very low price; one extra appeal was that they had a picture of Lenin under the back collar.

Thanks to the pioneering efforts of Polish-speaking retirees from this country and western Europe, Poland is a surprisingly open society for Eastern Europe. You can travel on your own, rent cars (expensive), or tour by bicycle, horse, or caravan. Unlike the situation in other communist countries, you do not have to stick with package tours. But you do need a visa. ❦

PORTUGAL

ATLANTIC OCEAN

• Porto

• Aveiro

• Coimbra

• Batalha

TAGUS RIVER

Estoril • LISBON

Cascais

• Evora

ALENTEJO

MONCHIQUE MTS.

CALDERAO MTS.

To AZORES

ALGARVE REG.

/ To Madeira

ATL. Oc.

MADEIRA

ATLANTIC OCEAN

AZORES

SPAIN

Portugal is beautiful, cheap, and relatively undiscovered by our fellow-Americans. The country is typically Mediterranean: a land of wheat and vines, olive trees and cork oaks, scrub pine and almonds. The food is based on the olive and the tomato; the drink is wine. The people are short and dark and speak a language descended from Latin. Houses are whitewashed or covered with tiles; donkeys still carry people and goods along tree-shaded narrow roads between dry stone walls. Pious old ladies dress from head to toe in black while the rest of the population swings. The only thing un-Mediterranean about Portugal is its geography. The country is bordered by Spain on the north and east, and by the Atlantic Ocean on the west and south. It is not actually on the Mediterranean, despite its Mediterranean culture.

The capital, **Lisbon**, was built on seven hills on the north shore of the mighty Tagus River. It contains one of the most perfect urban squares in Europe, which opens to the Tagus on the south. It is variously called **Black Horse Square** (by the British) because of its statue of King João riding a black horse; Praça de Comercio; or Terreno de Paço. Up river from here is the **Alfama**, the oldest quarter of Lisbon, huddled under the **Fort of St. George,** a good viewing point. Down river is the bridge finally built to cross the Tagus. Further west is **Belém,** seat of the government, site of the **Tower of Belem**, which used to command the entrance to the great port. Here, too, is the great **Jeronimos Monastery,** built in the peculiar Portuguese

EMBASSY: *2125 Kalorama Road N.W., Washington, DC 20008; (202)328-8610.*

SYSTEM OF GOVERNMENT: Parliamentary democracy.

ETHNIC GROUPS: Mediterranean stock; black African minority.

RELIGIOUS GROUP: Roman Catholics, 97%.

LANGUAGE: Portuguese.

POPULATION: 10.1 million.

AREA: 35,515 square miles (91,985 square kilometers); including the Azores Islands, Porto Santo, and Madeira. Comparable to Indiana in size.

CAPITAL: Lisbon (population 812,400 in 1981).

TERRAIN: Mountainous north of the Tagus River; rolling plains in the central-south region.

CLIMATE: Maritime temperate. Cool and rainy in the north; drier and warmer in the south.

TELECOMMUNICATIONS
  Country Code: 351.
  Time Zone: +6 hours Eastern Standard Time; Madeira Islands, +5 hours Eastern Standard Time.

Code of Capital: 1.

LOCAL/NATIONAL AIRLINES: TAP Air Portugal, *(800)442-5973;* **Trans World Airlines,** *(800)892-4141.*

U.S. CONSULATE IN COUNTRY: *av. das Forças Armadas, 1600 Lisbon; tel. (351-1)72-56-00.*

CURRENCY: Portuguese escudo. Travelers may import 5,000 escudos and export 5,000 escudos.

GROSS NATIONAL PRODUCT: $27.4 billion (in 1986).

WORK FORCE: Services and government, 44%; industry and commerce, 31%; agriculture, 24%.

OUR QUALITY OF LIFE RANKING: 61.18.

VISA REQUIREMENTS: Valid passports are required. Visas are required for stays longer than 60 days. To obtain a visa, contact the embassy or the consulate in New York, Boston, New Bedford, San Francisco, Providence, Rhode Island, or Newark.

TOURIST OFFICE IN THE UNITED STATES: Portuguese Tourist Office, *548 Fifth Ave., New York, NY 10036; (212)354-4403.*

version of Gothic called Manueline. The decor of Manueline architecture evokes the sea: there are carvings of waves, ropes, knots, and anchors. Since the Jeronimos Monastery was built in thanksgiving for the discoveries of Portuguese navigators, the symbols are apt. Here are buried Vasco da Gama, who first circumnavigated the globe, the princes who inspired the journeys of discovery (starting with Henry the Navigator), and the Portuguese bard who wrote their epic, Luis de Camoãs.

North of Black Horse Square is modern Lisbon, starting with the **Rossio,** center of night life and tourist shopping. From here the **Avenida da Liberdade** leads to the statue of the kingpin of 18th-century Portuguese liberalism, the Marquis of Pombal, who guards the entrance to the Lisbon town park, called **Parque Eduardo VII.** Farther north is the **Praça de Espanha,** off which is the great **Gulbenkian Museum.** Rather improbably, the Armenian multimillionaire left to Portugal his collection of 18th-century French furniture, Beauvais tapestries, oriental carpets, middle eastern antiquities, and great paintings by Turner Watteau, Corot, and Gainsborough. North of the city, too, is the airport; the sounds of airplanes landing or taking off is part of the Lisbon noise background.

Just west of the city, on the Atlantic, are the bedroom communities of the **Sintra Peninsula,** the most westerly point on the mainland of Europe. **Sintra** holds the neo-Gothic **Pena Palace,** with its steep and gloomy garden. Sintra square features great boutiques and restaurants and a tile fountain replica of a Portuguese astrolabe, a navigational instrument. Nearby **Queluz** has the former Royal Palace. **Estoril** has a beach and a casino. **Cascais** is on a lovely scenic road and a treacherous shore.

If you liked Jeronimos, you will want to see another great monastery at **Batalha,** north of Lisbon. Further afield to the north, aim for **Porto,** the town built upon the trade in fortified wine. Also see **Coimbra,** the picturesque home of the oldest Portuguese university, whose students wear mortarboards and gowns even when they are not graduating. And last but not least, see **Aveiro,** on the coast, a fishing town with canals and gondolas.

You have to take a ferry across the river to reach the railroad station for the southern half of the country. To the south, across the great bridge, is a huge statue, **Christo Rey,** the model for the one in Rio de Janeiro. South of the Tagus is **O Alentejo,** the region stretching from the sea to the Spanish border. It produces wheat, cork oaks for European bottles, and trouble; this is the region whose huge sharecropped estates bred revolution, most recently in 1976. Its best town is **Evora,** graced by a Roman temple and the prettiest hotel in Europe, the Pousada dos Loios. Cross the Calderão and Monchique mountains from the Alentejo and you are in the former independent Kingdom of the **Algarve,** featuring fishing ports with a North African look and the sunniest beaches in western Europe.

In the middle of the Atlantic are two farther outposts of Lusitania: **Madeira,** a beautiful tourist island, and the **Azores,** nine volcanic islands with a more temperate and rainy climate than the rest of Portugal. Some say it is the site of the mythical Atlantis.

Portuguese cuisine features goodies from the sea, both salt cod (*bacalhão,* which the Portuguese cook 365 different ways), fish and shellfish (try *gambas,*

168

large shrimp); *ameijoas na cataplana* (clams cooked in a primitive pressure cooker); or *carne de porco à alentejana* (pork with shellfish). *Calderada* is the Portuguese *bouillabaisse*, a fish stew that may have given its name to our own chowders. *Caldo verde* is the cabbage soup of the country. Portugal has lovely tomatoes, splendid chicken, and a variety of citrus fruits. The Portuguese also eat what we think of as soul food: turnip and mustard greens and corn bread. The best wines are local, rather than the rosé wines such as Mateus and Lancer's, which are made for the export market.

Shopping features things made by hand (because Portugal is still a cheap-labor country). Portugal is the only European country to grow cotton. Beware of shrinkage—they don't preshrink garments here. Other goodies include brass, pottery, leather goods, embroidered Madeira linens, crystal, and silver.

It's a good idea to learn Portuguese if you plan to spend much time here, although Portuguese is a tough language to learn. Many well-educated Portuguese do speak English, thanks to a historic link between the two countries. British families settled in Porto to deal in wine and many British retirees settle in the Algarve. Henry the Navigator had an English mother, and Charles the Second had a Portuguese wife who taught the British how to brew tea. ❦

SINGAPORE

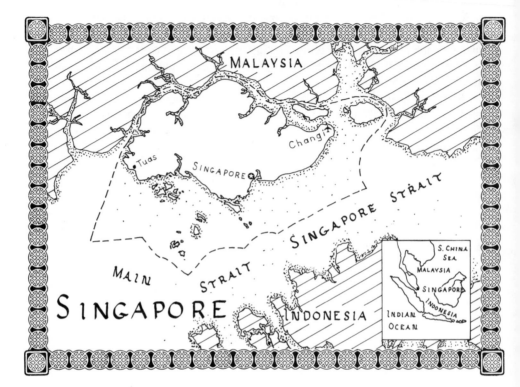

Singapore is a prosperous little island country covering 227 square miles. The prime minister, a British-educated Singapore Chinese, Lee Kuan Yew, heads the only legal party in the city-state. His party, called the People's Action Party, controls every seat of the Parliament. More than three-quarters of the population is Chinese, with the remainder Malay, Indian, and other. Among the government's recent actions is interfering in its citizens' right to read *The Wall Street Journal* or *The Far Eastern Economic Review*. (If you travel to Singapore, don't bring this guide with you, either.) People are given tickets for wearing their hair too long, for spitting on the street, or littering (you can get fined S$500 for dropping a cigarette butt on the street). Tourists with long hair or beards have been banned. So have many journalists. Talking about politics (as distinguished from saying how clean, well-organized, and prosperous Singapore looks) can get you into trouble.

A recent government campaign aims to persuade educated Singapore women of Chinese ancestry to have more children and to persuade educated Singapore men of Chinese ancestry to father these children. They are all then supposed to speak classic Mandarin rather than the South-Chinese dialect they are used to. And they are supposed to remove Straits slang and idioms from their English. The Malay minority and less educated Chinese are being persuaded to practice birth control with slogans like "Girls and boys: two is enough." This is enforced by a system of points for getting your children admitted to the primary school of your choice. Theoretically, a place is guaranteed only for the first two children of any family; a third child will be admitted only if the mother has been sterilized immediately after its birth. A special exception covers twins, and there are severe penalties for those who have a third child after one of the first two proved to be a boy. This follows the traditional Chinese cultural bias in favor of sons.

The island is hot, and it rains in the winter monsoon period. The airport, on the eastern end of the island at **Changi**, is the largest in Asia. It ruined what used to be Singapore's best beach. The airport's construction left a series of Malay villages or *kampongs* stranded on the sides of the road. They used to be fishing villages on the shore, but suffered from the landfill. **Marina Centre,** on reclaimed land, contains a wholly new tourist and shopping zone with three huge hotels.

Singapore split off from the surrounding territory now called Malaysia after it became independent in 1965. The city of Singapore was founded in 1819 by Sir

EMBASSY: *1824 R St. N.W., Washington, DC 20009; (202)667-7555.*

SYSTEM OF GOVERNMENT: One-party parliamentary democracy.

ETHNIC GROUPS: Chinese, 76%; Malays, 15%; Indians and Pakistanis, 7%.

RELIGIOUS GROUPS: Buddhists; Taoists; Moslems; Hindus; Christians.

LANGUAGES: Chinese; Malay; Tamil; Mandarin (all are official).

POPULATION: 2.586 million.

AREA: 238 square miles (618 square kilometers), including reclaimed land.

CAPITAL: Singapore.

TERRAIN: Lowland; 40 islands.

CLIMATE: Tropical.

TELECOMMUNICATIONS
   Country Code: 65.
   Time Zone: +13 hours Eastern Standard Time.

LOCAL/NATIONAL AIRLINES: Singapore Airlines, *(800)742-3333;* **Lufthansa,** *(800)645-3880;* **Pan Am,** *(800)221-1111;* and **Olympic Airways,** *(800)223-1226* or *(212)838-3600* in New York.

CURRENCY: Singapore dollar. No limit on import or export.

GROSS NATIONAL PRODUCT: $17.5 billion.

WORK FORCE: Commerce and services, 62.9%; Manufacturing, 25%; government, 16%; construction, 8.7%; agriculture and fishing, .7%.

OUR QUALITY OF LIFE RANKING: 48.28.

VISA REQUIREMENTS: Valid passports and onward/return tickets are required. Visas are not required for stays of up to 90 days.

TOURIST OFFICE IN THE UNITED STATES: Singapore Tourist Promotion Board, *342 Madison Ave., Suite 1008, New York, NY 10173; (212)687-0385.*

Stamford Raffles, after whom the most famous hotel was named. So was the pedestrian mall at Raffles Place. So was yet another booming new hotel-cum-office zone, Raffles City, off Orchard Road. For this British imperialist, the importance of Singapore was its control of the Straits, a passage between the Pacific and the Indian Oceans. Building on that geographical advantage, modern Singapore has developed its oil-refining and ship-building industries, as well as becoming a mercantile and financial center for the region.

Some of the harbor has been filled in to reclaim land for the bustling industrial and financial entrepôt that Singapore has become. Like Hong Kong and Taiwan, this is a showcase for Chinese entrepreneurship. But whether even prosperous folk will continue to put up with the Lee government is not certain.

The present population is 2.6 million enterprising and hard working people, most of whom are Buddhist. Among the Buddhist temples worth seeing are **Tau Pek Kong,** on **Kusu Island** in the middle of the harbor (take a *sampan* from Collyer Quay in town); **Twin Grove**, on Kim Keat Road; and the **Temple of 1,000 Lights,** on Race Course Road, where a 300-ton Buddha looks down on his flock. Or visit the Hindu temple of **Sri Mariamman,** with its colorful paintings, or the oldest Singapore mosque, **Kampong Malacca** (both are located in Chinatown, rather confusingly, since the Hindus and Moslems tend to be Indian and Malay rather than Chinese). Also interesting is the large **Sultan Mosque** on Arab Street.

When it gets too hot to walk, take a trishaw ride and imagine yourself in a Maugham novel. Apart from Chinatown there are separate market zones such as **Little India** and **Arab Street-Ophir Road,** which theoretically are dominated by the other ethnic groups. But despite the *souk* atmosphere and the screaming peddlers, the commercial scene has lost some of its liveliness, most of its danger, and many of its bargains because of the current government's clean-up and consumer protection campaigns. Little India boasts a **Thieves' Market** (Serangoon and Buffalo Roads). It has plenty of sari shops and places where you can buy joss sticks or Indian brass and gold, or Filipino *guayabera* shirts—but the crooks and fences have all been removed.

Shenton Way is the Wall Street of Asia, with hundreds of banks and foreign exchange dealers. This is the sort of merchant the government wants more of. The old **Change Alley,** which used to be where money changers worked, is now a more normal shopping street, full of multi-ethnic bustle and pushcarts. This used to be where sailors rolled on to shore to be ripped off.

Eating in Singapore is an ethnic mishmash. You will find good food in **Telok Ayer,** the octagonal-roofed market that sells a dozen kinds of noodles you eat with chopsticks. Chinatown features Chinese food you did not learn about at home, such as snakes and lizards. Singapore is Hong Kong's rival as the center for great Chinese cooking. It also has a great French restaurant in the Marco Polo Hotel. One of the best Indian restaurants is the **Rang Mahal** in the Oberoi Hotel. Singapore (like Hong Kong) is an exception to the rule that savvy travelers don't eat in hotels. The best hotel in Singapore is the **Mandarin Singapore,** *333 Orchard Road.* **Raffles** has style, but it's considered a bit seedy.

When you've had your fill of nosh, there is more shopping to do—even at night. **Pasar Malam** (the night market) moves to a different site every night of the week; you will find it at the Handicrafts Centre or on Sentosa Avenue. It offers smuggled batiks from Indonesia, pirate pop music tapes (don't buy without listening to the tape lest it turn out to be something other than the label advertises), pirated computer software, Japanese dolls, fake Rolex watches, and other symbols of Singaporean prosperity and vice. Singapore specialties include the contraband of its neighbors—something other mercantile centers such as Hong Kong lack. If you know your onions, this is the place to find smuggled antiquities from Southeast Asia (Buddhist statuary whose export Thailand has banned, for example). For real vice (overlaid with Singapore puritanism), head for **Bugis Street,** the well-patrolled red light district.

For modern shopping, using your credit cards, and getting your goods shipped home for you, you will probably do best in one of the malls or department stores. Best shopping for non-contraband goods is **Orchard Road** and environs. You are expected to bargain over prices except in the very chic boutiques. Here you will find Euro-goods, particularly clothing, at prices that would drive Bloomingdale's out of business.

What should you buy in Singapore? Don't bother with electronic goods, which are no cheaper than at a good U.S. discounter. As in Hong Kong, the People's Republic uses Singapore to sell its goods, and they are often a bargain. Consider a Chinese embroidered tablecloth and napkins, or a Chinese carpet. There are two carpet grades, by the way; some are no longer hand woven (you can spot them because they have a jute cover over the bottom of the carpet). Other handicrafts and curios from the PRC, Indochina, and the Malay-Philippine zone are also well-priced. Jewelry is said to be cheap, again if you know what you are doing. ❦

SPAIN

Spain, for too many tourists, is only Madrid, with perhaps a side trip to El Pardo Palace, Toledo, or the Valley of the Fallen. Once ruled by the centralization-minded Bourbons (who also left their mark on France), Spain has rediscovered regional particularism. So smart travelers will get into the Spanish heartland.

The Catalan language has come out of the closet in which it was confined by Franco and is now the most widely-spoken language in Spain's second- and third-largest cities, Barcelona and Valencia. The charming Basque region, home of Spain's highest mountains, the oldest Spanish representative body, and the oldest language in Europe, is the site of another cultural revival. The arid and depressed Spanish south is developing pride in its Moorish heritage, which once led the rest of the country to look down on Andalusia. A generation ago, talent for music (flamenco) or sports (bull-fighting) was the only way out of the south and getting out was the only way to get ahead. Even the stolid folk of the north coast, the *Gallegos*, who used to pride themselves on having produced Spain's *Caudillo*, now are discovering that they too have a regional dialect and special traditions.

In **Madrid**, the main sight is the **Prado Museum**, which houses all the great art that could be carted in from the rest of Spain and the Spanish territories (such as the Flanders of Brueghel and Rubens). Finally, the museum has modernized its lighting system so you can actually *see* the El Greco, Goya, Velázquez, Holbein, Murillo, and Zurbarán. A separate building houses the Picasso collection featuring the powerful *Guernica*, returned to Spain only after Franco was gone. Picasso

EMBASSY: *2700 15th St. N.W., Washington, DC 20009; (202)265- 0190.*

SYSTEM OF GOVERNMENT: Constitutional monarchy.

ETHNIC GROUPS: Mediterranean and Nordic peoples.

RELIGIOUS GROUPS: Roman Catholics, 82%; Protestants; Jews; Moslems.

LANGUAGES: Spanish; Catalan; Basque.

POPULATION: 40 million.

AREA: 194,884 square miles (504,750 square kilometers); comparable to Arizona and Utah combined.

CAPITAL: Madrid (population 3.217 million).

TERRAIN: High plateaus and mountains; lowlands in the south.

CLIMATE: Warm and dry; temperate in the northwest.

TELECOMMUNICATIONS
  Country Code: 34.
  Time Zone: +6 hours Eastern Standard Time.
  Code of Capital: 1.

LOCAL/NATIONAL AIRLINES: Council Charter, *(212)661-0311;* **Iberia,** *(800)221-9741;* **Sabena Airlines,** *(800)632-8050* (New York), *(800)645-3700* (East Coast), *(800)645-3790* (Southeast and Midwest), or *(800)645-1382* (West Coast); **Spantax Airlines,** *(212)582-8267;* **Tower Air,** *(800)221-2500* or *(718)917-8500* in New York; and **TWA,** *(800)892-4141.*

U.S. CONSULATE IN COUNTRY: *Serrano 75, Madrid 6; tel. (34-1)276-*

3400; **U.S. Consulates General,** *via Layetana 33, Barcelona; tel. (34-3)319-9550* or *Paseo de las Delicias 7, Seville; tel. (34-54)23-18-85.*

CURRENCY: Peseta. Travelers may import 100,000 pesetas and export 20,000 pesetas. Spanish banks are authorized to allocate to non-residents foreign currencies up to the equivalent of 80,000 pesetas.

GROSS NATIONAL PRODUCT: $227.2 billion (in 1986).

WORK FORCE: Services, 49%; industry and commerce, 34%; agriculture, 17%.

OUR QUALITY OF LIFE RANKING: 69.02.

VISA REQUIREMENTS: Valid passports are required. Visas are not required for stays of up to six months. Residence permits are required for stays longer than one year. Self-employed residents, including artists and writers, must obtain an annual identification card, which is granted to ensure payment of a negotiated tax on annual earnings. To obtain a visa, contact the embassy or the consulate in Houston, Chicago, Boston, Los Angeles, Miami, New Orleans, New York, San Francisco, or Puerto Rico.

TOURIST OFFICE IN THE UNITED STATES: Tourist Office of Spain, *665 Fifth Ave., New York, NY 10022; (212)759-8822.*

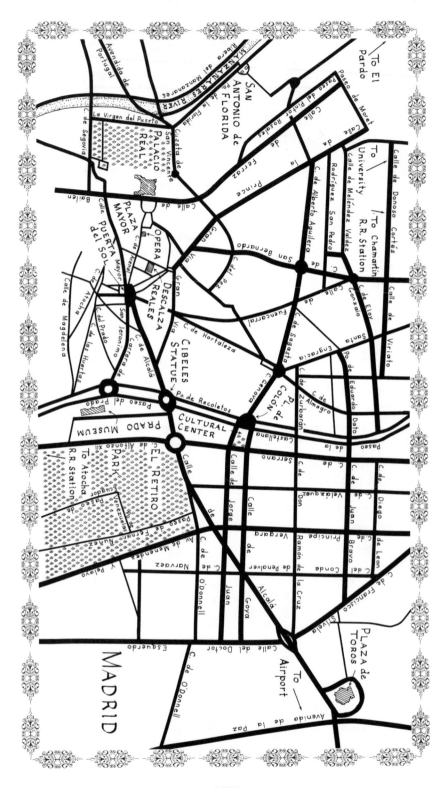

painted it in outrage at the bombing by Franco's forces of the historic center of Basque regional culture.

The main Madrid drag, the tree-lined and kiosk-studded **Paseo,** runs past the Prado Museum. Off it are famous sights such as the **Retiro Gardens** (with roses, lakes, and trees), the **Plaza de Cibeles** (Fountain of the Sibyls), and the **Plaza Colon,** with the **Cultural Center**. Madrileños still call the extension of the Paseo to the north the **Generalisimo**, an area graced with a series of ugly ministerial buildings. It becomes a red light district at night.

East of the Prado are Madrid's main centers. The **Puerta del Sol** is the center of popular life, shopping, and traffic congestion. It was built four centuries ago on the site of the ramparts of the town. The huge **Plaza Mayor,** once the political center of the Spanish empire, is now the place for a stroll among the arcades, an occasional snack or a drink, and people-watching. Farther to the east is the **Zarzuela**, the palace built on the site of the old Moorish alcazar, after which the Spanish form of vaudeville was named. Its gardens and throne room are worth a visit. West of the Paseo, along the **Calle Serrano,** are the big department stores, including Sears. Antique shopping is best along the **Alcalá,** which crosses the Paseo.

Barcelona is worth visiting for its **Picasso and Miró museums** and the extraordinary architectural wonders created there by Antoni Gaudi, notably the "art nouveau" **Sagrada Familia Cathedral,** which is still under construction. This is a must-see.

Toledo is worth more than the one-day side-trip from Madrid too many tour guides recommend. Beside the gloomy city itself, which on stormy days looks like a canvas by El Greco, sights include the **Monastery of San Juan de los Reyes,** built by Ferdinand and Isabella, and Toledo's great cathedral, with its El Greco sacristry, retable (a raised shelf behind the altar), and treasury. Also important are the great gates of **Bisagra** and **Budejar**, the much-restored **House of El Greco** and the **El Transito Church**, now returned to its original decor as a synagogue. (It was Christianized after the Jews and Moors were expelled from Spain in 1492.) Perhaps the most interesting sight in Toledo is the **Alcázar,** a fortress that looms over the city. El Cid, the 11th-century hero described in *El Poema del Cid,* lived here. It has been reconstructed and houses the Museum of the Spanish Civil War.

In **Seville**, the 300-foot tower called the **Giralda** (a minaret taken over by the cathedral) dominates the city. On one side is the cathedral, a vast structure built to overwhelm the former Moslem inhabitants of the town. On the other side is the former Moorish fortress, or **Alcazar,** with its Salon Arabe. The town is full of what people imagine Spain to be, particularly during Holy Week: ladies in *mantillas*, wrought-iron-trimmed houses with shuttered overhanging balconies, and narrow streets—which also are home of Spain's most vicious pickpockets.

Nearby **Granada** has the most extraordinary Moorish ruins in Europe, the **Alhambra.** As you stroll the beautiful gardens (which still benefit from the irrigation system built by the Moslems to bring water in from the snow-peaked Sierra Nevada Mountains), you encounter visitors from the Arab world who come to see what their ancestors created.

The third Andalusian city travelers should visit is **Córdoba**, whose cathedral stands cheek by jowl with the **Mezquita**, the former mosque complex, with its fountains for ritual ablutions and gardens. The mosque interior is a complex of pink and white striped stone pillars, with a magnificent *mithrab* (a niche indicating the direction of Mecca, to which Moslems face during their prayers). Córdoba also has the famous **Judería**, the former Jewish ghetto, which produced the greatest Jewish philosopher of the Middle Ages, Maimonides.

The Christians get their own back in the opposite, northwestern corner of Spain, at **Santiago de Compostela.** Cockleshell-carrying pilgrims of the middle ages trudged to this church to honor St. James the Apostle, whose body was supposed to have miraculously washed up here. The cathedral, with its huge Pórtico de la Gloria and the Pórtico de las Platerias, inspired Gothic architecture all over Europe. It also was the rallying point for the reconquest of the country from the Moors. The hilly town is picturesque, with narrow streets where students in medieval costumes serenade evening strollers with song and guitar.

There also are the **Balearic Islands, Cádiz,** walled **Valencia**, the **Canaries**, the **Costa del Sol, Málaga,** and my own special favorite, **Mérida**. But you get the idea: Leave Madrid.

Spanish bargains range from shoes and boots at every price to well-made counterfeit Louis Vuitton handbags and luggage, from chic ladies' clothing (Spanish chic is very wearable) to antiques, from espadrilles to pottery.

Spanish food is far more varied than most North Americans realize. Outside Valencia or Barcelona, you probably should not eat *paella*; and as for *gazpacho*, consider the version I ate in Córdoba, a soup made with grated almonds; a Spanish omelette in Spain contains potatoes. Other delicious meals I remember also reflect the country's newly revived regions: trout stuffed with ham and cheese in the foothills of the Pyrenees, tripe in Madrid, fish baked in a salt crust in Barcelona, rabbit with apricots in Seville. The most important Spanish food habit to get into is dining terribly late; keep going with *tapas*, little snacks served in bars (where you can also have a drink to keep you going). ❦

SWEDEN

Sweden is neutral, taxed beyond all reason for a full and growing welfare state, socialist, clean, and tidy.

The Swedes are big on modern architecture, ecology, and the ombudsman (who protects consumers and citizens). Its people are sports-minded and healthy (all that free medical care), but unfortunately plagued by a penchant for alcoholism and suicide. Some would say this is because their lives otherwise lack relish and risk; others blame the northern winters and lack of sunlight.

The Swedes are blessed with the first non-sexist constitutional monarchy. Under the 1980 Law of Swedish Succession, the eldest royal child (in fact Princess Victoria) succeeds to the throne regardless of its sex.

Sweden was not always so peaceful and just. It broke away from Denmark in the 16th century after a bloody war, and in the Thirty Years War its monarch was the scourge of Catholic Europe. The Swedes won considerable territory in what is now Finland, Germany, and Russia under the Treaty of Westphalia in 1648, which ended the Thirty Years War. They were only driven back to the north by the united armies of Russia, Poland, and Denmark after the Peace of Nystad (1721). Under Napoleon, a new dynasty was imposed, headed by Count Bernadotte whose wife, Désirée, may have been Napoleon's mistress. Norway finally gained independence

EMBASSY: *600 New Hampshire Ave. N.W., Suite 1200, Washington, DC 20037; (202)944-5600.*

SYSTEM OF GOVERNMENT: Constitutional monarchy.

ETHNIC GROUPS: Nordic groups; Lapps.

RELIGIOUS GROUPS: State Lutherans, 95%; Roman Catholics.

LANGUAGES: Swedish; Finnish.

POPULATION: 8.357 million (in 1986).

AREA: 173,731 square miles (449,964 square kilometers); slightly larger than California.

CAPITAL: Stockholm (population 653,000).

TERRAIN: Flat and rolling countryside; 25% of the land area is covered with mountains; several large lakes.

CLIMATE: Northern temperate. The winters last more than seven months.

TELECOMMUNICATIONS
   Country Code: 46.
   Time Zone: +6 hours Eastern Standard Time.
   Code of Capital: 8.

LOCAL/NATIONAL AIRLINES: Northwest Airlines, *(800)447-4747;* **Pan Am,** *(800)221-1111;* **Sabena Airlines,**

(800)632-8050 (New York), *(800)645-3700* (East Coast), *(800)645-3790* (Southeast and Midwest), or *(800)645-1382* (West Coast); and **Scanair,** *(305)665-8109.*

U.S. CONSULATE IN COUNTRY: *Strandvagen 101, Stockholm; tel. (46-08)63-05-20;* **U.S. Consulates General,** *Sodra Hamngatan 53, Goteborg; tel. (46-031)80-38-60.*

CURRENCY: Krona. No limit on import; travelers may export 6,000 kronor (in denominations less than 100 kronor).

GROSS NATIONAL PRODUCT: $127.8 billion (in 1986).

WORK FORCE: Services, 44%; industry, 30%; commerce and finance, 21%; agriculture, 5%.

OUR QUALITY OF LIFE RANKING: 79.39.

VISA REQUIREMENTS: Visas are not required for stays of up to three months (the period begins when you enter the Scandinavian area—Finland, Norway, Denmark, or Iceland).

TOURIST OFFICE IN THE UNITED STATES: Scandinavian Tourist Office, *655 Third Ave., New York, NY 10019; (212)949-2333.*

from Sweden in 1905. The Swedes began to legislate their welfare state in 1911 and went in for neutrality both in World War I and in World War II.

Stockholm, because of its many waterways and canals, is often called the Venice of the North. Swedes are great yachtsmen. Statistics show they own more yachts than cars.

The best way to see this water-lover's city is to take a boat tour. Stockholm is more like an American city than your usual European capital, because so much of it was built in the last two centuries. Little is left of medieval Stockholm, apart from **Gamla Stan,** the medieval quarter which contains the market square, **Riddarhuset** (The Hall of Nobles), and the **Royal Palace.** The **Royal Dramatic Theater** and the **Concert Hall** are both neo-baroque buildings of the last century. In the latter, the Nobel Peace Prizes are awarded.

Stockholm has one of the oldest museums in the world (built in 1794), the **National Museum,** which boasts works by Rembrandt, El Greco, Rubens, and Cézanne. The **Östasiatiska Muséet** contains the finest collection of Chinese antiquities outside China, collected by King Gustavus Adolphus. Matisse and moderns are found at the **Moderna Muséet,** which has works by Andy Warhol, Roy Liechtenstein, Calder, and the Cubists. The museum officials tore down a walk-in sculpture by Nikki de St. Phalle and Jean Tinquely called *She.* The suburban **Thielska Galleriet**, an art nouveau villa on **Djurgården Island** holds work by Munch and Strindberg (who was a painter as well as a dramatist).

On the island too is the **Skansen,** an outdoor museum of historic Swedish houses from all over the country, also used as a zoo, a dance hall, and a concert hall. And the Wasa, an excavated ship which sank on its maiden voyage in 1628 also can be seen on Djugården.

On another island, **Lidingö**, overlooking Stockholm is the sculpture garden of Carl Milles. Outside Stockholm you should see the **Drottningholm Royal Palace** on an island in Lake Mälaren, built in the Louis XIV style, with a perfect little theater. Sail on the lake.

More fierce is **Gripsholms Castle,** on the same lake, a 16th-century fortification with another tiny theater. Nearby is the restored historic town of **Mariefred.** You can reach it by coal-fired steamer from the Stockhold Stashusbron in the summer. The steamer, which dates from the turn of the century, is also called the *Mariefred.*

Very near Stockholm is **Uppsala**, the oldest Swedish university, which has the largest cathedral in Scandinavia. **Göteborg** on the south coast is a good destination for a steamer trip along the Göta Canal (350 miles long). The third Swedish city is **Malmö**, terminus of the ferry from Copenhagen, site of a university and surrounded by good dune beaches.

Another excursion might be to **Lapland**, the northern territory of Sweden (as well as of Norway, Finland, and part of the Soviet Union). The snow-covered **Mount Akka,** in Swedish Lapland, is beautiful. Lapps herd reindeer and drive dog sleds in colorful felt costumes.

Swedish food features the smorgasbord, which is good, and *Köttbullar* (meatballs), which are awful. The best things are from the sea, 57 varieties of

181

herring (try *matjesill* and—despite the odor—*surströmming*), salmon (*gravad lax*), and crayfish (*krøaftskiva*). Try *Jannsons frestelse* (Jannson's temptation), a casserole of anchovies, potatoes, sliced onions, and cream, the whole of which is greater than the sum of its parts. Drink is very expensive because of the anti-alcoholism tax, but you can still slosh back beer and an *akvavit* chaser.

Shopping teaches you how low the dollar has sunk. Besides tableware (crystal, wood, and silver), kitchenware (enamel and wood), good buys include fur and suede garments. ❧

SWITZERLAND

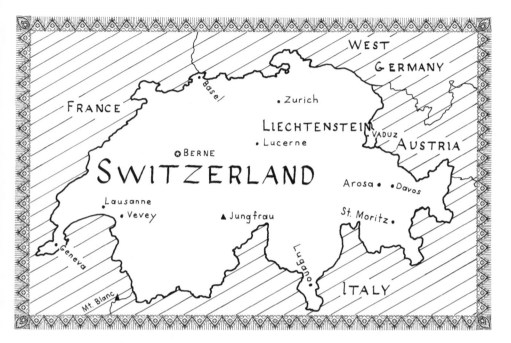

Switzerland has the highest mountains and the most stable currency in Europe. Its people would be boring if they were not so full of curious particularisms: From one little Alpine valley to the next, the dialects of spoken German vary so greatly that the Swiss can barely understand each other. In addition to a host of varieties of German, Swiss also speak French, Italian, and a fourth language spoken nowhere else, called Romansch, which is descended from Latin. Although this is the country that first adopted Calvin's Protestant teachings, it also has a substantial Catholic minority.

Under the Swiss system of initiative, referendum, and local government (which gives great power to the canton, or state, and the commune, or town meeting), every variety of particularism flourishes. In some ways, Switzerland's system is like what we would have had in this country had we not had a Constitutional Convention or a Civil War. Their system dates back to the revolt of the men of the valleys of Uri and Schwyz against the Hapsburg monarchy in the 14th century—the time of the famous William Tell. But curiously, until the beginning of this century, Switzerland was poor, its ill-paid population struggling to survive the icy winters by such cottage industries as watch-making, lace-making, and weaving. From the rich Alpine milk they made cheese and chocolate.

These provided the impetus for Switzerland's modern industry, which features pharmaceuticals and chemicals (an outgrowth of the dyes used by the cloth-makers) and precision instruments (an outgrowth of watch-making). In addition, thanks to the combination of a position smack in the middle of Europe, political neutrality in both World Wars, and laws protecting banking secrecy, Switzerland is a European tax haven.

The Swiss Alps brought mountain climbers, the earliest tourists. The **Jungfrau** (13,650 feet) was first climbed in 1911. The Alps, including the **Matterhorn** (known as "the killer Alp") and the **Jungfraujoch**, the highest point in Europe, make Switzerland the winter sports capital of the world. Here you can practice not only downhill and cross-country skiing, but also ice skating, bobsledding, dogsledding, and tobogganing. The **Cresta Run** in **St. Moritz** is the oldest and most dangerous sports toboggan run, a drop of 500 feet in its three-quarter mile tunnel-and-turn length. The slopes between **Davos** and **Arosa** are the highest and most dra-

---

EMBASSY: *2900 Cathedral Ave. N.W., Washington, DC 20008; (202)745-7900.*

SYSTEM OF GOVERNMENT: Federal state.

ETHNIC GROUPS: Germans; French; Italians.

RELIGIOUS GROUPS: Roman Catholics, 47.6%; Protestants, 44.3%; Jews.

LANGUAGES: German, 65%; French, 18%; Italian, 9.8%; Romansch, 1%.

POPULATION: 6.466 million (in 1986).

AREA: 15,943 square miles (41,292 square kilometers).

CAPITAL: Bern (population 182,000).

TERRAIN: Mountains and plateaus.

CLIMATE: Temperate; varies with altitude.

TELECOMMUNICATIONS
 Country Code: 41.
 Time Zone: +6 hours Eastern Standard Time.
 Code of Capital: 31.

LOCAL/NATIONAL AIRLINES:
Council Charter, *(212)661-0311;* **Pan Am,** *(800)221-1111;* **Sabena Airlines,** *(800)632-8050* (New York), *(800)645-3700* (East Coast), *(800)645-3790*

(Southeast and Midwest), or *(800)645-1382* (West Coast); and **Swissair,** *(800)225-3569.*

RAILROAD OFFICE IN THE UNITED STATES: Swiss Federal Railroads, *608 Fifth Ave., New York, NY 10020; (212)759-5944.*

U.S. CONSULATE IN COUNTRY: *Jubilaeumstrasse 93, 3005 Bern; tel. (41-31)437-011;* **U.S. Consulates General,** *Zollikerstrasse 141, 8008 Zurich; tel. (41-1)552-566.*

CURRENCY: Swiss franc. No limit on import or export.

GROSS NATIONAL PRODUCT: $142.4 billion (in 1986).

WORK FORCE: Services, 50%; industry and commerce, 39%; agriculture, 7%.

OUR QUALITY OF LIFE RANKING: 82.11.

VISA REQUIREMENTS: Tourist visas are not required for stays of up to three months. After three months, apply to the local police for a temporary permit.

TOURIST OFFICE IN THE UNITED STATES: Swiss National Tourist Office, *608 Fifth Ave., New York, NY 10020; (212)759-5944.*

matic in the Alps, and it is here that downhill skiing was first practiced a century ago. There were no ski lifts or gondolas. You simply hiked to the top and then put on your skis to ride down. The magnificence of the Alps from the top of a mountain on a clear day is hard to beat.

Switzerland's capital, **Berne**, is low-keyed, as you would expect in a country where localism is so strong, and where hardly anyone knows the president's name. It boasts a medieval clock tower, fountains and arcades along centuries-old streets, and a bear pit (the bear is the symbol of the city).

Geneva is on the lake of the same name, and boasts the **Palais des Nations** and many other buildings of the **United Nations** (it is headquarters of several U.N. bodies, and used to be the headquarters of the ill-fated League of Nations). Switzerland, has voted by referendum against becoming a member of the United Nations. A great statue of Calvin graces the **Promenade des Bastions Park** and there is a giant fountain in the lake near the city. The old town boasts the birthplace of Jean-Jacques Rousseau and the new town along the lake boasts the homes of Middle Eastern sheiks and international movie stars. Down the lake are **Lausanne**, **Vevey**, **Montreux** and the great medieval **Castle of Chillon**, subject of a poem by Lord Byron.

Lucerne's skyline is marked by the **Hofkirche's** twin spires. Parts of the church date back to 735. Its **Kapell-Brücke,** with paintings of Tell and other heroes, crosses the river on a diagonal. **Zurich** is the largest Swiss city, and its **Bahnhofstrasse** is the center of Swiss banking. The **Grossmünster,** a great church with oval domes, is the major landmark; another is the **Helmhouse Museum.**

Basel, is home of the central bankers' central bank, the **Bank for International Settlements,** and most of the chemical concerns. Its cathedral holds the tomb of Erasmus. Its slogan-decorated red town hall is a major site.

Travelers also like **Lugano**, an Italian-speaking town south of the Alps. It is on a palm-bordered lake.

Swiss food features the humble potato at its most marvelous: *Rösti*. It also features a calorie- and cholesterol-rich dish of veal in cream sauce called *Geschnetzeltes* (*Eminé de Veau à la Zurichoise* in French). Fondue is a mixture of cheeses, white sauce, and *Kirschwasser* (cherry brandy) into which you dunk chunks of bread. The Swiss invented *Muesli*. Swiss wines are usually light and white, and classified by varieties as in California, rather than by vineyard or location as in France. They do not travel well but taste fine in Switzerland.

Few Americans can still afford the shops interspersed with banks along Swiss streets. In fact, you may not want to order a glass of orange juice with your breakfast at a Swiss hotel ($12 at the Intercontinental Geneva!). There is hope left, however. It is called **Migros**. This is a Swiss chain of cheap supermarket-department stores that blanket the country and offer such goodies as throwaway watches (don't expect to ever repair these), T-shirts, souvenirs, and chunks of cheese and *aufschnitt* (cold cuts) for cheap meals. Luxury goods from other European countries are sold here tax-free at prices that beat airport duty-free levels. And there are always top-quality watches by Rolex and Vacherin Constantin, which you can buy for yourself, and hand down to your children and your grandchildren. ❦

TAHITI

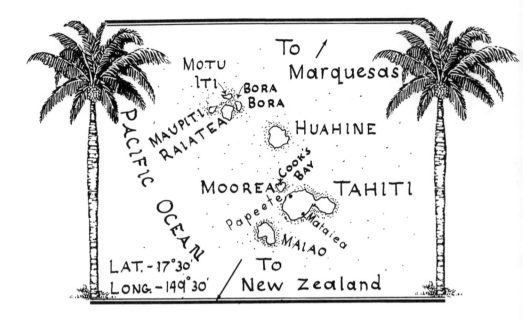

MOTU ITI
To / Marquesas
BORA BORA
MAUPITI
RAIATEA
HUAHINE
PACIFIC OCEAN
MOOREA
COOK'S BAY
TAHITI
Papeete
Mataiea
MAIAO
LAT. -17°30'
LONG. -149°30'
To New Zealand

    Tahiti is—still—*the* South Sea Island paradise, Arcadia, the garden of Eden, the Isles of Cythera, the Pleasant Valley. As Rupert Brooke wrote, "They are Calypso's and Prospero's isle, and the Hesperides." The beautiful natives can feed themselves with coconuts and breadfruit, which drop paradisaically from the trees. But in an attempt at modesty, the once bare-breasted Tahitian women now wear bras (often with nothing over the bra). They also eat Cheese Twisties, pay their electric bill, and buy gasoline for their motor scooter. The cool trade wind still blows to shore, but it is backed up by air conditioners. Where, oh where, are the idylls of yesteryear?

    Tahiti's present-day coconut palms, tropical flowers, and half-dressed maidens—now only nine hours by jet from Los Angeles—will never live up to those topless lasses immortalized by Paul Gauguin. The painter went to **Papeete** in 1891 to get away from his demanding wife and five children and his job as a stockbroker. He settled at **Mataiea** on the south coast (28 miles from Papeete) and took a 13-year-old "bride" named Tehuru. He also wrote for the newspapers and spent a few months as a civil servant before deciding that Tahiti was being ruined by civilization and setting sail for Hivaeoa in the Marquesa islands (600 miles to the northeast), where he died two years later, in 1903.

    The hotel nightclub dancers performing the *tamare* (hula) seem to lack the grace of Gauguin's Tehuru or Bloody Mary's daughter in *South Pacific*. King Pomar, who greeted Captain Bligh and the Bounty, is commemorated in the boulevard that skirts Papeete Bay. The lagoon is full of modern hotels and tourist resorts with steep prices, adding to our nostalgia for the Tahiti of yore. There's nothing like a $200 hotel room or a $5 beer to ruin paradise. These high prices reflect a combination of the effect of a falling dollar (the Pacific franc moves with the French franc) and the great distances that tourists and everything brought to please them has had to come.

Tahiti's first native Christian was Pomare II, an early 19th-century tribal chieftain who was driven by a rebellion out of the main Tahiti island to **Moorea**, the island across the lagoon. He sought to consolidate his power by winning over the white man. He sought both British and French help—but the French were more aggressive soldiers and the British missionaries got distracted by Australia and New Zealand. Pomare II's daughter, who became Queen Pomare IV after her brother's death, expelled the French priests, who sought to convert the riotous natives. In 1838 a French warship arrived to redress the insult and collect a fine. The Queen first agreed, and then had second thoughts. In 1842, a warship arrived to hoist the tricolor and drive her into exile. But in 1847 Queen Pomare was allowed to return and resume her rule. Upon her death in 1877, her second son, Pomare V, abdicated, and Tahiti became a French colony.

The capital of French Polynesia is Papeete (pronounced: pah-pay-ay-tay), a yacht harbor and fishing town with modern hotels and an international airport. It is

EMBASSY: None. Contact the **Embassy of France**, *4101 Reservoir Road N.W., Washington, DC 20007; (202)944-6000.*

SYSTEM OF GOVERNMENT: French territory.

ETHNIC GROUPS: Polynesians, 64%; Europeans, 11.2%; Asiatics, 5.4%.

RELIGIOUS GROUPS: Protestants, 55%; Catholics, 30%; Mormons, 6%.

LANGUAGES: French; Tahitian; English.

POPULATION: 95,000.

AREA: 1,544 square miles (2,470 square kilometers).

CAPITAL: Papeete.

TERRAIN: Mountainous islands.

CLIMATE: Subtropical.

TELECOMMUNICATIONS
Country Code: 689.

Time Zone: -5 hours Eastern Standard Time.

LOCAL/NATIONAL AIRLINE: UTA **French Airlines**, *(800)237-2747;* **Qantas**, *(800)227-4500* or *(213)646-9500* in California; and **Air New Zealand**, *(800)262-1234.*

CURRENCY: Pacific franc. No limit on import; travelers may export 50,000 francs.

GROSS NATIONAL PRODUCT: $1 billion.

VISA REQUIREMENTS: Valid passports are required. Visas valid for five years can be obtained upon arrival.

TOURIST OFFICE IN THE UNITED STATES: **French Government Tourist Office**, *610 Fifth Ave., New York, NY 10020; (212)757-1125.*

the center of the French administration of Polynesia. There is a considerable French population amidst the gorgeous natives: civil, naval, and military officials, bakers of baguettes (which, of course, everyone prefers to breadfruit), hotel owners, maître d'hôtels, sommeliers, chefs, and scuba diving instructors. It has supermarkets, Chinese tailors, stores, restaurants, and traffic jams. The best time to visit is for the July 14 Bastille Day celebrations, which go on all month. But the weather is even most of the year—unless there is a typhoon. Best avoided are the summer months of December and January, when it is hottest and most humid.

French Polynesia covers an area of 2 million square miles in the Pacific Ocean—about the size of Europe west of the Urals—on which stand 130 islands covering a total of 1,500 square miles. Close to a third of the population lives around the capital.

Tahiti's names still reek of romance. Take in the black sand beach at **Taharaa** and its pyramid-shaped hotel. Visit the lighthouse at **Point Venus** on **Matavai Bay,** where the seemingly friendly natives attacked the HMS Dolphin, captained by John Cook. (Cook named Cape Venus after the transit of that planet across the sun, which he had come there to observe in 1769.) The natives later befriended the men of the HMS Bounty. The sailors spent five months fraternizing with the locals, and then sailed only as far as Tonga before they mutinied.

Travel the island using the ubiquitous island form of transport, Le Truck. Or sail or fly to nearby islands of the Windward group. Visit Fletcher Christian's **Pitcairn** or the pretty town of **Fare** on **Huahine.** Or sail across the lagoon from Tahiti to **Moorea** across the **Reef Pass.** On Moorea are **Cook's Bay** and the beautiful peaks of mounts **Rotui** and **Moua Roa.** Here is the most beautiful yacht anchorage in the world, **Opunohu Bay.** Fly Air Tahiti, canoe, or hop a smelly copra freighter to **Bora Bora's** gorgeous **Matira Point.** Or set off from there to **Raiatea,** an out island with a rain forest, where canoe races are held in **Opoa Bay.** Raiatea natives still perform the fire dance barefoot on coals, except on Sundays when they go to the red-steepled church in **Uturoa.** Visit a *tapu* (sacred) *marae* (altar) such as **Taputapuatea Marae** in **Opoa, Raiatea** or the **Ti'i Statue** in the Tahiti botanical garden—ill-remembered relics of the islands' former pagan religion.

Eat breadfruit; Captain Bligh was in Tahiti to gather breadfruit seeds, which the British proposed to plant in the West Indies to feed the slaves they had transported there. You can also try papaya and taro. The markets abound in fish from the lagoons: ature, grouper, sea bass. Then there is all that good French food imported (along with the flour for baguettes) from France.

Shopping in Tahiti is frustrating, unless you want a *pareo* or a feather-and-bead headdress; almost everything is imported from France, Australia, or Japan. ❦

Tanzania

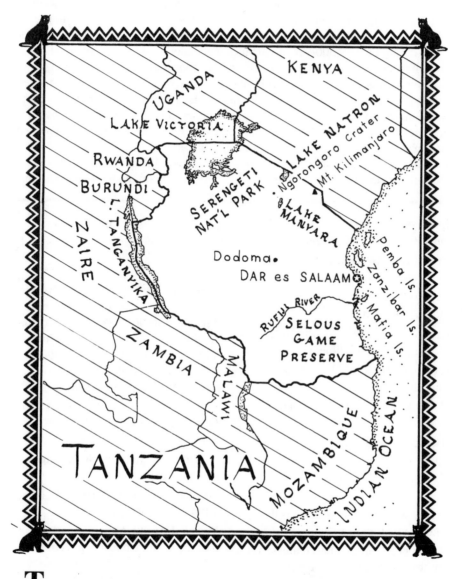

T anzania is a combination of what were formerly two separate republics, Tanganyika and Zanzibar. According to archeologist Louis Leakey, Tanzania was home to the earliest human beings over 14 million years ago. The 2 million-year-old fossil *Zinjanthropus Boisei* was discovered in **Olduvai Gorge**. Early man found an ideal climate in Tanzania's forested mountains in the north (the site of **Mt. Kilimanjaro**), its immense central plateau flanked by **Lake Tanganyika** in the west and lakes **Manyara** and **Natron** in the east, and its 500 miles of tropical coastland along the Indian Ocean.

The natives—composed of some 130 ethnic groups among which the legendary Masai is the most prominent—have been subject to the whims of foreign powers since the 10th century when Persia took control, spreading Islam and trade. It was during Persia's 500-year dominance that today's national language of Swahili emerged—an African language with Persian and Arab roots. (English, however, is spoken in most areas.) By the time Vasco da Gama and the Portuguese invaded in the early 16th century, the infamous East African slave trade was in full swing. Arabs reasserted control in the 18th century, only to be bought out by Bismarck's Germany. After the German defeat in World War I, the British moved in. Tanzania finally attained its independence in 1961.

Tanzania's topography and immensely varied wildlife are its main attractions. Most international flights fly to the capital, **Dar es Salaam**, on the Indian Ocean.

EMBASSY: *2139 R St. N.W., Washington, DC 20008; (202)939-6125.*

SYSTEM OF GOVERNMENT: One-party, independent, socialist state.

ETHNIC GROUPS: Bantus, 95%, Masai, various tribes.

RELIGIOUS GROUPS: Christians, 35%; Moslems, 35%; traditional beliefs, 30%.

LANGUAGES: Swahili (official); English.

POPULATION: 22.415 million (in 1986).

AREA: 364,900 square miles (945,087 square kilometers).

CAPITAL: Dar es Salaam.

TERRAIN: Mountainous, with a low coastal strip. Mt. Kilimanjaro is the highest in Africa.

CLIMATE: Tropical coastal areas; hot, dry central plateau; semi-temperate highland areas; lake region. The rainy season runs from November through December and from March through May.

TELECOMMUNICATIONS
  Country Code: 255.

Time Zone: +8 hours Eastern Standard Time.
  Code of Capital: 51.

LOCAL/NATIONAL AIRLINES: Air Tanzania, *(305)526-4300;* **Swiss Air,** *(800)225-3569;* **Lufthansa German Airlines,** *(800)645-3880;* and **Sabena Airlines,** *(800)632-8050* (New York), *(800)645-3700* (East Coast), *(800)645-3790* (Southeast and Midwest), or *(800)645-1382* (West Coast).

U.S. CONSULATE IN COUNTRY: *36 Laibon Road, P.O. Box 9123; tel. (255-51)37501.*

CURRENCY: Shilling. No limit on import or export.

GROSS NATIONAL PRODUCT: 4.1 billion (in 1984).

WORK FORCE: Agriculture, 94%; industry, commerce, and government, 6%.

OUR QUALITY OF LIFE RANKING: 17.70.

VISA REQUIREMENTS: Visas (valid up to six months) are required.

(A few fly directly to **Moshi** at the foothills of Mt. Kilimanjaro.) Dar is the only city in the country with a population over 1 million. Some 85% of the population still lives in rural areas. The government is in the process of building up **Dodoma** to shift the capital to a more central location. Dar's architecture reflects its past, with Arab mosques mixed in with wood-beamed German buildings and white British skyscrapers. The **National Museum,** near the **Botanical Gardens,** contains impressive anthropological and ethnographical collections. Despite these lures, the city's seediness and downright danger make anything but brief stays inadvisable. Locals in tattered clothes wander up and down filthy streets. Petty theft, robbery, and physical assault are not uncommon.

Before exploring the mainland, take an excursion to the islands off the coast: **Zanzibar, Pemba,** and **Mafia.** Zanzibar and its sister, Pemba, are both known as "the spice islands," with ubiquitous clove trees. Zanzibar's **Stone Town** reflects its Arab heritage, with winding streets, buildings with elaborately carved doors, and handicraft markets. The **Zanzibar Museum** features a noteworthy wildlife exhibit and various relics discovered by Dr. Livingstone, who settled here. The island also offers white sandy beaches shaded by coconut trees. Here, too, caution is in order. Women should avoid traveling alone and dress conservatively—though not necessarily to the extreme of Katharine Hepburn in *The African Queen.* Circumvent scheming taxi drivers by taking the government tour—especially since most tourist attractions require government approval. Pemba is worth a look if you're intrigued by bullfighting—a remnant of the Portuguese occupation. Forty minutes by air from Dar es Salaam, Mafia Island attracts big game fishermen who are after everything from barracuda and marlin to shark and red snapper. The prime fishing season extends from September to March.

Mt. Kilimanjaro, located near **Marangu** on the Kenyan border, is, at roughly 20,000 feet, the tallest mountain in Africa. It's the stuff of legends. Like many travelers, Ernest Hemingway was startled by its snow-capped peaks despite its location just three degrees south of the equator. He begins his "Snows of Kilimanjaro" by referring to the puzzling presence of a leopard's remains on its summit. Tanzania celebrates its independence every year by having a runner carry a burning torch up the mountain. The climb up to **Kibo Peak** and back down takes five days. (Experienced climbers might prefer the more challenging climb to **Mawenzi Peak,** which requires complete mountain-climbing gear.) Arrangements for guides, food, and lodging en route can be made at a hotel in Marangu. You will be following the historic path of the German Dr. Hans Meyer, who was the first to reach the top in 1889. At **Gillman's Point,** 19,000 feet up, look into the masses of ice inside the crater and write yourself into history—by signing the ledger containing the names of all those who have made the climb. The best months are January, February, September, and October because of the clear skies. Avoid April and May, the rainy season.

Located 225 miles west of the Kilimanjaro Airport, **Serengeti National Park,** spread out over 5,000 square miles, is home to a spectacular collection of wildlife—about 2 million animals in all. Best known for its lions, the park contains more than 35 species of game and 350 species of birds. The 1.8 million wildebeests and 200,000 zebras lead a fascinating migration. From December through May, they graze in the south end of the park. Then, followed by predators—lions, hyenas, and vultures—they divide into two migratory chains, one heading for the western and the other for the eastern lakes. In November, they join forces and head back south—completing the annual cycle. Towering above the eastern edge of the park is the world-famous **Ngorongoro Crater,** which covers 100 square miles. Ten thousand Masai and their 100,000 cattle and sheep share the crater floor with varied game such as elephants, lions, rhinos, leopards, and buffalo. Some 30 miles west of the crater is **Olduvai Gorge**, where the Leakey family first found prehistoric human fossils in the 1930s.

Just southeast of the Serengeti is the much smaller, yet no less striking, **Lake Manyara National Park**. The site is demarcated by the **Rift Valley**, from whose springs this saline lake flows—accounting for two-thirds of the park's area. An ornithologist's paradise, Manyara features over 350 species of birds and a breath-taking flamingo migration. As they flock from one East African lake to another, the flamingos pass through Manyara—forming a pink mosaic that shimmers on the water. Bird enthusiasts like to perch at the **Lake Manyara Hotel,** nestled among wild bushes and flowers about one and a half miles up the Rift Valley. Plains game and large mammals also inhabit some of the grasslands and swamplands—from baboons and buffaloes to velvet monkeys and zebras. The lions—perhaps because of the heat—can be viewed during the day sleeping on the limbs of Acacia trees, some 10 to 20 feet up. Traveling south from the northern wildlife areas, you might make a brief stop-over in central Tanzania to see the famous **Kondoa Irangi Rock Paintings.** Tribesmen from Stone Age cultures—presumably some 2,000 to 7,000 years ago—painted these hunting scenes (in red, brown, purple, and black) on their cave walls.

The **Selous Game Reserve**, traversed by the **Rufiji River**, spreads across some 20,000 square miles, making it the largest game reserve in the world. The vast park is not as densely populated as the others, and the animals are also harder to spot since they are wary of hunters—not allowed elsewhere. Over 1 million animals roam within its borders—most notably, over 50,000 elephants and 5,000 black rhinoceros. The weather is best for animal sightings from June to October; the reserve is shut down during the rainy season. The Tanzanian Tourist Corp. offers boat rides down the Rufiji and, for those brave enough to confront some of the wildlife face-to-face, these are walking safaris with armed guides.

Northern and western Tanzania are bordered by lakes—**Lake Tanganyika**, the second-deepest lake in the world, near the Zaire border, and **Lake Victoria,** the second-largest lake in the world, just south of the Ugandan border. Both lakes are served by steamers. The legendary site where Stanley met Livingstone at **Ujiji** on Lake Tanganyika is commemorated with a plaque. On Lake Victoria is **Mwanza**, a commercial center where, among other landmarks, you will find Bismarck Rock, unlike the statesman, is poised to fall, but never does.

Gourmet dining is available only in the capital and some of the larger hotels scattered around the country. Otherwise settle for fresh seafood or some of the local meat dishes: *wali na nyama* (beef curry), *ndizi na nyama* (bananas and beef), and *nyama ya mbuzi* (goat meat). The wine from Dodoma, the national beers, and the popular coconut drinks are also worth a try. You also won't have to fight your urge to shop: the only things that might capture your attention are animal woodcarvings, semi-precious stones set by local craftsman, and handbags and other goods made from animal skins.

Travelers should begin taking a prophylactic against malaria two weeks before departure. The medication should be continued until two weeks after the return home. It also is advisable to get inoculated against small pox, yellow fever, and cholera. Another caveat: You must declare all your cash at the border. If you lose your receipt, local authorities will have no compunction about confiscating all of your remaining cash. ❦

THAILAND

Thailand is an enchanting Southeast Asian kingdom equidistant from China and India. With its lush tropical scenery, golden-spired temples, peaceful Buddhas, exotic cuisine, and beautiful, friendly people, Thailand stimulates and delights the senses.

Larger than Spain but smaller than France, Thailand is divided into four regions: the mountainous North, where elephants still work the teakwood forests; the semi-arid northeast plateau, where one of the world's first civilizations flourished more than 5,000 years ago; the fertile, rice-growing central plains; and the tropical, jungle-covered isthmus.

Thailand has two distinct climates, tropical savannah from the Gulf of Thailand north, and a tropical monsoon climate to the south. There are three seasons: the hot season (March through May), the rainy season (June through October), and the cool season (November through February). In the hot season it is *very* hot.

The nation's history is still being written. Archeologists are studying finds in the northeast, where Bronze Age communities existed at the dawn of civilization. No one knows what happened to these prehistoric people. The Thai people originated in southern China about 4,500 years ago, migrating south and west through Burma and Laos, and established their first capital at **Sukhothai** by the 13th century. Here, the beginnings of a great culture developed, influenced by the art, technology, and ideas of China, India, and Kampuchea.

The Kingdom of Ayutthaya, known as Siam, expanded into Laos, Burma, Kampuchea, and Malaysia. Cultural, intellectual, and diplomatic relations were established with the rest of the world. In the 17th century, Ayutthaya had more residents than Paris or London, with beautiful canals, temples, and palaces. In

EMBASSY: *2300 Kalorama Road N.W., Washington, DC 20008; (202)483-7200.*

SYSTEM OF GOVERNMENT: Democratic monarchy.

ETHNIC GROUPS: Thai, 75%; Chinese, 14%; Vietnamese, 11%.

RELIGIOUS GROUPS: Buddhists, 95%; Moslems, 4%; Christians, 1%.

LANGUAGES: Thai; dialects.

POPULATION: 52.438 million (in 1986).

AREA: 209,411 square miles (542,373 square kilometers).

CAPITAL: Bangkok (population 4.875 million).

TERRAIN: Mountainous with flat plains; southern peninsula is covered with rain forests.

CLIMATE: Tropical with high humidity.

TELECOMMUNICATIONS
   Country Code: 66.
   Time Zone: +12 hours Eastern Standard Time.

Code of Capital: 2.

LOCAL/NATIONAL AIRLINE: Thai Airways, *(800)426-5204.*

U.S. CONSULATE IN COUNTRY: *95 Wireless Road, Bangkok; tel. (66-2)252-5040.*

CURRENCY: Thai baht.

GROSS NATIONAL PRODUCT: $42.6 billion (in 1984).

WORK FORCE: Agriculture and fishing, 62%; commerce and services, 19%; manufacturing, 8%; government, 5%; construction, 2%.

OUR QUALITY OF LIFE RANKING: 40.24.

VISA REQUIREMENTS: Visas are not required for stays of up to 15 days; you must show an onward/return ticket. To obtain a visa, contact the embassy or the consulate in Los Angeles, Chicago, or New York.

TOURIST OFFICE IN THE UNITED STATES: Thai Tourism, *5 World Trade Center, Suite 2449, New York, NY 10048; (212)432-0433.*

1767, however, the Burmese captured and destroyed the city. Eventually the Thais regained their land, establishing a third capital at **Thon Buri**, across the river from Bangkok. General Chakri, who became King Rama I, founded the present dynasty, and moved the capital to larger, and more easily defended, Bangkok. His descendant, King Bhumibol Adulaydej, is the present day-Rama IX.

Bangkok, the "city of angels," is sprawling, disorganized, chaotic...and fascinating. Erotic nightlife, excellent restaurants, beautiful palaces and temples, lovely canals, and eclectic markets are among its attractions. Broken sidewalks, horrendous traffic, hot weather, and great distances make it one of the world's least-walkable cities. Probably the best way to see Bangkok is to hire a car and guide (for a very reasonable fee) to take you around. You will encounter first-hand the friendly, easy-going nature of the Thai people. (Thailand, promoted by the tourist board as "the land of smiles," really has the most pleasant and polite people you are likely to meet anywhere.)

In Bangkok, visit the **Grand Palace**, a vast complex of royal buildings surrounded by a high, white crenelated wall. There are yards and yards of beautiful murals and incredible sculptures, shimmering golden buildings with elegant spires and glittering temples, including the famous **Temple of the Emerald Buddha** (it is actually made of jasper), fantastic monsters and oriental demons guarding the opulent courtyards and gates—not to mention the real live Thai soldiers, with M-16s slung loosely over their shoulders. Be sure to dress modestly (no shorts, or sleeveless shirts for men), and do not point your feet at the Buddha (or anyone else); it's considered impolite.

Other important sights include various *wats* (temples); the **Jim Thompson House**, with its superb collection of Asian *objets d'art*; the **Pasteur Institute's Snake Farm**, where poisonous snakes are fed and milked to make anti-venom serum; and the **Thieves', Floating, and Weekend markets.** Classical Thai dancing, Thai boxing, and a host of clubs, massage parlors, and bars may also be of interest to the traveler.

Nakhon Pathom, 37 miles west of Bangkok, boasts the world's largest and holiest Buddhist monument, the 380-foot-high **Phra Pathom Chedi**, marking the site of the Buddhist revelation over 2,000 years ago. This is said to be Thailand's oldest city, dating from 150 B.C. Farther west is **Kanchanaburi**, site of *The Bridge Over The River Kwai,* and a cemetery for soldiers who built the **"Death Railway"** during World War II. More than 16,000 Allied prisoners of war and 49,000 other slave laborers from Japanese-occupied countries died during its construction. The area is surrounded by what some consider the world's most beautiful mountains, rivers, jungles, waterfalls, and caves (once inhabited by Neolithic people). The **Erawan National Park** near **Kanchanaburi** has a spectacular waterfall descending seven levels, with deep green pools where you can swim. The park also has exotic wildlife (including elephants) and a natural underground cathedral with multi-colored formations—and bats.

To the north are the mountains of the hill tribes of Thailand, and the ancient city of **Chiang Mai,** a city founded in 1296 in a fertile valley 1,000 meters above sea level. It is known for its historic temples, mist-covered mountains, lovely

scenery, fruit orchards, cool weather, and beautiful people. The mountains surrounding Chiang Mai form the lower **Himalayas**. Here you can spend your days
smoking opium in the tents of members of the hill tribes.

In the south are lovely white sand beaches, palms, and clear green seas.
Largely unspoiled, the sunny resorts, deserted islands, and fishing villages are a
bargain for the traveler, offering inexpensive accommodations and excellent
cuisine. **Phuket Island** is the most developed of the resorts. It is Thailand's largest
island (approximately the size of Singapore), with gorgeous beaches, secluded
coves, hidden bays, and probably the best seafood from the Indian Ocean. An
interesting geological formation occurs northeast of Phuket, at **Phang Nga Bay**,
where limestone islands with caves and grottos rise perpendicularly, some more
than 300 meters high, from the clear, calm waters.

Hua Hin, on the west coast of the **Gulf of Thailand,** has been the royal
family's summer residence since the 1920s, and is Thailand's oldest beach resort. It
is peaceful and charming, with an old colonial-style hotel where most travelers
stay. South of Hua Hin is a quiet fishing village, **Prachuap Khiri Khan,** with a
scenic bay, a pagoda on the beach, and a resident monkey tribe.

For more exciting nightlife, the popular town of **Pattaya** is the place to go for
a weekend by the sea. Only 100 miles from the capital, on the east coast of the gulf,
Pattaya is easy to get to and offers a wide range of accommodations, restaurants,
nightlife, and outdoor activities including water skiing, parasailing, wind surfing,
scuba diving, and hang gliding—all at bargain prices.

Thai cuisine is sometimes described as a mixture of Szechuan and Indian—so
be careful about ordering. For those who like it hot, it is terrific, and for those who
don't, there are many dishes that are mild (try various noodle dishes). Most Thai
restaurants have huge menus, offering curries, *satays*, and rice and noodle dishes
made with fresh seafood, duck, chicken, beef, and pork, as well as more exotic boar
and snake. Try *gaeng ped ped yarng* (roast duck curry with coconut milk), *larb kai
svoey* (chopped cooked chicken with Thai herbs, spices, lemon, and greens) or
Siamese hors d'oeuvres (an assortment of fresh chunks of ginger, lemon grass,
cashew nuts, lemon slices, and very hot little green peppers). Wash it all down with
a good, cold Thai beer.

Thailand is also a shopper's paradise known for its indigenous goods. The best
buy here is beautiful, brightly colored Thai silk. Antiques, rattan, nielloware, lacquerware, bronzeware, ceramics, ivory, and woodcarvings are all well-priced. From
a reputable store, buy rubies from Thailand, Burma, Kampuchea, or Sri Lanka;
Thai black star and green sapphires, garnets from Africa or South America;
emeralds from Pakistan, India, and South America. Particularly good buys include
Australian opals and South American topaz. Among the more unusual objects
available in Thailand are stuffed cobras and mongooses, mounted butterflies and
scorpions, and some of the world's most beautiful artificial flowers. Bargaining
firmly, politely, patiently, and with a smile will get you the best prices, as well as
the respect of the Thai people. ❦

USSR

The Evil Empire having been declared to be good, what with Mikhail Gorbachev's *perestroika* and *glasnost*, tourists are heading for the banks of the Neva and Moskva Rivers. What they will find in the Soviet Union is a European culture that in some ways is very like our own. Like the United States, Russia was a country that consciously set out to copy Western Europe and improve on the model. Starting early in the 18th century, with Czar Peter the Great, Russia, like the United States, sought to bring in the best of the old world—and become a model for reforming it. Like our own country, Russia aimed to expand to a distant sea (theirs was to the east; ours to the west). It, too, is a big country, with bold ideas, huge prairies, and wide open spaces. Like our own country, theirs suffered from a fundamental injustice: not slavery, but the near-slavery of serfdom, abolished by Czarist *Ukase* (decree) during the very period of our own Civil War.

But even the most reform-minded Czars were held back by the weight of the old court system, with nobles instead of elections, with an established Orthodox church that banished dissident sects, with a bureaucracy that sent people with democratic ideas to Siberia. The rulers were limited by the need to defend borders and meddle in European wars and diplomacy. Moves toward liberalism and the free play of ideas were squelched by the bureaucracy and frequently reversed when the next Czar succeeded. The system was toppled by Russia's losses in territory,

---

EMBASSY: *1125 16th St. N.W., Washington, DC 20036; (202)328-3225.*

SYSTEM OF GOVERNMENT: Communist dictatorship.

ETHNIC GROUPS: Russians, 52%; Ukrainians, 16%; Uzbeks, 5%; Byelorussians, 4%.

RELIGIOUS GROUPS: Atheists, 70%; members of the Russian Orthodox Church, 18%; Moslems, 9%; Jews, 3%; Protestants; members of the Georgian Orthodox Church; Roman Catholics.

LANGUAGES: Russian, 58.5% (official); Ukrainian.

POPULATION: 280 million.

AREA: 8.65 million square miles (22.402 million square kilometers).

CAPITAL: Moscow (population 8.396 million).

TERRAIN: Varied; low mountains, prairies; and tundra.

CLIMATE: Varied; generally long, cold winters and short summers.

TELECOMMUNICATIONS
    Country Code: Must go through the international operator.
    Time Zone: +8 hours Eastern Standard Time (Moscow).

U.S. CONSULATE IN COUNTRY: *Ulitsa Chaykovskogo, 19/21/23, Moscow; tel. (096)252-2451;* **U.S. Consulates General,** *Ulitsa Petra Lavrova 15, Leningrad; tel. (814)274-8235.*

CURRENCY: Ruble. Travelers may not import or export currency.

GROSS NATIONAL PRODUCT: $734 billion (in 1984).

WORK FORCE: Industry and commerce, 29%; services and government, 21%; agriculture, 19%.

OUR QUALITY OF LIFE RANKING: 44.78.

VISA REQUIREMENTS: Passports and visas (which are valid for three months and free of charge) are required. Make travel arrangements through a travel agency that has a contract with Intourist. A travel agent can handle your application for a Soviet visa.

TOURIST OFFICE IN THE UNITED STATES: Intourist, *630 Fifth Ave., Suite 868, New York, NY 10111; (212)757-3884.*

FINLAND

Tallinn

Leningrad

ESTONIA

Rīga

Volga River

Gorki

LATVIA

LITHUANIA

Podolsk

Moscow

Kaunas

Vilnius

Dniepr R.

Minsk

POLAND

BYELORUSSIA

SOVIET UNION

Chernobyl

Kiev

UKRAINE

Dniepr River

MOLDAVIA

Odessa

ROMANIA

Yalta

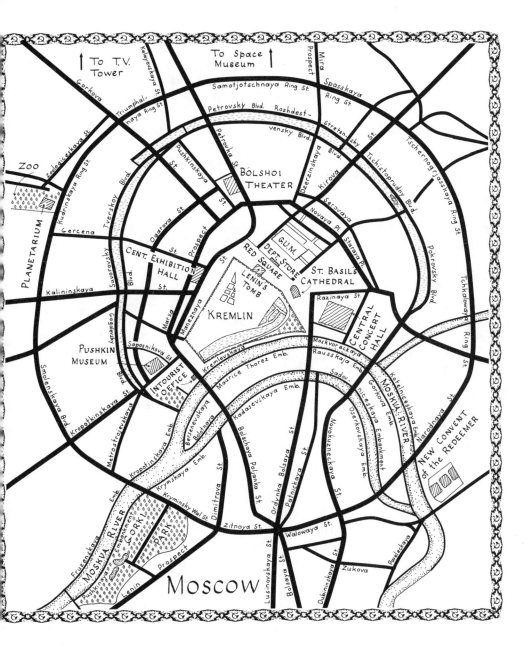

economic might, and lives during World War I. This bad situation was exploited by Vladimir Ilyich Lenin, who led the Russian (October) Revolution of 1917 and became head of state. Lenin's death led to a power struggle eventually won by Joseph Stalin, who wiped out his opponents in the Great Purge, and forcibly collectivized agriculture at the expense of millions of lives. Millions were exiled to the salt mines of Siberia for disagreeing with government policies.

Despite a treacherous pact by Stalin with Adolf Hitler, the Soviet Union was invaded by Germany in 1941. For the remainder of World War II, the Soviet Union was allied with the United States and Britain against the Axis powers. The Soviet people suffered occupation and famine, atrocities and great loss of life (20 million Soviet citizens died). But the Nazis were turned back in their drive toward the southern oil wells and wheat fields at the great battle of Stalingrad, one of the turning points of the war. In 1945, American GIs and Soviet troops embraced in the conquest of Berlin.

Then Stalin's mounting ambition and paranoia resulted in the effective annexation of much of Eastern Europe, now controlled by the Soviets through the Warsaw Pact. Russia built an atom bomb, ending the U.S. monopoly of nuclear weapons. The United States reacted by building up its own alliances to protect Western Europe and other vital areas. A political and ideological Iron Curtain separated East and West. The Cold War began, which flared into hot war in Korea and Vietnam. Meanwhile, the Soviet monolith was challenged from within, successfully, by Yugoslavia, and with only indirect success by East Germany, Hungary, Poland, and Czechoslovakia. But dissidents were still sent to Siberia. On the Chinese border, clashes broke out.

Until the most recent years, Stalin's successors were like the czars, never daring to challenge the bureaucracy and institute liberal policies or representative government for fear of unrest. Even today, Mikhail Gorbachev has to worry about the number of internal threats: the growing force in atheistic Russia of religion (particularly among Jews and the growing Moslem minority); the rise in monolithic Russia of linguistic minorities such as the Armenians, Latvians, Estonians, and Ukrainians; the challenge from writers and intellectuals to go faster in opening Soviet society; the vodka-drinkers' lobby; and the die-hard masochistic Stalinists.

Moscow is the older of Russia's two famous cities, having been founded 800 years ago. **The Kremlin** is the center of the oldest part of the city, its name meaning fortress. In **Cathedral Square** are three famous churches—the best loved monuments of godless Moscow—**St. Michael the Archangel, Annunciation,** and **Assumption**, with their gilded onion domes. Towering over it all is the 256-foot **Belfry of Ivan the Terrible.** Its *kolokola* (bells) ring out the hours.

Other Kremlin sights include the **Armory**, a collection of Czarist coaches, costumes, and jewelry; the **Palace of Facets** (Granovitaya Palata), the **Church of the Deposition,** and the **Spasskaya** (Savior) **Tower**. On **Red Square,** just outside the walls, huge silent Russian lines wait to pay their respects at **Lenin's Tomb**. Across the square is the largest department store in Russia, **GUM**. On Red Square is another great Christian edifice, St. Basil's or the **Cathedral of the Intercession,** put up by a character the Russians call Ivan Groznyi (Ivan the Great), whom we call—with reason—Ivan the Terrible. When St. Basil's was completed in 1560, Ivan put out the eyes of the builder lest he create another building of comparable beauty.

Moscow University Tower is a great place from which to view the capital. Among the advantages of this vista is the fact that from the tower you cannot see the tower itself, a monumental piece of Stalinist neo-baroque. The **Moscow Metro** is a marvel, decorated so as to bring beauty to the masses in the form of marble statues, stained glass, and crystal chandeliers. There are two must-see art galleries amidst the museums dedicated to the Russian view of themselves (skip the **Lenin Museum**, the **Central Revolution Museum**, the **History Museum**, and the **Economic Achievement Exhibition**). The **Tretyakov Museum** is dedicated to Russian artists and artisans from icons to Socialist Realism (except for Andrei Rublev, who has a separate museum of his own in the former **Andronikov Monastery,** also worth visiting). The great **Pushkin Museum** contains six Rembrandts, a wonderful Impressionist collection (the Russians, like the Americans, were big collectors of the Impressionists), Ruben's *Bacchanalia,* Monet's *Boulevard des Capucines,* and various Picassos. **The Glinka** is a museum of musical instruments; the homes of Pushkin, Lermantov, Tolstoy, Checkhov, and Mayakovsky are museums to their works; and the **Ostankino Palace,** built by serfs in the 18th century entirely of wood, is a museum of art by serfs.

Excursions outside Moscow can take you to **Vladimir** or **Suzdal,** both great historic monasteries and museums; **Arkhangelskoe,** a beautifully restored 18th-century estate; **Tchaikovsky's Home; Tolstoy's Estate** in **Yasnaya Polyana**; and houses where Lenin lived in **Gorki** or **Podolski.** Save one night for the **Bolshoi Ballet.**

Leningrad was founded as Peter the Great's new, west-facing capital, which he called St. Petersburg, and has always been a rival for Moscow (which won back primacy after the Revolution of 1917). The historic center is beautiful and perfectly 18th-century, with broad streets and bridges linking the 100 islands on which the city is built. The main thoroughfare is called the **Nevsky Prospect.** From here, the **Winter Palace**, the **Summer Palace**, the **Smolny Palace** (where the revolutionaries had their headquarters), and the pastel-colored stucco city can be viewed. The baroque **St. Isaac's Cathedral,** with its beautiful malachite interior and its pastel painted dome is worth visiting. In the harbor is the cruiser **Aurora**, which fired the shots that started the revolution. The old Czarist jail, **Peter-and-Paul Fortress,** on a hexagonal island in the river, is the first stone building Peter had erected, as well as the burial site of the Czars and a museum. Here, too, a surviving wooden building, called the **Museum Lodge**, can be visited—it is an architectural museum.

The most important art museum in Russia is in Leningrad, the **Hermitage State Museum,** with 3 million works, housed in the Winter Palace and adjacent buildings. Peter the Great and his successor, Catherine the Great, were collectors of works by Rembrandt, Van Dyck, Brueghel, Rubens, Watteau, Poussin, Raphael, Tintoretto, Titian, Caravaggio, Da Vinci, and El Greco. And—thanks to more recent donations—the museum also has a collection of works by Picasso. There are also museums devoted to such subjects as the navy, the 1917 Revolution, Russian ethnology, Pushkin, Chaliapin, atheism (the former **Kazan Cathedral**), applied arts (Summer Palace), the theater, the Siege of Leningrad (during the Second World War), and Dostoyevsky. Outside the city, you can visit **Catherine the Great's Château** at Pushkin (formerly Czarskoe Selo) and other palaces at **Petrodvorets** (Peter's rival to Versailles), **Lomonosov** (formerly Oranienbaum, home of Peter's pal Menshikov), and **Pavlovsk**. The best nearby monastery town is **Novgorod**, which is rich in art. It was the capital of the very first Russian kingdom. The **Maly Theater** offers ballet (to put things into perspective, Leningrad's Maly means small; Moscow's Bolshoi means big).

Russia's third most important city, **Kiev**, is capital of the formerly separate Ukraine, and near **Chernobyl** and **Babi Yar** (sight of a major German atrocity which is subject of a famous poem by Yeutushenko). Founded in the fifth century, Kiev was the dominant town of eastern Europe by the year 1000. It was sacked by the Tartars and the Germans (both World Wars) and has been extensively restored. Parts of the city, on the Dniepr River, date back to the 11th century (such as Uspensky Cathedral and St. Cyril's Church). Other sights, such as the ugly statue commemorating World War II, are modern.

If you can get to one of the formerly independent Baltic states (Latvia, Lithuania, or Estonia) you will see some of the prettiest cities in Europe. **Estonia's Tallinn** is a medieval treasure; **Lithuania's Vilnius** (formerly Vilna), **Kaunas,** and **Trakai** are well-restored old castle towns; and **Latvia's Riga**, with a 13th-century cathedral and health resorts, is another Hanseatic beauty spot. Note also that these formerly independent Soviet republics offer better food than Moscow or Leningrad.

Or you can try to head for another formerly independent kingdom, closed to tourists as of this writing, **Armenia**, where thanks to climate and the entrepreneurship of the population, the food is almost to European standards. In the mountainous capital of Armenia, **Yerevan** (the oldest Soviet city, founded in 782 B.C.), you can view great fortresses, manuscripts, icons, miniatures, monasteries, and churches of incredible antiquity. At **Echmiadzinis,** a fourth-century church, founded in the early years of Christianity. At **Garni** ,you can visit a pagan temple. Or visit the **Caucasus—Baku, Tbilisi, Telavi,** and the **Black Sea** towns of **Sebastopol, Odessa,** or **Sochi Beach**—the Soviet deep south.

For a different culture head east, in the footsteps of Marco Polo (take the Trans-Siberian railroad) to fabled **Samarkand, Ashkhabad, Alma-Ata, Ulan Bator, Bukhara, Frunze, Tashkent** or the vale of **Dushanbe**. Here, the golden domes are on mosques rather than Orthodox churches, and the towers are minarets. The monasteries are sometimes Buddhist. The Russian expansion eastward followed the old silk route and sought to impose the culture of the dominant Russians on the exotic natives—with less success than our own experience with the Indians. The Asian and Moslem Soviet Republics and the "independent" republic (**Inner Mongolia**) have the fastest-growing population in the Soviet Union and threaten to outnumber the Russians in a few years.

Among the things advised to take to Russia are toilet paper and Kleenex, a rubber ball to serve as a sink stopper, and blue jeans. Food in the Soviet Union is stodgy, starchy, and boring. Furthermore it is slowly, erratically, and sullenly served. The country survives on good bread backed up by potatoes, soups, pickles, and vegetable dishes featuring beets, cabbage, cucumbers, and more potatoes. Fruits, vegetables, and tender meat are in scant supply. Most menus list foods that are not available. If you can, try *borscht* (beet soup), *kvass* (sour bread soup), *trikadelkami* (sour cucumber soup), blini with caviar, *pirozhki*, chicken Kiev or Poyarsky, or stroganoff (beef stew, in theory). Try to get Armenian, Azerbaijani, or Uzbek food—available in these republics and in Moscow or Leningrad. *Morzhenoe* (ice cream) is very good. But Soviet sodas are vile. Beer is barely better since Mikhail Gorbachev cracked down on the hard stuff, drink good southern wines.

Russian ladies always have a string bag with them and join any line that seems to be forming. That tells you the secret of shopping in Russia: if you want it, buy it right away, because you may not find it again tomorrow. Special shops and arrangements favor those holding foreign currency or traveler's checks. Apart from fur coats and hats for both sexes (in Russia they are almost a necessity in winter), bargains include Ukrainian or Uzbek embroidery, wooden *matroshka* dolls (the doll opens up to reveal another doll, which opens up to reveal another doll, etc.), records of Cossack and Red Army choruses, and black boxes and broaches painted in brightly colored traditional designs with a hair-fine brush. ❦

VENEZUELA

V enezuela compares with Venice, with Switzerland, with Los Angeles—improbable as that combination may sound.

Venezuela's capital, **Caracas**, has the cheapest gasoline and some of the worst traffic jams in the world. This is thanks to the man whom you might call the second father of Venezuela, Rómulo Betancourt, who was one of the leaders in founding the OPEC oil cartel.

Venezuela was conquered by the Spanish in 1499. The first father of Venezuela was Simón Bolívar, who from 1817 to 1830 led the rebellion against the Spanish in Venezuela (as well as present-day Colombia, Panama, and Ecuador); he was proclaimed The Liberator. Apart from a bloody coup in 1958, the republic proclaimed by Bolívar has functioned since 1830.

Caracas, a set of suburbs looking for a city center, with traffic-choked *autopistas*, and a lot of modern architecture, reminds one of nothing so much as Los

Angeles. The center of downtown is graced with a not-very-distinguished art museum in a pretty park, **Parque Los Caobos**. There are some much better art galleries, and a grandiose **Capitol** (built in 1873), whose Salón Elíptico is decorated with heroic paintings. Around the **Plaza Bolívar** which is graced by a splendid statue of the Liberator on a rearing horse, there are some nice buildings (which house government offices). In an old quarter called **La Pastora** is the

---

EMBASSY: *2445 Massachusetts Ave. N.W., Washington, DC 20008; (202)797-3800.*

SYSTEM OF GOVERNMENT: Representative federal republic.

ETHNIC GROUPS: Mestizos, 69%; Caucasians, 20%; Negroes, 9%; American Indians, 2%.

RELIGIOUS GROUPS: Roman Catholics, 96%.

LANGUAGES: Spanish; local dialects, 2%.

POPULATION: 17.5 million.

AREA: 352,143 square miles (912,050 square kilometers).

CAPITAL: Caracas (population 3 million).

TERRAIN: Low extensions of the Andes in the north; plains and forests in the southeast; basin of Lake Maracaibo in the west. South of the Orinoco River are the Guiana Highlands, which are largely unexplored.

CLIMATE: Varied, depending on the altitude. The rainy season is from April through November. The average temperature in Caracas in January is 69 degrees Fahrenheit; the average temperature in July is 74 degrees Fahrenheit.

TELECOMMUNICATIONS
Country Code: 58.
Time Zone: +1 hour Eastern Standard Time.

Code of Capital: 2.

LOCAL/NATIONAL AIRLINES: Pan Am, *(800)221-1111;* **Air Panama,** *(800)225-3569;* and **Viasa Airline,** *(800)327-5454.*

U.S. CONSULATE IN COUNTRY: *avenida Francisco de Miranda* and *avenida Principal de la Floresta, Caracas; tel. (58-2)284-7111; telex 25501 AMEMB VE.*

CURRENCY: Bolivar. No limit on import or export.

GROSS NATIONAL PRODUCT: $50 billion (in 1985).

WORK FORCE: Industry and commerce, 35%; services, 26%; agriculture, 15%.

OUR QUALITY OF LIFE RANKING: 57.20.

VISA REQUIREMENTS: Passports, onward/return tickets, and visas or tourist cards are required. You can obtain a tourist card (valid for 60 days) from carriers at no charge. To obtain a visa (valid for 60 days), you must appear in person before a consulate (consulates are located in Boston, Baltimore, New York, New Orleans, Chicago, Philadelphia, Houston, Miami, San Francisco, and San Juan). All travelers except tourists must pay an $18 exit tax.

National Pantheon, which looks like an elongated top-heavy Spanish mission church (it used to be the Iglesia de la Santisima Trinidad, and dates from the late 18th century). It houses Bolívar's tomb. The Spanish city includes some much-restored old churches, notably **St. Francis Church** and the cathedral, which were founded by the conquistadors. From **Mount Avila,** reachable by cable car, you get a good view of the city. In **Parque de Este**, orchids hang from the trees, giving Venezuela one of its national symbols, the climbing orchid (commemorated in jewelry). The **Casa Natal,** where Bolivar was born in 1783, can be visited. The **Museo Bolivariano,** next door, is one of the few colonial mansions standing. Another is **Hacienda de San Bernardino**, a former colonial mansion outside town. The **Consejo Municipal** (right on Bolivar Square) holds the **Raul Santa Museum,** which explains the creole way of life with costumes, tools, dioramas, and skits.

Modern architectural wonders include the university and the **Centro Simón Bolívar,** a huge ministerial complex with its own underground road system. Another wonder is the highway to Columbia, which climbs through passes 12,000 feet high in the Andes. Another is the great port of Caracas, **La Guaira**.

Maracaibo, the oil port town, is, if anything, even more modern than Caracas. When the Spaniards arrived and saw the Indians' canoes and their houses built on stilts, they were reminded of Venice. Poetic license. From the Venetian parallel the name of Venezuela derives. Maracaibo is the center of Venezuelan oil wealth and no longer picturesque.

The third largest city, **Valencia**, retains a genuine Spanish colonial center, featuring a cathedral and a theater. The largest cable railway in the world runs from **Merida**, a cool mountain city, at the foot of the Sierra Novada de Merida to the top of the mountain, **Pico Bolívar**. This is the high point of the snow-covered **Sierra Nevada,** the winter-sports region of Venezuela. The second highest mountain, **Pico Humboldt,** is next to a lake full of trout. The area, which Venezuelans claim looks like Switzerland, is part of the **Parque Nacional de la Sierra,** one of the dozen national parks in the country. Merida also has the best carnival—although some argue that there is an even better pre-Lenten celebration in **Carúpano** on the **Paria Peninsula.**

Puerto Cabello is a pretty palm-fringed harbor where pirates used to hang out, now the wonderfully-scented coffee-export port. Tourists often head for the cheap Venezuelan Caribbean island of **Margarita**, 15 miles off the coast. This is the center of the cult of the *Virgen del Valle*, one of the most colorful of the fiestas.

Salto Angel (also called Churún-Merú) is the tallest waterfall in the world. The **Canaima** area of the Andes Range where it is located, is a beautiful mountain zone with tourist developments. Other lovely waterfalls are located along the **Orinoco** and and **Paraguay** riverbanks in the mountainous eastern part of Venezuela. This area has two more national parks (**La Llovizna** and **Chachamay**) and a preserved colonial town called **Ciudad Bolivar,** or **Angostura**. Here you can see the **Zamuro Fortaleza,** the site of the ill-fated Angostura Congress (which represented the four countries Bolívar liberated), the first printing plant in the country which produced the pro-Bolívar newspaper, a fine old cathedral, and old churches. Another natural wonder is **Cueva del Guacharo** in Monagas State, with its caverns and grottoes.

There are few surviving Indian customs or handicrafts apart from palm weaving and blanket making. Most of the culture is Spanish, right down to bull-fights, should they take your fancy. **Colonia Tovar,** a 130-year old German colony, offers its own folklore, with chalet-style houses amidst the mountains, sauerkraut restaurants, and lots of non-German flowers and birds.

Shopping in Venezuela should not only focus on the watered-down Indian products such as *mantas* (blankets), straw hats, and hammocks. If you must buy this stuff, buy it in the east or on Margarita Island. In Ciudad Bolívar (and to an increasing extent in other areas) you can buy lovely charms in the shapes of an orchid, an Andean daisy (*espeletia* or *failejon*), or a bird. These are available in gold or silver made into pins, necklaces, or earrings.

Venezuelan food features a native fast food, the *arepa*, a filled cornmeal roll, sold by *arepera* stands. You usually choose the filling yourself. *Quesillos* are cheese-filled tortillas; *hallacas*, served around Christmas, are spicy tortillas filled with rice and steamed in banana leaves. A *parrillada* is a beef barbecue. Beer, rum, and coffee are excellent; so are *merengada* (milk shake) and *batido* (fruit juice drink). 🐛

WEST GERMANY

Many travelers from the United States still approach Germany with mixed feelings. To many Americans, Germany means Adolf Hitler and sauerkraut, *Hogan's Heroes* and Volkswagen, lederhosen and Mercedes Benz. Many start their tour with the traditional trip down the Rhine past romantic villages and medieval castle ruins. Here a legendary mermaid, the Lorelei, was the first "rock singer" to lure hormone-crazed youths into the dangerous depths. Scenic vineyards along the steep banks of the river connect famous and "typical" towns like **Bacharach**, **Rüdesheim**, and **Coblenz**, home of medieval legends and commercialized *Gemütlichkeit*.

Following the course of the river, you encounter **Bonn**, the capitol. Rumor has it Bonn is half as big as Chicago's Central Cemetery—but twice as dead. This is the birthplace of Beethoven and the German *Bundestag* (Parliament), and the site of the **Rhineland Museum**, with the remains of the world-famous Neanderthal man. Other Rhineland-born major figures include Heinrich Heine, who was born in

---

EMBASSY: *4645 Reservoir Road N.W., Washington, DC 20007; (202)298-4000.*

SYSTEM OF GOVERNMENT: Federal republic.

ETHNIC GROUPS: Germans.

RELIGIOUS GROUPS: Roman Catholics, 45%; Protestants, 44%.

LANGUAGE: German.

POPULATION: 60.734 million (in 1986).

AREA: 95,996 square miles (248,630 square kilometers); comparable to Wyoming.

CAPITAL: Bonn (population 300,000).

TERRAIN: Lowlands in the north; uplands in the central area; mountainous Alpine region in the south.

CLIMATE: Moderate, but changes in the weather are frequent. Average temperature in January is 30 degrees Fahrenheit; average temperature in July is 63 degrees Fahrenheit.

TELECOMMUNICATIONS
   Country Code: 49.
   Time Zone: +6 hours Eastern Standard Time.
   Code of Capital: 228.

LOCAL/NATIONAL AIRLINES: American Trans Air, *(800)225-9920;* **Condor,** *(312)951-0005;* **Delta,**

(800)221-1212; **Icelandair,** *(800)223-5500;* **KLM Royal Dutch Airlines,** *(800)777-5553;* **LTU German Lines,** *(800)888-0200;* **Lufthansa German Airlines,** *(800)645-3880;* **Northwest Airlines,** *(800)447-4747;* **Sabena Airlines,** *(800)632-8050* (New York), *(800)645-3700* (East Coast), *(800)645-3790* (Southeast and Midwest), or *(800)645-1382* (West Coast); and **TWA,** *(800)892-4141.*

U.S. CONSULATE IN COUNTRY: *Diechmanns Avenue, 5300 Bonn 2; tel. (49-228)3391.*

CURRENCY: Deutschemark.

GROSS NATIONAL PRODUCT: $901.6 billion (in 1986).

WORK FORCE: Industry and commerce, 42%; services, 42%; and agriculture, 6%.

OUR QUALITY OF LIFE RANKING: 78.39.

VISA REQUIREMENTS: Visas are not required for stays of up to three months. For longer stays, you can obtain a temporary residence permit from the local Alien Office.

TOURIST OFFICE IN THE UNITED STATES: German National Tourist Office, *747 Third Ave., New York, NY, 10017; (212)308-3300.*

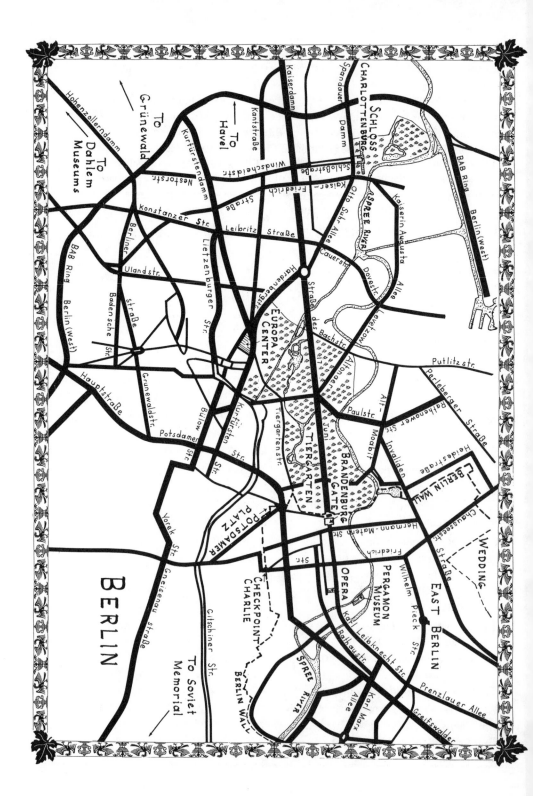

Düsseldorf, and Karl Marx, a local boy from Trier. Continuing the trip along the Rhine, whose colors might have changed from dark brown to bright red or green in between—due to sewage "accidents" of adjoining chemical industries—you will finally arrive in **Cologne**. The Gothic silhouette of the cathedral's famous twin towers is contrasted by the post modern building of the new **Roman-Germanic Museum,** which contains an excellent collection of archeological artifacts and mosaics from the Roman and Frankish periods of Cologne's past. The weak local *Kölsch* beer (the original "light" beer) is usually served in small test-tube like glasses. The **Bergisches Land** east of Cologne is full of cozy little inns offering local specialties.

Another center for the American tramp abroad is **Heidelberg**, famous for its colorful student life and the musical, *The Student Prince,* whose famous refrain, "Drink, drink, drink!" still inspires the collegians. Through Heidelberg's alleys the noise of modern mass tourism drowns most traces of nostalgia one might expect to find in Germany's oldest university town.

For more authentic student life, you might want to visit **Coburg** or **Würzburg**—both are centers for student conventions (roughly comparable to the U.S. universities' descent on Fort Lauderdale at Easter), which take place six weeks after Easter, one weekend before Pentecost.

In Northern Germany the old Hanseatic cities of **Bremen, Hamburg,** and **Lübeck** still preserve the brisk business-like air their Protestant inhabitants had acquired in centuries of sea commerce. Hamburg would not be Hamburg without the **Reeperbahn** and **Herbertstrasse** and their notorious peep shows, street prostitution, and night clubs, which provide a source for moral outrage for the one side and cheap voyeuristic amusement for the other. Hamburg is also Germany's greatest sea port, site of the discovery of the Beatles, and home to renowned operas, musicals, and theater. The famous *Fischmarkt* is a lusty, noisy affair starting at 5 a.m. close to the Altona docks.

The center of **Bremen** is marked by Hanseatic half-timbered houses surrounding a statue of Roland. Lübeck produced another famous German writer, Thomas Mann, and features a 15th-century gateway. In this area, a fine dish to order in the summer is *Rote-Grütze*, a mixture of berries and cherries served with vanilla sauce. Another speciality is marzipan, sold in a variety of shapes and colors.

Catholic South Germany, with its Baroque churches and picturesque castles, is the lively counterpart to the sober North, yet it is in this supposedly less serious part of Germany that they make the Porsche, the Mercedes, and the BMW. **Munich,** capital of Bavaria, is famous for its **Hofbräuhaus, the German (science) Museum,** and its art museums. Its closeness to the Alpine winter sports centers such as **Garmisch-Partenkirchen,** and romantic (and, alas, 19th-century) castles makes it one of the most popular cities in Germany. Many of these castles were built by the German equivalent of Walt Disney, the mad king of Bavaria, Ludwig II, who ultimately drowned mysteriously in the lake below one of the fantasy castles on which he squandered his tax receipts. (He also was a patron of the composer Wagner.) Every autumn, Munich features the **Oktoberfest** on the Theresienwiese, with streams of beer and wagonloads of pretzels. Hangovers can be cured by walks in the **Hofgarten**, the **Englischer Garten,** or through the parks of **Nymphenburg Palace**, the Bavarian kings' summer residence. **The Antiquarium** (within the **Residenz**) has a collection of Greek and Roman art. On **Marienplatz**, the **Viktualienmarkt** and the double towers of the **Frauenkirche** are a must for travelers.

West Berlin, a democratic island in the middle of East Germany, is fully integrated into the judicial and financial system of West Germany. With 1.9 million inhabitants, it is the largest German city, and in spite of its isolated position it has lost nothing of its metropolitan vitality. The cultural (and counter-cultural) "scene" of Berlin ranges from little cabarets and experimental theaters to the internationally renowned **Deutsche Oper** and **Schiller Theater**. The **Kurfürstendamm** provides miles of first-class shops, including the **KaDeWe**, Europe's biggest department store. Sites include **Charlottenburg Palace** (which faces a Roman museum on one side and an Egyptian museum with the beautiful head of Nefertiti on the other) and the **Gedächtniskirche**, whose ruined towers are an anti-war monument. The **Olympic Stadium** evokes ambivalent memories of the 1936 games. The most notorious site is the **Berlin Wall,** which has been separating the city from East Berlin and East Germany since 1961.

The museums in **Dahlem**, an area on the southwestern edge of the city near the Free University, includes art museums featuring Rembrandt's *Man with a Golden Helmet*, a collection of Dürer engravings, and an ethnographical museum with important African masks and Asian pottery.

Across the border in **East Berlin**, the **Pergamon Museum** features the rebuilt Pergamon Altar which originally stood in Asia Minor, the **Ishtar Gate** from Babylon, and an extensive collection of ancient and Islamic treasures. In East Berlin, visitors may want to visit Bertolt Brecht's old theater to take in a show by the **Berliner Ensemble**. You can also see a goose-stepping East German honor guard at the **War Memorial.**

Germany is no longer a bargain center for American-dollar shoppers. But you can still pick up goodies like wooden toys, cuckoo clocks, "Trachten" (Bavarian costumes), which often are attractive and un-peasanty, *Lebkuchen* (the German version of Christmas gingerbread), and small leather goods.

German food can be heavy and greasy. *Königberger Klopse* are meatballs in sweet-and-sour sauce. White asparagus (*Spargel*) is a spring treat (unless you prefer new cabbage, named like the chancellor, Kohl). *Weisswurst*, a sausage made of veal and pork, simply boiled and served with *Senf* (mustard), is the traditional Bavarian second breakfast (about 11 a.m.). If fresh, you can eat it all day. Dessert is what saves German food: try *Schwarzwälder Kirschtorte*, a lovely confection of chocolate cake, cherries, and lots of whipped cream; *Frankfurter Kranz*, a layer cake lathered with jam and butter-cream; and *Apfelstrudel*. In Germany you can drink beer (the purest in the world) or wine. Try to get away from *Liebfraumilch*. Try *Frankenwein* in its special bottle with a rounded shoulder. Or a light sweet wine from the Mosel Valley or Baden-Württemberg. *Edelzwicker* is a dry white wine from the French border. In Berlin you should try *Weisse mit Schuss*, light beer mixed with raspberry syrup, refreshing on a hot summer day. North German beer, such as Jever or Flensburger Pils, tends to be strong and bitter; the lighter Bavarian brews are closer to the American taste. 🐑

YUGOSLAVIA

Yugoslavia has six republics, four languages, three religions, and two alphabets. The republics are Bosnia-Herzegovina, Croatia, Macedonia, Montenegro, Serbia, and Slovenia, but there are also two autonomous provinces, Kosovo and Slovenia. The languages are Yugoslavian (or Serbo-Croatian), Macedonian, Slovene, and Albanian; the religions Roman Catholicism and Eastern Orthodoxy; the alphabets Roman and Cyrillic.

As a result of this mish-mash, Yugoslavia, the land of the South Slavs, created after World War I out of former Hapsburg territory, is a federation. Its monarchy was discredited by links with fascism. Out of the resistance movement during

World War II (when Yugoslavia was divided up by Italy, Germany, Bulgaria, and Hungary), a pro-Communist force led by Josip Broz Tito emerged and liberated the country.

Tito was one of the few post-war Communist leaders who actually had a power base separate from the Russian Army, and he resisted the attempt by Stalin and the Communist International to limit Yugoslavian sovereignty. This resulted in a break with Russia in 1948, after which Yugoslavia followed its own path toward communism based on worker management of enterprises. In theory, this means workers

---

EMBASSY: *2410 California St. N.W., Washington, DC 20008; (202)462-6566.*

SYSTEM OF GOVERNMENT: One-party, Communist.

ETHNIC GROUPS: Serbians, 42%; Croatians, 24%; Slovenes, 10%; Macedonians, 5%; Albanians, 4%.

RELIGIOUS GROUPS: Members of the Eastern Orthodox Church, 41%; Roman Catholics, 32%; Moslems, 12%.

LANGUAGES: Serbo-Croatian; Slovene; Macedonian (all official).

POPULATION: 23.284 million (in 1986).

AREA: 98,766 square miles (255,804 square kilometers).

CAPITAL: Belgrade (population 1.3 million).

TERRAIN: Four-fifths of the land area is mountainous; plains in the northern region; 1,050 islands.

CLIMATE: Continental in north and central regions; Mediterranean along the coast.

TELECOMMUNICATIONS
Country Code: 38.
Time Zone: +6 hours Eastern Standard Time.
Code of Capital: 11.

LOCAL/NATIONAL AIRLINES: Yugoslav Airlines, *(212)246-6401;* and

Lufthansa German Airlines, *(800)645-3880.*

U.S. CONSULATE IN COUNTRY: *Kneza Milosa 50, Belgrade; tel. (38-11)645655; telex 11529;* **U.S. Consulates General,** Brace Kavurica 2, *Zagreb; tel. (38-041)44-48-00; telex 21180.*

CURRENCY: Yugoslavian dinar. Travelers may import 80,000 dinars and export 80,000 dinars (in denominations of 100 dinars or less).

GROSS NATIONAL PRODUCT: $49.2 billion (in 1984).

WORK FORCE: Industry, 70%; agriculture, 30%.

OUR QUALITY OF LIFE RANKING: 49.97.

VISA REQUIREMENTS: Visas (which are valid up to 90 days) are required. To obtain a visa, contact the embassy or the consulate in Chicago, San Francisco, New York, Cleveland, or Pittsburgh. You can obtain a permit for a 30-day visit at any entry point.

TOURIST OFFICE IN THE UNITED STATES: **Yugoslav State Tourist Office,** *630 Fifth Ave., Suite 280, New York, NY 10111; (212)757-2801.*

elect delegates to run the economic system and decide on factory wages and the price of goods produced; in practice, it means something considerably less democratic. Yugoslavia also became a leader of the non-aligned countries.

Most travelers don't bother going inland—which means they miss reconstructed **Belgrade**, the capital. Its great fortress, **Kalemegdan** (its ramparts turned into a garden), controls the confluence of the **Sava River** with the **Danube**. Its **National Museum** is worth visiting. Its Bohemian-cum-gypsy quarter, **Skadarlija**, is popular with tourists seeking a *kafana* (low bar), where they can soak up a local brew.

The overdeveloped heart of the craggy and beautiful Dalmatian Coast is **Dubrovnik**, a perfect walled city founded as a Venetian fortress called Ragusa. Its old fountains and shops (including a functioning medieval pharmacy), its towers, its markets, and its synagogue (the third oldest in Europe) help make up for the overwhelming tourist mob.

Yugoslavia is cheap for European sun-seekers as well as for Americans, and the government is eager to stuff them in and collect their foreign exchange. The palpable greed of the tourist industry in Dubrovnik can be extremely off-putting. Things are not much better in **Split**, which was the favorite vacation home of the Roman Emperor Diocletian. His palace has been divided up to create homes and shops in the old town. Other destinations include **Hvar** (which offers a purpose-built tourism complex) **Porec Umag** and the islands of **Rab** and **Krk**. (You won't be able to pronounce the latter—but it is reputedly one of the most beautiful seaside sites in the world.) Always with an eye to the foreign exchange they get from tourism, the Yugoslavs have so departed from Socialist prudery as to encourage naturist beaches, and **Koversada** is the largest nudist colony in the world. Centered around **Opatija** north of here is the **Croatian Riviera**, the former sea resort of the Hapsburg Empire, with many traces of former luxury amidst the campsites.

Still farther north, in **Slovenia**, is the great Euro-invasion route into Yugoslavia, which can be abominably crowded in the summer. This area does offer lovely mountains. Local winter sports centers are off the beaten track and are recommended for mountaineering, trout-fishing, and absorbing culture and history in the off-season. Try **Kranj, Planica, Kanin,** or **Velika Planina**. If you go farther than Croatia to the south, off the coast in the **Republic of Montenegro**, is the Yugoslavian version of Mont St.- Michel, called **Sveti Stefan**, a pilgrimage site cut off from the mainland by tides. It is picture-perfect, a result achieved by luring the former inhabitants of the island, fishermen, from their old homes into modern accommodations, and then converting the fisher cottages into suites and apartments for holiday-makers. Other seaside resorts include **Herreg-Novi** and its region; or you can visit the mountains, taking in **Kolasîn** or **Durmitor**. Head for **Lake Skadar** (on the border with Albania, which, as a result, is shunned by tourists).

A little-known attraction of the Adriatic coast is spelunking. The largest cave is **Postoinska Yama**, near the Italian border. The most dramatic is **Zlavaskiya**, a blue grotto you enter by rowboat from the sea (shades of Capri). But there are hundreds more. Caves are a great way to get away from the sun, the heat, and the crowds.

Shopping should focus on handicrafts. Buy a *guzzela* (a gorgeously carved

218

single-string fiddle), a peasant blouse, a woven woolen shoulder bag, or a small oriental carpet. Serbian or Montenegran *naif* paintings (based on icons but sometimes showing secular subjects) can be a good buy. Look for pottery, metalwork, and gold and silver jewelry based on ancient designs (it is much cheaper here than from designers in Greece).

Yugoslavia has great wines; my favorite is *zilavka*, a slightly fizzy white wine. The coffee tends to be Turkish, brewed from a powdery mixture of coffee and sugar. The food is Balkan: stuffed cabbage; good lamb dishes; goulash; and moussaka-like eggplant dishes. Try the lovely salad made of eggplant, tomatoes, zucchini, and red peppers. *Cevapcici* are spicy meatballs, which can be delicious. Or, in Belgrade, you can go to the first McDonald's in Eastern Europe. ❦

CONTINENT MAPS

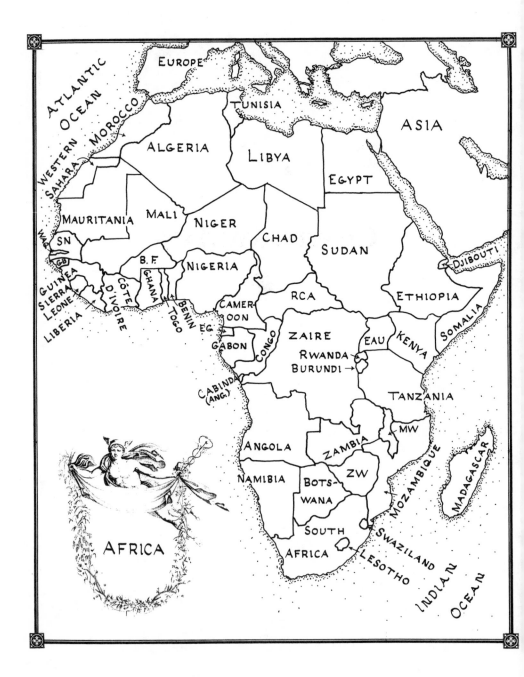

AFRICA

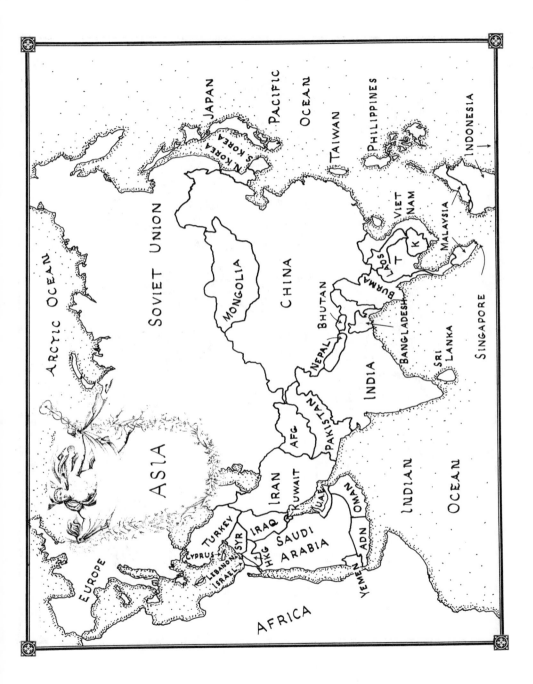

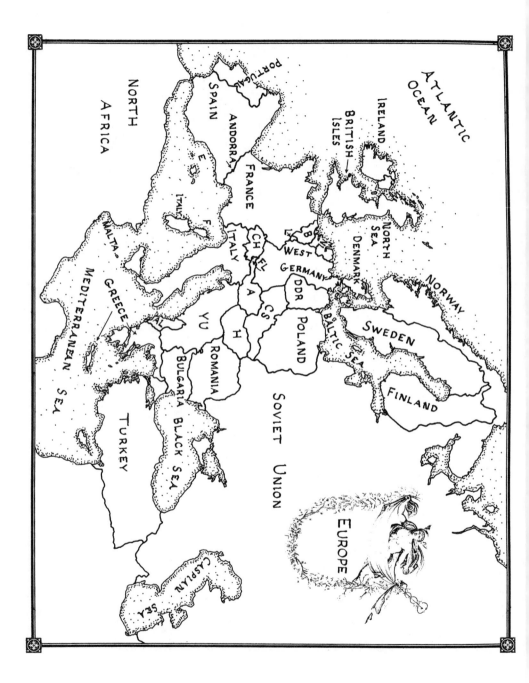

ATLANTIC
OCEAN

NORTH
AFRICA

PORTUGAL

SPAIN

ANDORRA

FRANCE

IRELAND

BRITISH
ISLES

NORTH
SEA

DENMARK

NORWAY

WEST
GERMANY

DDR

POLAND

BALTIC SEA

SWEDEN

FINLAND

MALTA

MEDITERRANEAN SEA

GREECE

ITALY

CH

FL

A

CS

H

YU

ROMANIA

BULGARIA

BLACK SEA

TURKEY

SOVIET UNION

EUROPE

CASPIAN SEA

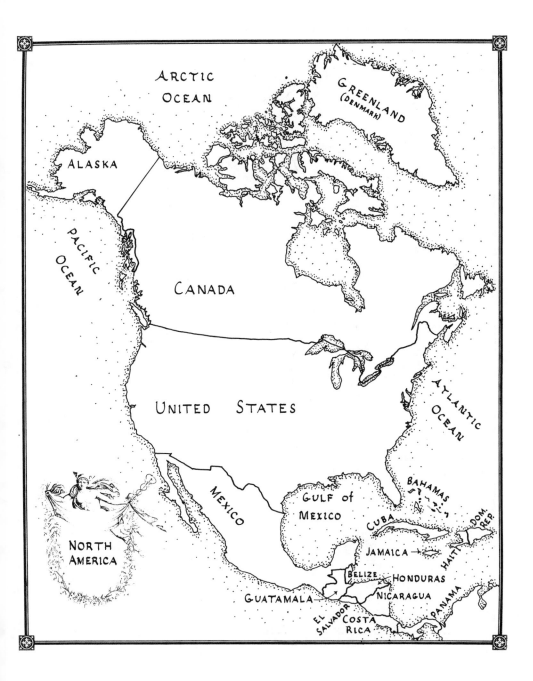

ARCTIC OCEAN

GREENLAND
(DENMARK)

ALASKA

PACIFIC OCEAN

CANADA

UNITED STATES

ATLANTIC OCEAN

NORTH AMERICA

MEXICO

GULF of MEXICO

BAHAMAS

CUBA

DOM. REP.

JAMAICA

HAITI

BELIZE

HONDURAS

GUATAMALA

NICARAGUA

PANAMA

EL SALVADOR

COSTA RICA

ATLANTIC OCEAN

VENEZUELA

GUYANA

SURINAME

FRENCH GUIANA

COLOMBIA

ECUADOR

AMAZON RIVER

PERU

BRAZIL

BOLIVIA

PARAGUAY

CHILE

URUGUAY

PACIFIC OCEAN

ARGENTINA

SOUTH AMERICA

Key for Map Abbreviations

Afghanistan	AFG	Finland	SF
Albania	AL	France	F
Algeria	DZ	French Guiana	F
Andorra	AND	French Polynesia	F
Argentina	RA	Gambia	WAG
Australia	AUS	Germany (Dem. Rep.)	DDR
Austria	A	Germany (Fed. Rep.)	D
Bahamas	BS	Ghana	GH
Bahrain	BRN	Gibralter	GBZ
Bangladesh	BD	Greece	GR
Barbados	BDS	Grenada	WG
Belgium	B	Guadeloupe	F
Belize	BH	Guatemala	GCA
Benin	DY	Guyana	GUY
Botswana	RB	Haiti	RH
Brazil	BR	Hong Kong	HK
Brunei	BRU	Hungary	H
Bulgaria	BG	Iceland	IS
Burma	BUR	India	IND
Burundi	RU	Indonesia	RI
Canada	CDN	Iran	IR
Central African Republic	RCA	Iraq	IRQ
Chile	RCH	Ireland	IRL
Colombia	CO	Israel	IL
Congo	RGB	Italy	I
Costa Rica	CR	Ivory Coast	CI
Cuba	C	Jamaica	JA
Curaçao	NA	Liechtenstein	FL
Cyprus	CY	Luxembourg	L
Czechoslovakia	CS	Madagascar	RM
Denmark	DK	Malawi	MW
Dominica	WD	Mali	RMM
Dominican Republic	DOM	Malta	M
Ecuador	EC	Martinique	F
Egypt	ET	Mauritania	RIM
El Salvadore	ES	Mauritius	MS
Ethiopia	ETH	Mexico	MEX
Fiji	FJI	Monaco	MC

Morocco	MA	Sweden	S
Japan	J	Switzerland	CH
Jordan	HKJ	Syria	SYR
Kampuchea	K	Taiwan	RC
Kenya	EAK	Tanzania	EAT
Korea (Rep.)	ROK	Thailand	T
Kuwait	KWT	Togo	TG
Laos (People's Dem. Rep.)	LAO	Trinidad & Tobago	TT
Lebanon	RL	Tunisia	TN
Lesotho	LS	Turkey	TR
Liberia	LB	Uganda	EAU
Libya	LAR	United Kingdom	GB
Namibia	SWA or ZA	Uruguay	ROU
Netherlands	NL	USSR	SU
New Caledonia	F	Venezuela	YV
New Zealand	NZ	Viet Nam	VN
Nicaragua	NIC	Western Samoa	WS
Niger	RN	Yemen (People's Dem. Rep.)	ADN
Nigeria	WAN	Yugoslavia	YU
Norway	N	Zaire	ZRE
Pakistan	PAK	Zambia	Z
Panama	PA	Zimbabwe	ZW
Papua-New Guinea	PNG		
Paraguay	PY		
Peru	PE		
Philippines	RP		
Poland	PL		
Portugal	P		
Romania	RO		
Rwanda	RWA		
San Marino	RSM		
Senegal	SN		
Seychelles	SY		
Sierra Leone	WAL		
Singapore	SGP		
South Africa	ZA		
Spain	E		
Sri Lanka	CL		
St. Lucia	WL		
St. Vincent	WV		
Suriname	SME		
Swaziland	SD		